Modern Microcomputers
Second Edition

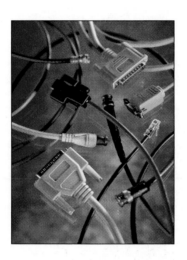

FRITZ J. ERICKSON

Millersville University of Pennsylvania

JOHN A. VONK

University of Northern Colorado

IRWIN

Chicago • Bogotá • Boston • Buenos Aires • Caracas
London • Madrid • Mexico City • Sydney • Toronto

Irwin Book Team

Publisher: *Tom Casson*
Sponsoring editor: *Garrett Glanz*
Project editor: *Jean Lou Hess*
Production supervisor: *Dina L. Genovese*
Manager, Prepress Purchasing: *Kimberly Meriwether David*
Senior designer: *Heidi J. Baughman*
Cover and interior designer: *Ellen Pettengell*
Coordinator, graphics & desktop services: *Keri Johnson*
Photo researcher: *Randall Nicholas*
Compositor: *GTS Graphics, Inc.*
Typeface: *10/12 Century Light*
Printer: *Webcrafters, Inc.*

**Times Mirror
Higher Education Group**

Library of Congress Cataloging-in-Publication Data

Erickson, Frtiz J.
    Modern microcomputers / Fritz J. Erickson, John A. Vonk. — 2nd ed.
      p.   cm.
    ISBN 0-697-27798-4
    1. Microcomputers.   I. Vonk, John A.   II. Title
  QA76.5.E667 1996   95–45503
  004.16—dc20

Printed in the United States of America
1 2 3 4 5 6 7 8 9 0 WC 1 0 9 8 7 6

Hi Mom

Preface

COMPUTERS AS TOOLS

Not so long ago, the use of a computer to solve a problem was big news. Today, however, computers affect so many aspects of our daily activities that we sometimes hardly notice their benefits. This is not to say that the world of computing is no longer interesting; hardly! The pace of innovation and potential applications make the study of computers more exciting than ever. The goal of this text is to share that excitement with students by showing them the far-reaching effects of computers and technology, and the applications that computers have to their own lives.

THE TOOLS FOR UNDERSTANDING CONCEPTS

Students are motivated by success. By introducing ideas in manageable doses, this text allows students to succeed with each topic, building confidence to move to the next. In addition, we have created the following learning system to help students effectively comprehend computer concepts.

- *Extensive examples.* Throughout every chapter, each example is designed to encourage student interest and motivation and support topics presented in the text. These examples have been chosen for their relevance and interest to freshman or sophomore students.
- *Emphasis on microcomputers.* With more efficient microprocessors available each year, the microcomputer is the dominant tool of the end-user. To reflect this shift away from mainframes, we have focused exclusively on microcomputers (PCs and Macs) and their relevance to the college student and professional.
- *A brief history.* History adds flavor and personality to most disciplines. Computing is no exception. Unfortunately, few instructors can devote significant class time specifically to the history of computers. That is why we have included a special appendix highlighting the most interesting aspects of computing history. Students will learn about the evolution of computing and the people behind the changes.
- *Easy-to-understand language.* We made a considerable effort to make technical information comprehensible to the student. We made no assumptions about jargon, technical terms, or industry names. As a result, students will be less intimidated and will understand more.

Interesting marginal notes

special keys often perform specialized input tasks. Other input devices include a mouse, which manipulates a pointer on the computer screen for giving commands and entering data; a scanner, which reads graphic images and pages of text and sends them to the computer; and a modem, which receives data over phone lines.

Once data is in a microcomputer, it is **processed** by the microprocessor and its associated integrated circuits. Microprocessors perform all calculations and manipulations necessary to transform data into meaningful information. Associated with the processor is the computer's memory, which is used for storing data and programs while they're being used by the processor.

Getting processed data out of the computer is the job of **output devices.** Most often computers display data on a monitor. There are several types including color or monochrome, flat panel or picture tube, desktop or portable. You can also send data to a printer or plotter to make a paper copy, use the modem to send the data over a phone line to another computer, or use any number of specialized output devices.

Easy-to-understand language

What do you do if you want to keep the data in a permanent form? Use a **storage device.** Storage devices hold data for later retrieval. Microcomputers typically store data magnetically on disks or tape. Each type of disk is used by its corresponding disk drive to read and write information. Floppy disks are used for easy, portable

COMPUTERS AND NATURAL DISASTERS

Scientists at Livermore Labs in California used computerized wind and weather data to guide Air Force pilots through volcanic ash clouds as they evacuated people from the vicinity of erupting Mount Pinatubo in the Philippines. Over 20,00 people were evacuated. Every 12 hours scientists sent their predictions—which later were confirmed by satellite photos—to Air Force pilots. Earlier, the scientists had computed the path of clouds of radiation released by the explosion of the Soviet nuclear reactor at Chernobyl, which sent plumes of radiation up to 50,000 feet into the atmosphere. More recently, the same team of scientists provided forecasts of the dense clouds made by oil wells set on fire by the Iraqi army as it began fleeing Kuwait during the Gulf War.

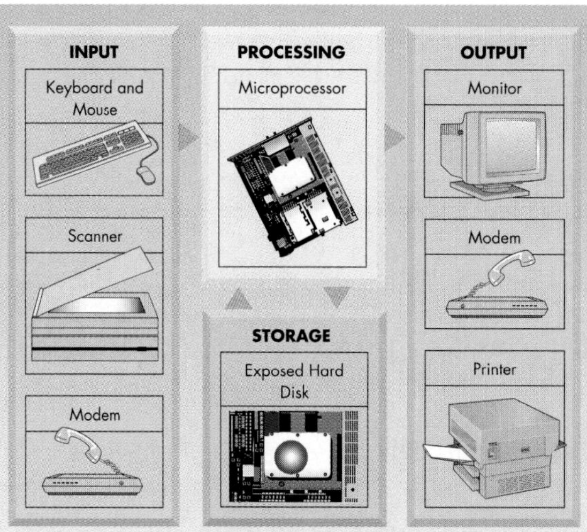

Figure 1-6
The computing cycle. The microprocessor (CPU) receives data from input devices, processes it, and sends the data to output devices for display, printing, or communication. Along the way, the CPU stores data temporarily in memory or permanently on a storage medium such as magnetic disk, tape, or optical disk.

Clear illustrations and descriptions

EXTENSIVE END-OF-CHAPTER RESOURCES MAKE THE TEXT A TRUE LEARNING TOOL

Another application for which businesses have found great use is presentation graphics. Whether you are selling an idea or product to your boss or to a potential customer, presentation graphics software can help get your point across. These programs give you a great deal of power to create and format charts, graphs, and accompanying text.

SUMMARY   Recaps critical concepts

- Computers can be broadly classified as special purpose or general purpose.
- Special-purpose computers, such as an ATM at the bank, accept only certain types of input and present a narrow range of outputs.
- This book focuses on a type of general-purpose computer, the microcomputer.
- The computing cycle includes four kinds of hardware devices: input, pro-

KEY TERMS   Provides a list of important topics for student review

application	input
application software	mainframe computers
computer	microcomputers
computing cycle	minicomputers
desktop publishing (DTP)	modem
E-mail	operating systems
general-purpose computers	output devices
hardware	processed

REVIEW QUESTIONS   Promotes discussion and critical thinking

1. Is a calculator a general-purpose or special-purpose computer? Why? Explain your reasoning.
2. How might you use a word processor, spreadsheet program, and database program in your classes?
3. Even if minicomputers and mainframe computers were inexpensive, why is it unlikely that a person would buy one for home use?
4. What is a scanner? a mouse? a modem? What functions does each serve?
5. If you wanted to create a professional-looking brochure to advertise your carpentry business, what kind of application software would you use?
6. How could you use database software to help write a term paper?
7. Describe the individual processes of the computing cycle.
8. What are the major types of application software?

Allows students to practice for tests or exams ➤

SELF-QUIZ

1. Computers can remember information on a short, temporary basis by using
   - *a.* magnetic tapes.
   - *b.* magnetic disks.
   - *c.* hard disks.
   - *d.* memory circuits.
2. Early microcomputers (about 1975) were largely used by
   - *a.* accounting firms.
   - *b.* hobbyists.
   - *c.* large industry.
   - *d.* scientists.
3. Hardware consists of
   - *a.* application programs.
   - *b.* operating systems.
   - *c.* virtual devices.
   - *d.* physical devices.
4. Because their meanings are very similar, the terms software and _____ are often used interchangeably.
   - *a.* hardware
   - *b.* operating system
   - *c.* input device
   - *d.* program
5. The six most common types of application software are word processing, graphics, spreadsheet, database, desktop publishing, and _____ software.
   - *a.* communications
   - *b.* games
   - *c.* utility
   - *d.* drawing

Encourages students to question and explore the world of microcomputers ➤

SIMULATIONS

So you think you know something about computers. Maybe. Maybe not. Answer the following questions as truthfully as possible. Do not look anything up. Do not ask a friend. If you do not know an answer then write "I don't know." Honesty is always the best policy.

1. Right now could you write a 10-page term paper on a word processor that contained headers and footers?
2. Describe one use of Internet.
3. What is a font, a style, and point size?
4. What is the difference between a formula and a function?
5. What is the difference between bit-mapped and object-oriented graphics?
6. Have you ever taken a computer class before? If so, what did you do and what did you learn?
7. What are two types of networks?
8. What is the difference between RAM and ROM?
9. What is Internet?
10. What are the three components that make up any computer system? Can you provide an example of each?

Expands student interest with practical assignments ➤

HANDS-ON COMPUTING

1. How can computers make your life easier? In this chapter we examined how computers were used to help create this book. Think of the tasks that you do on a somewhat regular basis. Can computers make completing those tasks easier? Create a list of computing possibilities.
2. Of course computers are everywhere. They are at banks, in the grocery store, at the registrar's office. Keep a list of every place where you have had contact with a computer for one week. Don't limit yourself to just microcomputers but think about the special computing devices that affect your everyday life.
3. What do you like to do? Are you a train buff? Are you a bike rider? Do you play an instrument? Do you like baseball cards? Computers are most often useful for hobbies and interests. For example, if you are a baseball fan, there are computer programs that help you track, organize, and evaluate baseball cards. There are train programs that help you set up a model-train layout. What can you find? Take a trip to the local software store and see what type of software is available for your particular interest or hobby.
4. Computers are very much part of the popular media. In fact, many movies feature computers in a major role. Create a list of movies where computers play a central character. Here are a few to get you started—*2001: A Space Odyssey, The Lawn Mower Man, War Games.*
5. Become a futurist. Ten years ago, it was difficult to imagine the impact

- *Active learning.* Computing is a hands-on experience. At the end of each chapter are sections called Simulations and Hands-On Computing. Simulations provides you with real-life examples of computer uses. Hands-On gives you the opportunity to use computers to learn about computers.
- *Pedagogy.* Each chapter contains an Introduction, Vignettes, Learning Objectives/Outlines, Chapter Summaries, List of Key Terms, Discussion Questions, Self-Quiz, and Study/Review Questions.
- *Marginal notes.* Throughout the text, interesting marginal notes include tips on avoiding microcomputer problems, stories about historical figures in computing, and real-life applications of the chapter subject.

ANCILLARY MATERIALS

Knowing that modern microcomputers is just one component of the course, we have developed several instructional tools with utility and value in mind.

- *PowerPoint Presentation Software:* Consists of PowerPoint slides and animated graphics that enhance the classroom presentation of computer concepts.
- *Instructor's Manual with resource disk:* Available to instructors only, this manual contains lecture outlines, solutions to end-of-chapter questions and exercises, teaching tips, and additional test questions. The disk is in ASCII format, so it's easy to modify, add additional material, or print sections as needed.
- *Test bank:* This test bank contains many different questions, including true/false, multiple choice, fill-in, and short essay questions. Also included are a sample mid-term and a final exam, along with answers to all questions.
- *Computest:.* Irwin's popular, user-friendly computerized testing software contains test bank questions and allows instructors to customize test sheets, entering their own questions and generating review sheets and answer keys.
- *Videos:* 21 videos from the acclaimed PBS series, *Computer Chronicles,* are available that cover topics ranging from computer speech to the Internet.
- *Instructor's data disks:* For instructors using the lab tutorials for software education, these diskettes contain files used in the DOS- and Windows™-based software labs.
- *Phone and fax instructor support service:* Irwin's College New Media Department offers telephone-linked support services to instructors using Irwin software.

CUSTOMIZE YOUR TEXT

Custom Packaging

If you find that none of the titles in the Erickson/Vonk series meets the needs of your course exactly, Irwin will create a book especially for you. Simply call your sales representative, choose the exact content necessary for your course, and we'll do the rest. Your students will receive a text custom-fitted to your course needs. You can even include your own materials. The materials you select (including course-specific materials) are available in several different formats:

- Shrinkwrapped
- Wirecoil binding
- Comb binding
- Perfect bound

Within a week of the time we receive your selection, you can see the material you are considering for adoption in the custom-bound format.

ACKNOWLEDGMENTS

One of the joys of working on this book was having the very capable assistance of editors, students, and colleagues. Although they are too numerous to mention by name, we are grateful for their help and guidance throughout the development of this project; their unselfish contributions made this book possible. Our special gratitude goes to the efforts of editors Garrett Glanz and Paul Ducham, and the entire book team at Irwin. We are also indebted to Jean Lou Hess for her friendly voice and dedication to keeping this project on track and on time. Most of all we would like to thank our families. No author could develop a project of this nature without the loving tolerance of family members. Thanks, Jan, Jenna, John, Arlo, Parker, Petie, Jennifer, Julie, Jacqui, Joey, Clancy, Torrie, and Riley.

Lastly, we would like to extend a special thanks to those who took the time to review this book:

Bonnie Bailey
Morehead State University

Robert Sadler
Culver-Stockton College

Melinda White
Santa Fe Community College

Dan Codespoti
*University of South Carolina—
   Spartanburg*

Susan Finch
Pima Community College

Edouard Desautels
University of Wisconsin—Madison

Kate Goelz
Rutgers University

Photo Credits

Contents

Modern Microcomputers
SECOND EDITION

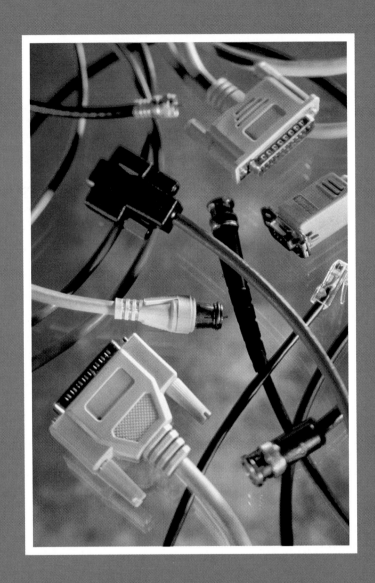

CHAPTER 1

Introduction to Microcomputers

FOCUS

The introduction of the microcomputer in 1975 revolutionized the world of computers and in the process has brought about vast changes in the way people live and work. Microcomputers have developed from toys for hobbyists to powerful and versatile tools.

In this book, you will look at the fundamental nature of microcomputers: the hardware devices that make up the physical machine; the operating systems and the six major types of application software that make microcomputers the profoundly useful tools they have become; and some of the issues surrounding microcomputer use today. Along the way, we will explore innovative ways to use microcomputers and understand some of the most important events in the development of microcomputers.

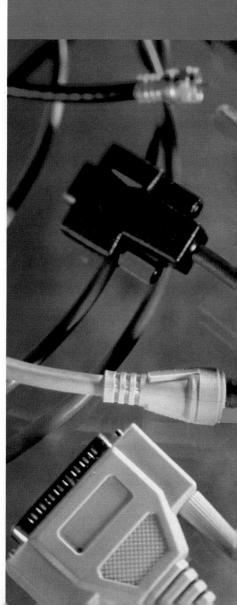

WHAT IS A MICROCOMPUTER?

There are many different kinds of computers. Different computers operate at banks, in your car, and at grocery stores. These computers are **special-purpose computers;** that is, they serve specific functions. There are also **general-purpose computers,** versatile enough to handle all kinds of tasks. The existence of all these different types of computers raises an important question: What *is* a computer? A **computer** is simply a device that processes raw data into useful information. But from that perspective, a typewriter, a calculator, or even an abacus could be called a computer. Three basic characteristics distinguish a computer from other information-processing devices:

- A computer is electronic. That is, all its processing functions are carried out with electrical signals.
- A computer can remember information and retain it for future use. Computers do this on a temporary basis with memory circuits and permanently with storage devices such as magnetic disk and tape.
- A computer is programmable. Unlike other devices built to perform a single function or limited range of functions, you can instruct a computer to do a variety of tasks. This opens up a vast realm of possibilities for computers to solve everyday problems: at home, at school, and at work.

The most common kind of general-purpose computer in use today is the personal computer or microcomputer. It gets the name **microcomputer** from the tiny electronic device, called the *microprocessor,* that does the actual processing (Figure 1–1). The use of personal computers has grown greatly during the last 15 years. Only a few million personal computers were in use a decade ago. Then microcomputers were a relative novelty. Today there are well over a hundred million in this country alone and growing.

Microcomputers form the most common of the four classes of general-purpose computers; the other three classes are minicomputers, mainframe computers, and supercomputers. Microcomputers are the smallest and are generally designed for a single or limited number of users (Figure 1–2). Minicomputers, mainframes, and supercomputers all use processors built from a large number of components and are designed for use by multiple users with large storage and processing capabilities. **Minicomputers,** larger than microcomputers (up to the size of a refrigerator), are generally intended for small- to medium-sized groups of users; minicomputers have processing abilities that are more robust

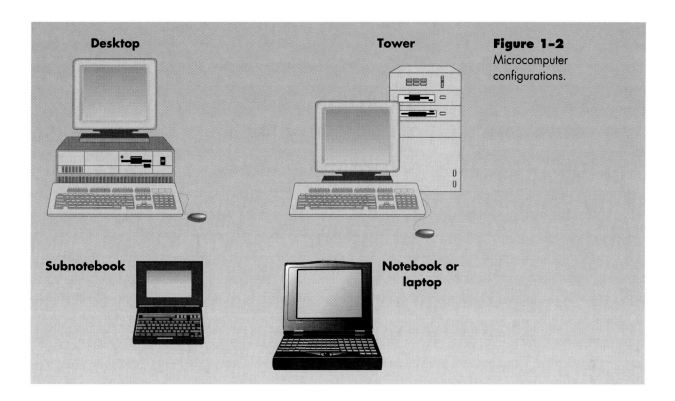

Desktop

Tower

Figure 1-2
Microcomputer
configurations.

Subnotebook

Notebook or laptop

than those of microcomputers. **Mainframe computers** can take up a whole room and can handle the needs of many users simultaneously while processing large volumes of data; they are most often used in large organizations and institutions. **Supercomputers,** the most sophisticated computers, are designed for extremely high-speed processing of huge amounts of data, often using multiple processors working together. They are most often used for performing complex computations by government, research, and large industrial groups.

WHY FOCUS ON MICROCOMPUTERS?

Fifteen or 20 years ago, most books on computers focused on mainframes, because mainframes were the most common. Today, you are more likely to use a microcomputer. The first micros were sold to computer hobbyists in 1975 (Figure 1–3). In 1977, Apple Computer, Inc., which started in a garage, introduced the Apple II, and it quickly grew into a major computer company. In 1981 IBM introduced its first microcomputer, known as the IBM-PC. A few years later, in 1984, Apple Computer, Inc., released the Macintosh. During the 1980s, literally hundreds of manufacturers began making microcomputers. The competition kept prices down, and millions of people bought micros.

As the microcomputer industry grew, computer makers constantly tried to lure new customers with more powerful computers. The typical microcomputer sold today can work with much more data than the first IBM-PC, Apple, or Macintosh. Today's microcomputers can work with data hundreds and even thousands of times faster. In fact, many of today's laptop (Figure 1–4) and desktop microcomputers are more powerful than the minis and mainframes that dominated the market only 15 or 20 years ago.

Figure 1-3
The MITS Altair 8800 was the first microcomputer, announced on the cover of the January 1975 *Popular Electronics.* It was based on the Intel 8080 microprocessor and was sold as a kit. Notice there is no keyboard. Instructions are issued by flipping the series of switches on the front panel.

Figure 1-4

It's a long way from the Altair to modern laptop computers based on the latest micro-processors: these have more processing power than many mainframes of 15 or 20 years ago.

Figure 1-5

A typical microcomputer.

The power of the modern microcomputer enables it to be used for all kinds of tasks. For a few thousand dollars, you can buy a computer and use it to write papers, perform mathematical computations and analyses, and conduct research. At home, you can use the same computer to communicate with friends, play games, buy airline tickets, and keep track of finances. The same computer can be used again at work for correspondence, financial analysis, compiling and analyzing data, communicating with clients, and a thousand other tasks. Today's computers do all of these tasks faster, easier, and more efficiently than the expensive minis and mainframes of yesterday (Figure 1–5).

HARDWARE AND THE COMPUTING PROCESS

All computers are made up of physical devices known as **hardware.** This includes the computer itself, disk drives, keyboards, monitors, and any other related physical devices. But computers are of little value without instructions. Instructions, known as software, tell computers what tasks to perform and what information to work on. Software also allows you, the user, to ultimately tell the computer what work to perform.

All computers use the same basic techniques for carrying out the tasks. Computers take in data through input devices, manipulate data according to instructions, then output the results of the processing, and store the data for later use. These four processes together are known as the **computing cycle** (Figure 1–6).

Input is the process of entering data into a computer. The most common microcomputer input device is the keyboard. Computer keyboards include many special command and function keys as well as the usual typewriter layout. These

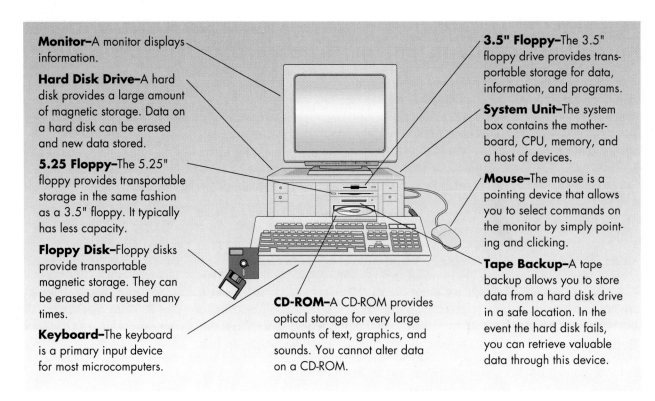

Monitor–A monitor displays information.

Hard Disk Drive–A hard disk provides a large amount of magnetic storage. Data on a hard disk can be erased and new data stored.

5.25 Floppy–The 5.25" floppy provides transportable storage in the same fashion as a 3.5" floppy. It typically has less capacity.

Floppy Disk–Floppy disks provide transportable magnetic storage. They can be erased and reused many times.

Keyboard–The keyboard is a primary input device for most microcomputers.

CD-ROM–A CD-ROM provides optical storage for very large amounts of text, graphics, and sounds. You cannot alter data on a CD-ROM.

3.5" Floppy–The 3.5" floppy drive provides transportable storage for data, information, and programs.

System Unit–The system box contains the motherboard, CPU, memory, and a host of devices.

Mouse–The mouse is a pointing device that allows you to select commands on the monitor by simply pointing and clicking.

Tape Backup–A tape backup allows you to store data from a hard disk drive in a safe location. In the event the hard disk fails, you can retrieve valuable data through this device.

special keys often perform specialized input tasks. Other input devices include a mouse, which manipulates a pointer on the computer screen for giving commands and entering data; a scanner, which reads graphic images and pages of text and sends them to the computer; and a modem, which receives data over phone lines.

Once data is in a microcomputer, it is **processed** by the microprocessor and its associated integrated circuits. Microprocessors perform all calculations and manipulations necessary to transform data into meaningful information. Associated with the processor is the computer's memory, which is used for storing data and programs while they're being used by the processor.

Getting processed data out of the computer is the job of **output devices.** Most often computers display data on a monitor. There are several types including color or monochrome, flat panel or picture tube, desktop or portable. You can also send data to a printer or plotter to make a paper copy, use the modem to send the data over a phone line to another computer, or use any number of specialized output devices.

What do you do if you want to keep the data in a permanent form? Use a **storage device.** Storage devices hold data for later retrieval. Microcomputers typically store data magnetically on disks or tape. Each type of disk is used by its corresponding disk drive to read and write information. Floppy disks are used for easy, portable

COMPUTERS AND NATURAL DISASTERS

Scientists at Livermore Labs in California used computerized wind and weather data to guide Air Force pilots through volcanic ash clouds as they evacuated people from the vicinity of erupting Mount Pinatubo in the Philippines. Over 20,00 people were evacuated. Every 12 hours scientists sent their predictions—which later were confirmed by satellite photos—to Air Force pilots. Earlier, the scientists had computed the path of clouds of radiation released by the explosion of the Soviet nuclear reactor at Chernobyl, which sent plumes of radiation up to 50,000 feet into the atmosphere. More recently, the same team of scientists provided forecasts of the dense clouds made by oil wells set on fire by the Iraqi army as it began fleeing Kuwait during the Gulf War.

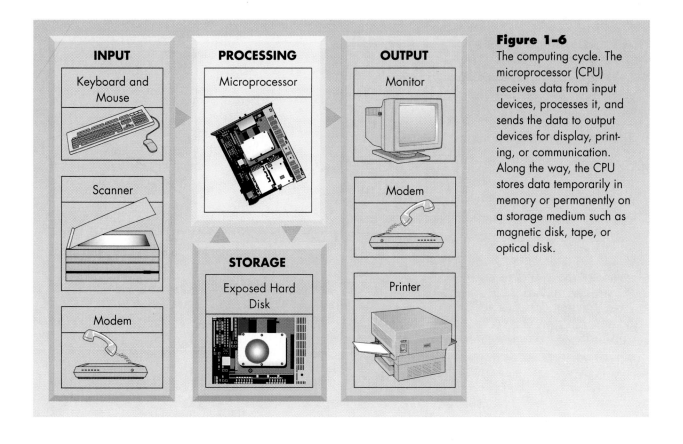

Figure 1-6
The computing cycle. The microprocessor (CPU) receives data from input devices, processes it, and sends the data to output devices for display, printing, or communication. Along the way, the CPU stores data temporarily in memory or permanently on a storage medium such as magnetic disk, tape, or optical disk.

THE LANGUAGE BARRIER

One of the most difficult hurdles facing multinational companies is the language barrier. But software companies face an extremely unusual challenge with the Japanese language because of its complex alphabet. English uses only 26 letters. The Japanese written language uses over 6,000 separate symbols. Also, it takes twice as much memory and storage space to hold each Japanese character as it does to hold each English character.

The difficulties of translating such a complex language into computerese have been both a help and a hindrance to the Japanese computer market. Their software market has developed slowly because the first computers used English ASCII code. But the Japanese have been way ahead in graphics displays, largely because of the problems associated with displaying complex characters clearly.

TALKING BOOKS

Thanks to the rapidly increasing storage capacity of hard disks, as well as the expanded capabilities of CD-ROM, more and more reference books, such as Grolier's Encyclopedia, which has over 33,000 articles and 10 million words, are being used in electronic format. Many of the electronic reference books are more than just books to be read on screen instead of on paper. They utilize computer technology to enhance their effectiveness: *Webster's New Collegiate Dictionary* can pronounce 160,000 root words. A complete edition of Shakespeare's works is available with texts in both Elizabethan English and modern English versions. Numerous style guides and collections of quotations, literature, and philosophy, as well as databases of historical events, can be accessed in a variety of ways. That's the good news. The bad news is that you still have to write your own term papers.

storage. Built-in hard disks typically are used to store larger amounts of data and programs with the computer system for fast access. Another common storage device is the optical disk (such as the CD-ROM).

SOFTWARE

A **program** is a set of instructions designed to control a computer. **Software** can be a single program or a group of programs that work together. Because their meanings are very similar, the terms *software* (or *a piece of software*) and *program* are often used interchangeably.

Two types of software (operating system and application software) are necessary to make the computer capable of performing useful work. **Operating systems** software contains basic instructions that tell the CPU how to use other hardware devices, where to find data, and how to load and keep track of programs in memory. Because it includes basic instructions that are vital to the internal functioning of the computer, the operating system is the first program to be processed when the computer is turned on. The operating system remains in memory until the computer is turned off.

For a computer to perform useful tasks, it needs application software (Figure 1–7) in addition to the operating system. An **application** is a job that a computer can perform, such as creating text documents, manipulating sets of numbers, creating graphic images, and communicating with other computers. **Application software** is the term used to describe programs that tell the computer how to perform such jobs. The six most common types of application software are

- Word processing software.
- Graphics software.
- Desktop publishing software.
- Spreadsheet software.
- Database management software.
- Communications software.

Application software is what makes a computer a useful tool for performing tasks at school, at home, or at the office.

HOW APPLICATION SOFTWARE WAS USED TO MAKE THIS BOOK

Because of the variety of application software available, microcomputers are much more than just flexible tools. In many cases they can be integrated into every aspect of a complex endeavor. Take the production of this book, for example. Virtually every step of the way, we used microcomputers. To give you a

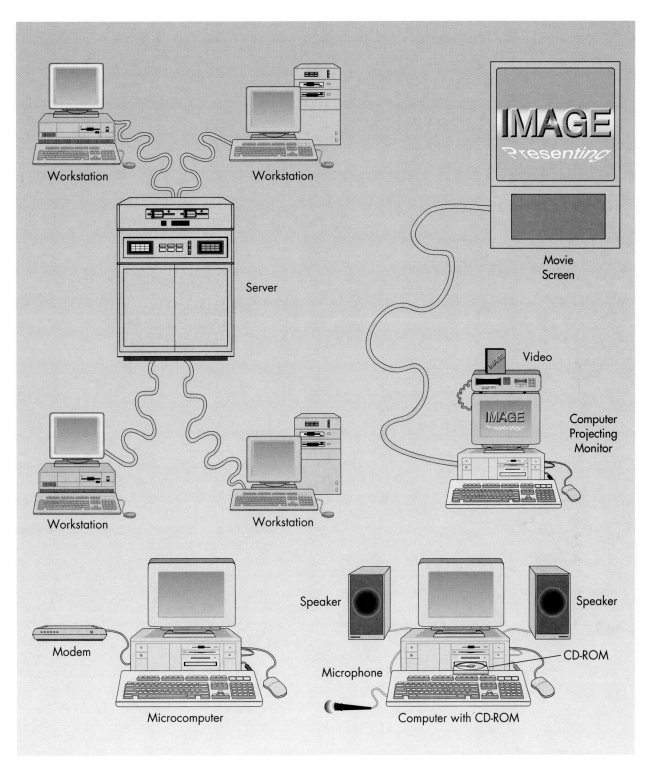

Workstation

Workstation

IMAGE
Presenting

Movie
Screen

Server

Video

Computer
Projecting
Monitor

IMAGE
Presenting

Workstation

Workstation

Modem

Microcomputer

Speaker

Microphone

Computer with CD-ROM

CD-ROM

Speaker

better sense of how a complex process can be accomplished using microcomputers, we'll describe the four stages of producing a textbook: planning, research, development, and production.

Planning

Like any other business, producing books requires financial planning. Before officially launching the project, the publisher of this book had to project

Figure 1-7
Modern multimedia classrooms are more than a few computers placed in the back of the room. They include workstations, a server, a data projection device, Internet connections, speakers, and a CD-ROM.

revenue and costs from the proposed book in a budget. Twenty years ago, budgets were created entirely by hand—an unpleasant task considering how many individual expenses had to be figured in. Even worse was revising the budget. Usually, a budget has to be manipulated and fiddled with for quite a long time before the numbers are acceptable. Each time the numbers are changed, all totals need to be recalculated. Doing budgets by hand was like getting an arithmetic assignment that took a week to finish.

Spreadsheet software helped our publisher calculate the budget for this book. The publisher still had to estimate each cost, enter it into the budget, and then plug in the formulas that were needed. But the computer, with instructions from the spreadsheet application, did all the math. If the totals weren't acceptable, the publisher decided where costs could be cut and then changed the numbers. The totals were calculated again automatically. A recalculation that would have taken a person with a calculator an hour to figure out probably took the computer less than a second.

Once the budget was complete, it was time for the publisher to draw up contracts for the authors. Here again, the publisher had application software to make the job easier: in this case, word processing software. The publisher did not even have to do much typing, because most authors' contracts are similar. All the publisher had to do was to personalize a generic contract by filling in the names, some figures, and the dates.

Research

With contracts in our hands, we were ready to get to work. Time was of the essence, and we had a schedule to keep. But you can't just sit down and write a textbook off the top of your head. You need to do some research. Fortunately, you can do a lot of research in your home or office with a microcomputer, a modem, and communications software. A **modem** is a hardware device that lets your computer communicate with another computer over the phone lines. Communication programs are application software you use to control a modem.

We used Procomm to control our modems. With these tools we accessed information services and bulletin boards, where we could ask questions of other microcomputer users and gain valuable information. If we found information that might be useful, we used the modem to pull the information into our computers. Not only did we save a lot of time this way, but we also saved a good deal in mailing costs.

The database software called Paradox also saved us time in our research. The only way to keep up with the ever-changing computer industry is to read a lot of newspapers and magazines. Every time we found an interesting or useful article, we entered data about the article in a database. When it came time to write about, say, graphics software, we were able to search our database for all the articles on the subject.

Development

With enough research amassed, it was time to start writing the manuscript. This is where we really put our word-processing software to work. We outlined,

Steve Roberts decided to create a life out of his three passions: travel, technology, and bicycling. The result is the world's smartest bike, the 350-pound Behemoth (big, electronic, human-energized machine, only too heavy), which comes complete with stereo, refrigerator, solar power, and a word processor. The keyboard is built into the handlebars of the bicycle and doubles as a musical instrument. Actually, there are about a half-dozen computers on board, one of which allows Roberts to hook into the Navstar satellite system and pinpoint his location within 50 feet. There is also a top-notch security system. If the bike is stolen, it can alert the police, and if anything is not functioning properly, it can alert Roberts. What else could a self-confessed "yuppie hobo" want?

wrote, revised, wrote some more, outlined again, and revised again. Whenever one of us finished a chapter, he used the modem to send the chapter to the other to check and revise the work. With the help of the word-processing program, WordPerfect for Windows, we streamlined much of the writing process. For example, we checked our spelling electronically, thus avoiding the embarrassment of sending the publisher a manuscript full of typos and misspelled words.

Each time we finished a chapter, we used another application software called Grammatik, which is a grammar checker. It searched our prose for nonstandard usage, bad sentences, and all kinds of other problems.

After completing about half the manuscript, we printed it out and sent it to a group of reviewers who teach classes like the one you are taking now. While the reviewers critiqued our work, we plunged ahead with the rest of the manuscript. When the reviews came back, we went back to the same word-processing files to revise our work. We went through the same process a second time, with the second half of the manuscript.

Production

As soon as we were done writing the manuscript, production began and a lot more people—and computers—got involved. This book was produced using the techniques of **desktop publishing,** or **DTP.** Desktop publishing is a process in which microcomputers, high-quality printers, and advanced text and graphics software are used to produce complex professional documents, such as books, advertisements, pamphlets, and magazines. The techniques of DTP have literally revolutionized the book-publishing industry. Books such as this one can now be produced in far less time and for less money than is required by traditional book-making practices.

A STREET MAP FOR THE WHOLE COUNTRY

Not all databases are filled with information about companies, business transactions, or scientific research. Some are filled with graphic images, and one new application for such graphic databases involves maps. Street Atlas USA from Delorme Mapping Company comes on a single CD-ROM and has street maps for the entire country—over 1,000,000 maps in all. The maps include the address ranges along each street, ZIP codes, and area codes, as well as names of mountains, rivers, lakes, and other geographical features, all in full color. Users can search all this data for specific geographical names or street addresses, use a zoom feature to display various levels of detail, and even copy sections of maps onto other documents.

As production began on this book, a production manager took over the job of coordinating everyone's efforts and keeping everyone on schedule. To help her in her work, she used project management software called Microsoft Project. Project management software keeps track of schedules, budgets, and vendors. Not only does it help the manager, but it also helps vendors get paid on time.

The first group of people to be hired by the production manager were the copy editors, an input editor, and proofreaders. The copy editors wrote corrections on the manuscript to make it logical, consistent, and grammatically accurate. The input editor entered the changes into the word processing files, and proofreaders checked the input editor's work.

While the copy editors, input editor, and proofreaders were working on the text, an illustrator and a photo researcher were making or finding all the illustrations you see in this book. The illustrator worked with a graphics program called Adobe Illustrator to create the line drawings and another program called Hijaak to create the screen captures. The photo researcher used a database of photos, listed by subject matter, that she created with a program called FoxPro.

When proofreaders, the illustrator, and the photo researcher were done, the manuscript went into page makeup. In this stage, the word processor files and the electronic illustrations were imported into desktop publishing software.

WHERE IN THE WORLD IS— WHO?

Carmen Sandiego, that's who, a now-legendary crook who does things like attempting to steal the Taj Mahal or the original copy of the Magna Carta. She's glamorous, hip, and thanks to the fact that children interact with her on their computers in a series of best-selling games (sales of over 1 million), she can travel anywhere in the world and visit any time. Oh, and yes, along the way children learn a lot about geography, history, and a variety of other subjects. And that's the real purpose of the games from Broderbund Software. Each player is a detective from Acme Detective Agency and must capture all of Carmen's gang to win. Each game comes with a reference book, appropriate to the storyline, which provides clues. Kids love the games, and parents love the fact that their children are learning—schools even have Carmen Sandiego Day, complete with an actress dressed as the crook arriving by helicopter. No one is saying where the next Carmen Sandiego game will be set, but there are a lot of people who can hardly wait to find out.

Desktop publishing software is a powerful tool for formatting pages that are used in books, pamphlets, ads—anything that needs to look professional. Word processing software contains some of the same features as desktop publishing software, but the latter specializes in text formatting and the ability to combine text and graphics on the same page.

Page makeup was the last major phase of production before printing, although the phase includes several cycles before it is completed. Each cycle is called a *pass*. After the production team members finished each pass, they printed out copies of the book's pages on a laser printer. Different types of quality checks were performed each time a new pass was printed.

Finally, after the last quality check, the book was printed. Even this step involved computers. The laser printer that printed the different passes produced a print of quality high enough to check for errors, but not high enough to print books from. Book printing required projecting the electronic page makeup files onto photographic film. The film was then passed through an offset printer, the printed pages were cut, and the book was bound. Voilà! You see the result before you.

MANY USERS, MANY USES

Publishing, of course, isn't the only business that uses microcomputers extensively. If you look closely, you will find that almost every business has been, at the very least, affected by their use. Equally important are the effects the microcomputer has had on homes and schools.

In the Schools

You have undoubtedly seen a few of the ways in which computers are used on campus. For writing papers, typewriters are becoming a thing of the past. Most students find that using a word processor is much faster and far more convenient, especially when it comes to editing and revising. But in addition to a word processing program, what other types of application software do students use in their studies?

In writing papers, another useful tool is hypermedia software, such as HyperCard for the Macintosh. Hypermedia programs are similar to database programs but are less rigidly structured. HyperCard, for instance, allows writers to create a set of electronic note cards and then create links between them. Using such a tool, a writer can work out the structure of an argument or presentation before writing it.

The most widely used application after the word processor is the electronic spreadsheet. In addition to helping students keep track of finances, spreadsheets are invaluable as research tools. This is especially true in science, where empirical evidence is often numeric. For example, if you are conducting a psychological study, the quality of your research depends largely on the number of people in your study. But as your sample size grows, the amount of math involved in analyzing your study grows too. Spreadsheet software makes this kind of work easier. Most programs, in fact, have statistical functions built in. Not only does the software speed the numeric calculations, but with a few commands you can also generate graphs and charts that summarize your data or analyses.

Another common application used in research is database software. In much the same way that we collected data about articles we read during the research phase of this book, students use databases to organize their own research. Whereas spreadsheets are good for organizing numeric data, database software is excellent for collecting many kinds of data, including numbers, text, graphic images, and even sound. Once you have collected a large body of data, you can use the software to search, organize, and retrieve specific subsets of related data.

Computer graphics software is also used in the arts at school. Fine arts majors can create startling images using computers. They can even combine more traditional formats with electronically generated material.

At Home

The first place microcomputers appeared was in the home. Today, applications geared for the home market are more diverse than ever. One popular type of software helps you calculate your taxes. For people who own a home, or work at home, or have outside investments, these programs can help identify items on which taxes must be paid and where deductions can be listed. Tax software can save you incredible amounts of time and money.

Games are also popular on home computers. Some of the best-selling types are adventure games, flight simulators, and sports games such as golf and football.

Databases have proven to be invaluable home software. People find it very convenient to organize data about their books, their recipes, or their collections (such as stamps). Insurance companies encourage their customers to keep a careful inventory of their valuables in case of fire or theft, and database software is an excellent way to do it.

In addition, people at home use the same types of software as they do at school or at the office. They use word processors to write letters, spreadsheets to keep track of finances, and communications software to access information services.

At the Office

The biggest market for application software is the office, and the uses for microcomputers are as varied as the businesses that use them. As in schools, the most widely used applications are word processors and spreadsheets. Creating documents (correspondence,

GRANDMASTER COMPUTER

The age-old question, Which is smarter, man or machine? has just been answered, at least when the application involves a chess game. The computer can now beat the grandmaster. Since computers are faster at calculating, they can test every possible move and every possible outcome from any given position of pieces on the board. Although a grandmaster has more familiarity with what may work and what may not, a human cannot exhaust every possibility each time it is his turn. But does the computer enjoy the game?

COMPUTERIZED TRAVEL GUIDES

Let's say you are visiting New York City for the first time and would like to visit a Thai restaurant that offers dancing and nearby parking, is close to your hotel, and allows two people to enjoy an evening for under $50. Thanks to a computerized version of the famous Zagat travel guides, you can key in your requirements, and if such an establishment exists, the computer lets you know. And if you need directions from your location to the restaurant, a little red Porsche zooms around the screen to show you the way. CityGuide (as the computer guide is known) currently offers help for three cities—New York, Los Angeles, and Chicago. Guides to 27 other U.S. cities should be available soon, with Europe and Japan following—as will CD-ROM versions of the information. Random House is converting its famous Fodor's travel books onto software that can be used with handheld computers. The Official Airlines Guides, published monthly, is now available on diskettes and CD-ROM. Some software suppliers are even looking ahead to a guide with an electronic voice for car computers so that the driver doesn't have to look at the map.

reports, and so on) and managing finances are the two most commonly pursued tasks in an office.

Another application that has steadily grown with microcomputer use is electronic mail, or **E-mail.** E-mail lets one computer user send a message to another user on the other side of the building—or the other side of the planet. As long as both users have access to a common computer network or Internet, they can communicate. Using E-mail is a lot like using a modem, except that the two users don't have to be using their computers at the same time. With E-mail, a businessperson just types a message to a client or associate and sends it. When the recipient next accesses the E-mail application, the message will be there waiting. Businesses have found that this type of communication can save large amounts of time and money.

Another application for which businesses have found great use is presentation graphics. Whether you are selling an idea or product to your boss or to a potential customer, presentation graphics software can help get your point across. These programs give you a great deal of power to create and format charts, graphs, and accompanying text.

SUMMARY

- Computers can be broadly classified as special purpose or general purpose.
- Special-purpose computers, such as an ATM at the bank, accept only certain types of input and present a narrow range of outputs.
- This book focuses on a type of general-purpose computer, the microcomputer.
- The computing cycle includes four kinds of hardware devices: input, processing, output, and storage devices.
- To be capable of performing useful work, a computer also needs two kinds of software: the operating system and application software.
- The six most common types of application software are word processing, graphics, desktop publishing, spreadsheet, database, and communications software.
- Microcomputers are used in thousands of ways at school and in homes. At school, students use them to write papers and conduct research. At home, they are used to figure taxes, play games, keep inventories, write letters, and keep track of finances.
- Businesses also use microcomputers in countless ways. The two most common applications are word processing and spreadsheets.
- E-mail is a growing application at home, in school, and in business.
- Presentation graphics are used to convey ideas. In all these ways and more, microcomputers are becoming a permanent part of our world.

KEY TERMS

application	input
application software	mainframe computers
computer	microcomputers
computing cycle	minicomputers
desktop publishing (DTP)	modem
E-mail	operating systems
general-purpose computers	output devices
hardware	processed

program
software
special-purpose computers

storage device
supercomputers

REVIEW QUESTIONS

1. Is a calculator a general-purpose or special-purpose computer? Why? Explain your reasoning.
2. How might you use a word processor, spreadsheet program, and database program in your classes?
3. Even if minicomputers and mainframe computers were inexpensive, why is it unlikely that a person would buy one for home use?
4. What is a scanner? a mouse? a modem? What functions does each serve?
5. If you wanted to create a professional-looking brochure to advertise your carpentry business, what kind of application software would you use?
6. How could you use database software to help write a term paper?
7. Describe the individual processes of the computing cycle.
8. What are the major types of application software?

SELF-QUIZ

1. Computers can remember information on a short, temporary basis by using
   a. magnetic tapes.
   b. magnetic disks.
   c. hard disks.
   d. memory circuits.
2. Early microcomputers (about 1975) were largely used by
   a. accounting firms.
   b. hobbyists.
   c. large industry.
   d. scientists.
3. Hardware consists of
   a. application programs.
   b. operating systems.
   c. virtual devices.
   d. physical devices.
4. Because their meanings are very similar, the terms software and _____PROGRAM_____ are often used interchangeably.
   a. hardware
   b. operating system
   c. input device
   d. program
5. The six most common types of application software are word processing, graphics, spreadsheet, database, desktop publishing, and _____ software.
   a. communications
   b. games
   c. utility
   d. drawing
6. The most common of the four classes of general purpose computers is the
   a. microcomputer.
   b. minicomputer.
   c. mainframe computer.
   d. supercomputer.
7. The two types of software necessary to make the computer capable of performing useful work are
   a. application software and utility software.
   b. utility software and operating system software.
   c. application software and operating system software.
   d. application software and word processing software.
8. The most common device used for input on the microcomputer is the _____KEYBOARD_____?
9. _____INPUT_____ is the process of entering data into a computer.

10. For a computer to perform useful tasks, it needs _APPLICATION_ software.
11. Computers that only perform specific functions are referred to as _SPECIAL PURPOSE_ computers.
12. A(n) _PROGRAM_ is a set of instructions designed to control a computer.

SIMULATIONS

Scenario 1:   What Do You Know?

So you think you know something about computers. Maybe. Maybe not. Answer the following questions as truthfully as possible. Do not look anything up. Do not ask a friend. If you do not know an answer then write "I don't know." Honesty is always the best policy.

1. Right now could you write a 10-page term paper on a word processor that contained headers and footers?
2. Describe one use of Internet?
3. What is a font, a style, and point size?
4. What is the difference between a formula and a function?
5. What is the difference between bit-mapped and object-oriented graphics?
6. Have you ever taken a computer class before? If so, what did you do and what did you learn?
7. What are two types of networks?
8. What is the difference between RAM and ROM?
9. What is Internet?
10. What are the three components that make up any computer system? Can you provide an example of each?
11. Name the most popular graphical user interface for MS-DOS–based computers.
12. In word processing, what is the rule of return?
13. What is multimedia?
14. What is the role and function of an operating system?
15. What is it that you want most out of this class?

Scenario 2:   Time to Explore

You have not decided on a major. This means one of two things. Either you can't decide on a major because you are interested in so many things or nothing is interesting to you. You thought about teaching, but this is a hard decision. Your friends think that those who can do, do and those that can't, teach. Your significant other wants you to become an accounting major because you will make more money. Your aunt likes the idea of your teaching because teachers impact the future, and she would like you around in the summers to paint her house. Your parents are just hoping you graduate from college and don't really care about your major.

Part of the fun of being undecided is that you can explore. This scenario gives you that opportunity. Your assignment is to begin the process of examining as much software as possible. If computer labs are available, look at a variety of software. As you explore, keep a list of all the software you examine on this sheet of paper. You may want to include some brief comments but they are not required.

Software Title   Publisher   Comments

HANDS-ON COMPUTING

1. How can computers make your life easier? In this chapter we examined how computers were used to help create this book. Think of the tasks that you do on a somewhat regular basis. Can computers make completing those tasks easier? Create a list of computing possibilities.

2. Of course computers are everywhere. They are at banks, in the grocery store, at the registrar's office. Keep a list of every place where you have had contact with a computer for one week. Don't limit yourself to just microcomputers but think about the special computing devices that affect your everyday life.

3. What do you like to do? Are you a train buff? Are you a bike rider? Do you play an instrument? Do you like baseball cards? Computers are most often useful for hobbies and interests. For example, if you are a baseball fan, there are computer programs that help you track, organize, and evaluate baseball cards. There are train programs that help you set up a model-train layout. What can you find? Take a trip to the local software store and see what type of software is available for your particular interest or hobby.

4. Computers are very much part of the popular media. In fact, many movies feature computers in a major role. Create a list of movies where computers play a central character. Here are a few to get you started—*2001: A Space Odyssey, The Lawn Mower Man, War Games.*

5. Become a futurist. Ten years ago, it was difficult to imagine the impact computers would have on us. Ten years from now, our uses of computers may be very much different. Write a brief statement of your vision of computer use 10 years from now.

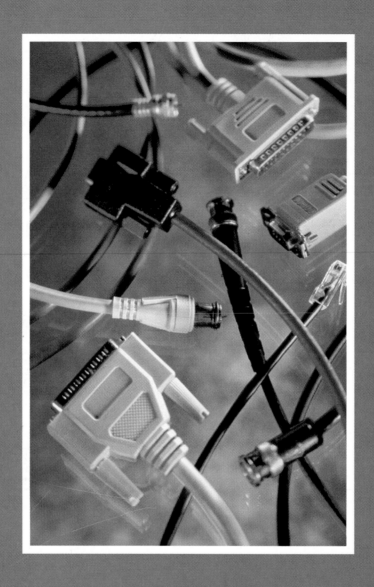

CHAPTER 2

Microcomputer Processors and Memory

FOCUS

Computer hardware is the physical part of a computer system—the devices that we can see and touch. The hardware for a typical microcomputer includes the microprocessor itself; the associated processing and memory circuits; storage devices, such as hard and floppy disk drives; and peripheral devices for input and output, such as a keyboard, a mouse, a monitor, and a printer.

Despite the many sophisticated tasks computers are capable of performing, they all use a simple set of electrical signals; all a computer has to know is whether a given circuit is on or off. Using only these two choices, a computer can manipulate information in a variety of ways to solve a problem or perform a task.

Microcomputers use many specialized hardware devices for completing the tasks of a computing cycle: input, processing, memory, and output. This chapter focuses on two critical elements of the computing cycle: processing and memory. However, processing and memory do not operate in isolation. Therefore, we will examine some of the basic elements of input/output and secondary memory. We will look at a number of devices to understand what they do and how they work together in the computing cycle. The discussion of input/output and secondary memory continues in Chapter 3.

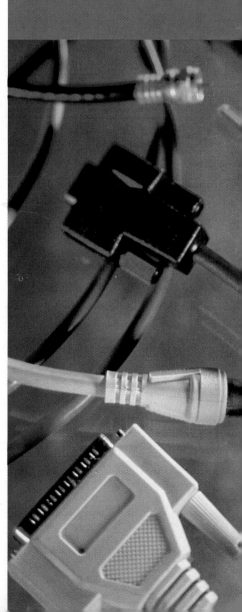

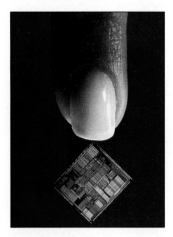

Figure 2-1
An integrated circuit chip has millions of tiny circuits photographically etched into silicon.

THE COMPUTING CYCLE: A CONCEPTUAL OVERVIEW

Computing is a process of integrating four key ingredients. It does not matter what type of computer you are using. It may be a microcomputer used in a home, in the office, or at school. It may be a computer used by the IRS to track tax records or a computer used at a university to register students and keep track of student records. Each of these computers uses the same four-step process—input, processing, memory, and output.

Input

To a human, data consist of a series of complex thoughts and ideas. To a computer, data are made up of a series of electrical signals. To convert data that a human can use into a form a computer can understand, each number, letter, or any other symbol must be converted into a specific combination of electrical signals. These electrical signals are presented to the computer in a binary format.

A signal in **binary format** instructs the computer that an electrical impulse is either on or off, connected or not connected, opened or closed. The binary system used by a computer uses only two values, zero and one, to represent all numbers, letters, or other symbols. This binary system is perfect for computers, which can understand only two states. The number zero represents an off signal and the number one represents an on signal. The number three in the binary system consists of two ones—11, that is, a series of two on electrical signals. Similarly, one on and one off electrical signal convert to a one followed by a zero. This binary number 10 is equal to the number 2 in the base-10 numbering system.

What about all the letters, punctuation marks, keystrokes, and so on? Computer code simply combines each of these into a unique combination of ones and zeros.

Each zero or one, the smallest piece of data used by the computer, is known as a **bit**—short for binary digit. Data from an input device enter the computer in groups of bits called a **byte.** For this reason, computer code generally assigns each letter, number, and symbol a unique combination of zeros and ones.

For example, the word HELLO, typed on the keyboard, enters the computer as five separate bytes—one for each letter. The following example uses an eight-bit series for each byte.

Byte	*Character*
01001000	H
01000101	E
01001100	L
01001100	L
01001111	O

CHANGING KEYS

When the typewriter was first invented in 1867, the letters on the keyboard were arranged to slow down the typist. Why? If typists went too quickly, the keys would jam, so letters that were usually next to each other in a word were placed far apart on the keyboard. However, when the electronic typewriter was introduced this was no longer a problem. This led to a new keyboard, called the Dvorak. It had the letters that normally followed each other next to one another. But the Dvorak keyboard did not catch on for the simple reason that generations of typists were accustomed to their QWERTY system (named for the first six letters on the typewriter keyboard). Now a new keyboard has been developed to help users avoid carpal tunnel syndrome. A common, debilitating malady for many people who use a keyboard over an extended period of time, carpal tunnel syndrome is caused by the continuous flexing of the wrist. To avoid this, the new keyboard splits the traditional keyboard into two sections, one for each hand. It also has an extended lip for the wrist to rest on. Will it replace the entrenched QWERTY keyboard? That depends on the users.

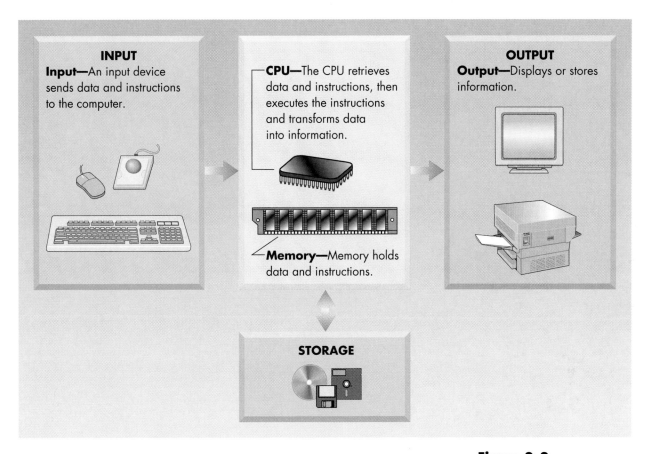

INPUT
Input—An input device sends data and instructions to the computer.

CPU—The CPU retrieves data and instructions, then executes the instructions and transforms data into information.

Memory—Memory holds data and instructions.

OUTPUT
Output—Displays or stores information.

STORAGE

Figure 2-2
The CPU controls the flow of data from input devices to output devices and storage.

Several binary codes exist; however, the most common code, which all popular U.S. microcomputers can use, is the American Standard Code for Information Interchange (**ASCII**). Table 2–1 shows the ASCII code, which includes letters, punctuation marks, other keystrokes, and control codes.

The **computing cycle** begins with input from any one of a series of devices. Input devices include a keyboard, a mouse, light pens, touch screens, scanners, and modems. While input devices differ, the function is the same—to send data into the computer for processing in binary form.

Processing

After data are converted into a binary form, they are available for processing. The central processing unit (**CPU**) performs this activity in conjunction with memory and storage (Figure 2–2). The CPU, the "brains" of the computer system, consists of a control unit and an arithmetic/logic unit (**ALU**).

- The control unit manages the computer system, acting like a traffic cop directing the flow of data throughout the system.
- The ALU performs all mathematical and logical functions.

One of the fundamental components linked to the CPU is memory. Just as a human requires memory to perform meaningful tasks, so does a computer. Memory is the area of the computer that stores data for processing. It comes in two forms, random access memory (**RAM**) and read only memory (**ROM**). RAM

Decimal	Character	Decimal	Character	Decimal	Character	Decimal	Character
0	NUL	16	DLE	32	(SP)	48	0
1	SOU	17	DC1	33	!	49	1
2	STX	18	DC2	34	"	50	2
3	ETX	19	DC3	35	#	51	3
4	EST	20	DC4	36	$	52	4
5	ENQ	21	NAK	37	%	53	5
6	ACK	22	SYN	38	&	54	6
7	(BEL)	23	ETB	39	'	55	7
8	(BS)	24	CAN	40	(	56	8
9	(HT)	25	EM	41	)	57	9
10	(LF)	26	SUB	42	·	58	:
11	VT	27	(ESC)	43	+	59	;
12	(FF)	28	FS	44	,	60	<
13	(CR)	29	GS	45	·	61	=
14	SO	30	RS	46	.	62	>
15	SI	31	US	47	/	63	?

Table 2-1
ASCII Codes

(discussed later in more detail) temporarily stores the data needed for the current processing task. When power to the computer is turned off, data in RAM vanish. We call RAM user memory. It is the memory where your term paper resides when you write it with word processing software. ROM (also discussed later in more detail) is permanent memory that provides the basic set of instructions for starting the computer. It contains the instructions that give meaning to keys on a keyboard, basic sounds, and access to storage devices.

Output

The result of processing is called **output.** Just as there are several input devices to convert human data into a form usable by the computer, there are also several output devices that convert computer information into a form usable by humans. Figure 2–3 on page 24 shows some of the more popular types of output devices: monitors, printers, plotters, speakers, and modems.

Storage

Because RAM is volatile (it is erased whenever you turn off the computer), you must store the contents of RAM in a more permanent form. This is the function of **storage** (sometimes called secondary memory). Typically, storage works in close conjunction with RAM. For example, you may type a 30-page term

Decimal	Character	Decimal	Character	Decimal	Character	Decimal	Character
64	@	80	P	96	'	112	p
65	A	81	Q	97	a	113	q
66	B	82	R	98	b	114	r
67	C	83	S	99	c	115	s
68	D	84	T	100	d	116	t
69	E	85	U	101	e	117	u
70	F	86	V	102	f	118	v
71	G	87	W	103	g	119	w
72	H	88	X	104	h	120	x
73	I	89	Y	105	i	121	y
74	J	90	Z	106	j	122	z
75	K	91	[	107	k	123	{
76	L	92	\	108	l	124		
77	M	93	]	109	m	125	}
78	N	94	^	110	n	126	.
79	O	95	-	111	o	127	

paper into RAM, but unless you store it somewhere (typically a disk), you will lose your work. Therefore, saving the contents of RAM to a disk is a vital part of the computing cycle (Figure 2–4 on page 25).

How the Computing Cycle Works

The computing cycle consisting of input, processing, output, and storage involves several steps in the flow of data. Data typically flow through the system in the following manner.

1. The control unit of the CPU directs the transfer of data from an input device to memory or storage. For example, the text that appears on the screen as you type goes into random access memory.

2. Data in storage remain in storage until needed for the next processing task. Then the control unit transfers data from storage to memory. When you select a spreadsheet program and a budget report, for example, they are loaded from storage to memory.

3. The control unit sends the required data from memory to the arithmetic/ logic unit. For example, the formula and data you need to calculate the return on an investment are placed in the ALU.

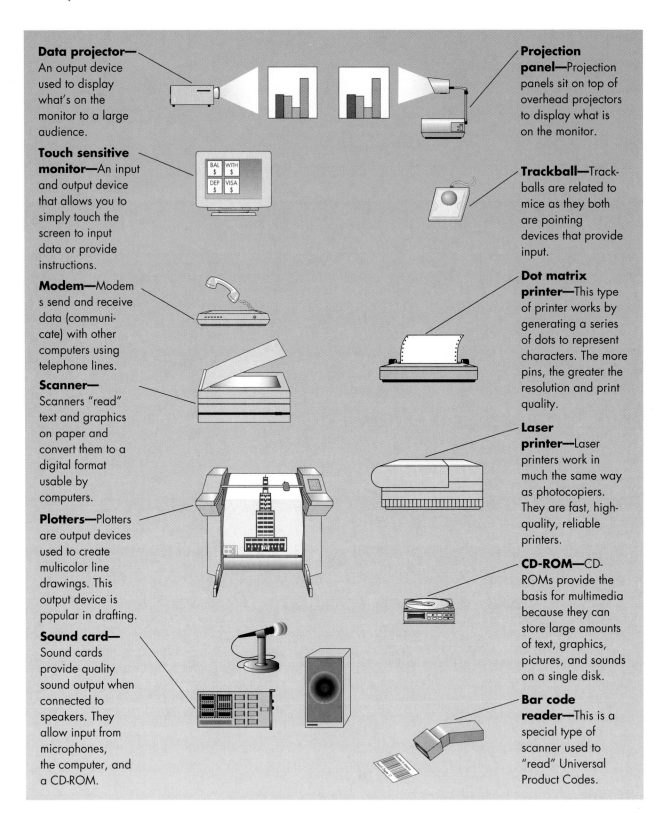

Data projector— An output device used to display what's on the monitor to a large audience.

Touch sensitive monitor— An input and output device that allows you to simply touch the screen to input data or provide instructions.

Modem— Modems send and receive data (communicate) with other computers using telephone lines.

Scanner— Scanners "read" text and graphics on paper and convert them to a digital format usable by computers.

Plotters— Plotters are output devices used to create multicolor line drawings. This output device is popular in drafting.

Sound card— Sound cards provide quality sound output when connected to speakers. They allow input from microphones, the computer, and a CD-ROM.

Projection panel— Projection panels sit on top of overhead projectors to display what is on the monitor.

Trackball— Trackballs are related to mice as they both are pointing devices that provide input.

Dot matrix printer— This type of printer works by generating a series of dots to represent characters. The more pins, the greater the resolution and print quality.

Laser printer— Laser printers work in much the same way as photocopiers. They are fast, high-quality, reliable printers.

CD-ROM— CD-ROMs provide the basis for multimedia because they can store large amounts of text, graphics, pictures, and sounds on a single disk.

Bar code reader— This is a special type of scanner used to "read" Universal Product Codes.

Figure 2-3
Popular peripherals.

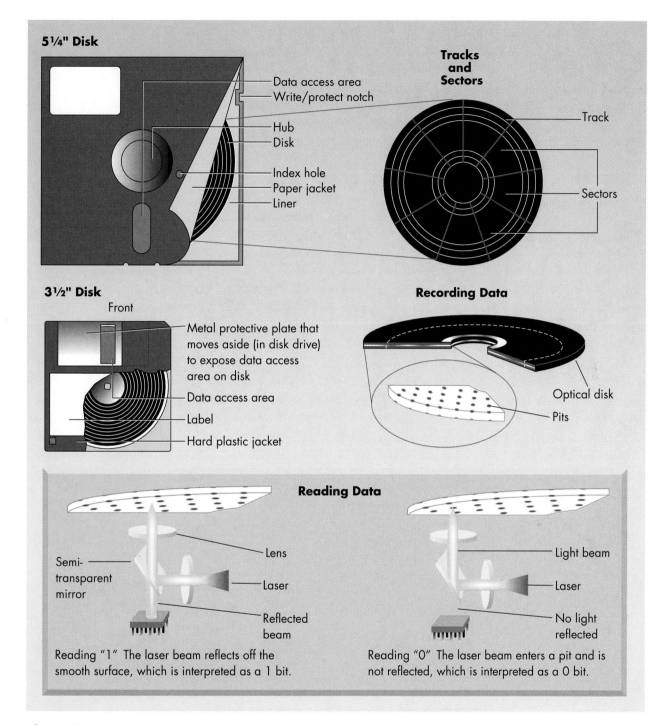

5¼" Disk

Data access area
Write/protect notch
Hub
Disk
Index hole
Paper jacket
Liner

Tracks and Sectors

Track
Sectors

3½" Disk

Front

Metal protective plate that moves aside (in disk drive) to expose data access area on disk
Data access area
Label
Hard plastic jacket

Recording Data

Optical disk
Pits

Reading Data

Lens
Laser
Reflected beam

Semi-transparent mirror

Reading "1" The laser beam reflects off the smooth surface, which is interpreted as a 1 bit.

Light beam
Laser
No light reflected

Reading "0" The laser beam enters a pit and is not reflected, which is interpreted as a 0 bit.

Figure 2-4
Storage devices can be both magnetic (disk drives) and optical (CD-ROM and Interactive Video Disk). Magnetic devices are relatively small and erasable. Optical storage is rather large but permanent.

Figure 2-5

Interactions among computer hardware: the CPU's control unit orchestrates the computing process, accepting data from input devices, giving instructions to the arithmetic/ logic unit, storing data temporarily in memory and permanently on storage devices, and sending data to output devices.

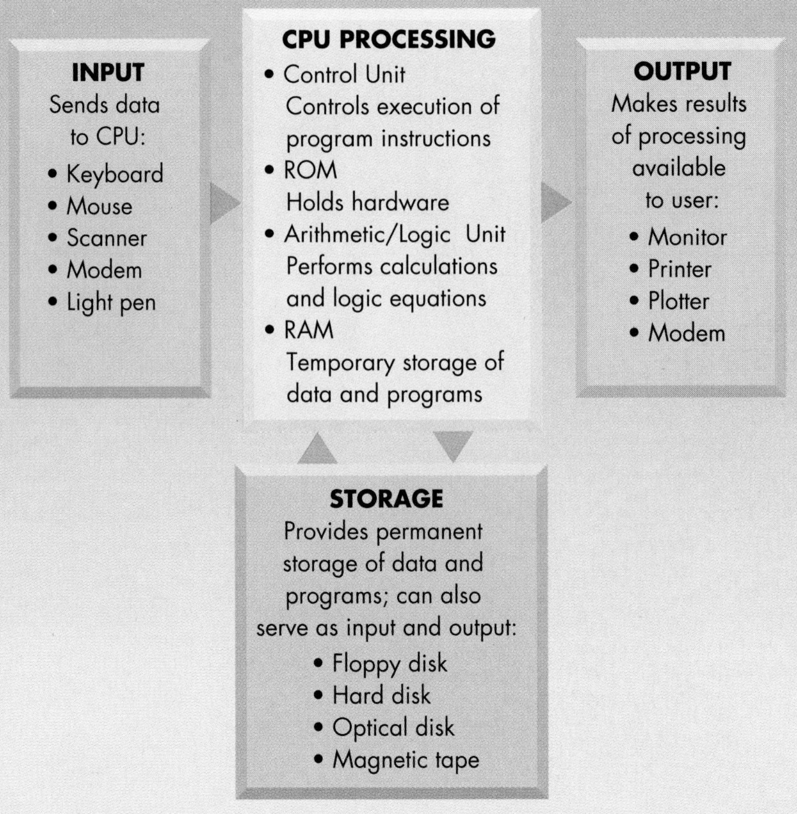

INPUT
Sends data
to CPU:
- Keyboard
- Mouse
- Scanner
- Modem
- Light pen

CPU PROCESSING
- Control Unit
  Controls execution of
  program instructions
- ROM
  Holds hardware
- Arithmetic/Logic Unit
  Performs calculations
  and logic equations
- RAM
  Temporary storage of
  data and programs

OUTPUT
Makes results
of processing
available
to user:
- Monitor
- Printer
- Plotter
- Modem

STORAGE
Provides permanent
storage of data and
programs; can also
serve as input and output:
- Floppy disk
- Hard disk
- Optical disk
- Magnetic tape

4.   The ALU makes the necessary mathematical and logical computations as you enter data and formulas.

5.   When all calculations are completed, the control unit sends the results to memory (RAM).

6.   The control unit sends the output from memory (RAM) to a monitor and/or printer.

7.   The control unit can also send all or part of the contents of memory (RAM) to storage (disk) for future use. The control unit can also erase data from memory when instructed to do so or when power to the computer is turned off.

MICROCOMPUTER PROCESSORS

The system unit, sometimes called the "box" or the processing unit, houses processing devices, various electronic circuits, and other components (Figure 2–6).

Chips, Printed Circuit Boards, and Slots

Many of the operating parts of a computer, such as the CPU and memory, consist of tiny silicon chips, also called semiconductors or integrated circuits (IC). Chips are enclosed by a carrier package called a **DIP** (dual inline package). Users commonly do not distinguish between DIPs and chips; generally, the entire enclosed package is referred to as a chip.

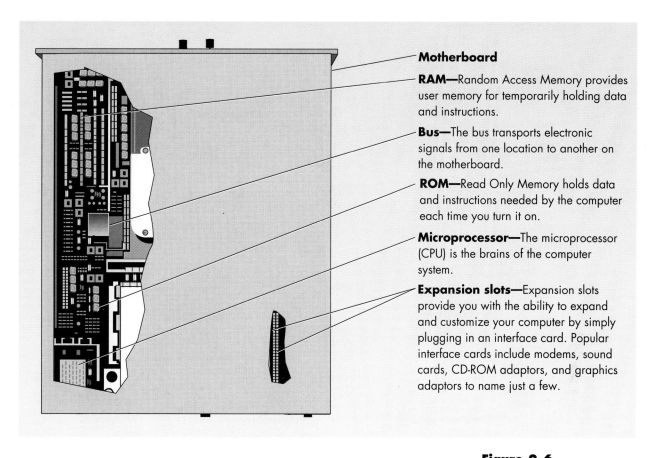

Motherboard

RAM—Random Access Memory provides user memory for temporarily holding data and instructions.

Bus—The bus transports electronic signals from one location to another on the motherboard.

ROM—Read Only Memory holds data and instructions needed by the computer each time you turn it on.

Microprocessor—The microprocessor (CPU) is the brains of the computer system.

Expansion slots—Expansion slots provide you with the ability to expand and customize your computer by simply plugging in an interface card. Popular interface cards include modems, sound cards, CD-ROM adaptors, and graphics adaptors to name just a few.

Figure 2-6
Inside the processing unit.

Each enclosed chip plugs into a socket on a printed circuit board (PC board, sometimes called a card). A series of metallic lines are embedded on each board that act like wires; these provide the hard-wired (directly connected) connections between different circuit elements (Figure 2–7).

The printed circuit board containing the CPU is called the system board or motherboard. A motherboard on a microcomputer can have a number of slots built into the board. These slots are called **expansion slots.** Each of these expansion slots can hold an additional **printed circuit board.** The additional printed circuit boards are called expansion boards, plug-in boards, or cards and can hold several different types of chips. When computer manufacturers allow users to open the box and add components, it is called **open architecture.** Computers with an open architecture allow users to add their own expansion boards and add new chips with different functions.

The Central Processing Unit

As stated earlier, microcomputers use a CPU for controlling the process within a computer system. The CPU has three components—one for controlling the computer, called the control unit; one for performing arithmetic and logical operations, called the arithmetic logic unit; and one for storing data immediately prior to and following an operation, called registers.

The control unit manages the computer system using a four-step process: fetching, decoding, executing, and storing. Before the ALU can perform an arithmetic or logical operation, it must first have an instruction. **Fetching** is the process of retrieving an instruction from memory. It places the instruction in a special type of memory internal to the CPU called a register. After an instruction

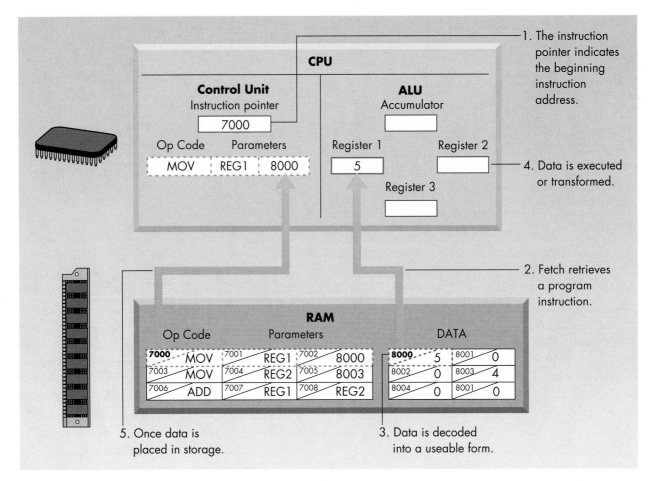

Figure 2-7
The instruction cycle.

is retrieved and placed in a register, it must be translated into a format the ALU can use. This process is known as **decoding. Executing** is the actual process used by the ALU to execute the command. Finally, when the ALU completes the execution of a command, the control unit uses storage to move data from the ALU back to memory. The control unit repeats this process for every operation in the computing cycle.

The Fetch, Decode, Execute, and Storage Process
1. Fetch an instruction from memory and store it in a register.
2. Decode the instruction into a form usable by the ALU.
3. Send a command to the ALU to execute the decoded instruction.
4. Send the results of the executed instruction to a register.
5. Move the results to memory.
6. Repeat the process for the next instruction.

The ALU does all the work in a binary representation (zeros and ones). This is the reason that decoding is an important function with the control unit. The ALU is capable of changing a zero to a one and a one to a zero. It is actually a simple process in which the ALU performs one task at a time, but at a very high speed.

Registers are high-speed storage areas directly linked to the ALU and managed by the control unit. In many cases, there are several different types of registers. For example, some storage registers temporarily hold data prior to it being executed by the ALU. Address registers hold only the address locations of the data the ALU needs to perform an operation. An accumulator register holds data processed by the ALU. Instruction registers hold instructions for the control unit. Finally, there are program-counter registers that hold the address of the next executable instruction. Each register exists to guide the flow of data and instructions to and from the ALU.

Microprocessor Chips

The fundamental difference between a microcomputer and a mainframe computer is that a microcomputer's CPU (ALU, control unit, and registers) is contained on one chip. This chip is called a microprocessor. Various manufacturers produce microprocessors with differing capabilities and capacities. A microprocessor's capacity is based on the number of bits it can process at one time and the speed with which it performs operations.

The number of bits a CPU can process at one time is known as a computer word. The number of bits held by registers and processed together make up the computer word. For example, a microprocessor which uses a 4-bit word has registers that allow 4 bits to be processed together by the ALU. A 64-bit microprocessor contains registers that allow 64 bits to be processed by the ALU.

Computer words are important because they affect the speed and performance of the computer system. If everything else is the same between two CPUs, a 32-bit CPU will process twice as much data as a 16-bit CPU in the same amount of time. In theory, a 64-bit CPU is twice as fast as a 32-bit CPU, which is twice as fast as a 16-bit CPU, which is twice as fast as an 8-bit CPU.

R ESPONDING TO THE MASTER'S VOICE

Computer technology has often improved the quality of life for those who are disabled, but simply using the computer can sometimes be a problem. The introduction of the graphical user interface put blind people at a distinct disadvantage; how to operate a computer that graphically displayed options? One solution is to use a voice synthesizer to describe icons. And rather than a mouse, keyboard commands can direct the computer.

However, this approach will not work for everybody. Consider Dennis Muchen, a counselor who is blind, wheelchair-bound, and missing some fingers. He first used a computer with a speech output that read back his work to him, but the state of his hands made his work slow and difficult. He now uses a desktop microphone to verbally command his computer to dictate letters and reports. The computer reads them back so he can verbally edit and format them.

Types of Intel Microprocessors

Processor	Date	Word*	Instructions Per Second
4004	1971	4-bit	60,000
8080	1974	8-bit	290,000
8086	1974	16-bit	333,000
8088	1978	8/16-bit	333,000
80286	1982	16-bit	2,000,000
80386	1985	32-bit	7,000,000
80486	1989	32-bit	15,000,000
Pentium	1992	64-bit	100,000,000+
Pentium Pro	1995	128-bit	200,000,000+

* Word is based on other factors in addition to CPU word capabilities.

System Bus

As data move through the computer system, they travel along paths on the PC boards in a prescribed format. The electrical pathway used to transport data from one location to another is called a **bus** (also called a **system bus** or bus line) (Figure 2–8). The bus consists of a series of parallel wires on the motherboard that connect the CPU with memory, other control chips, and expansion

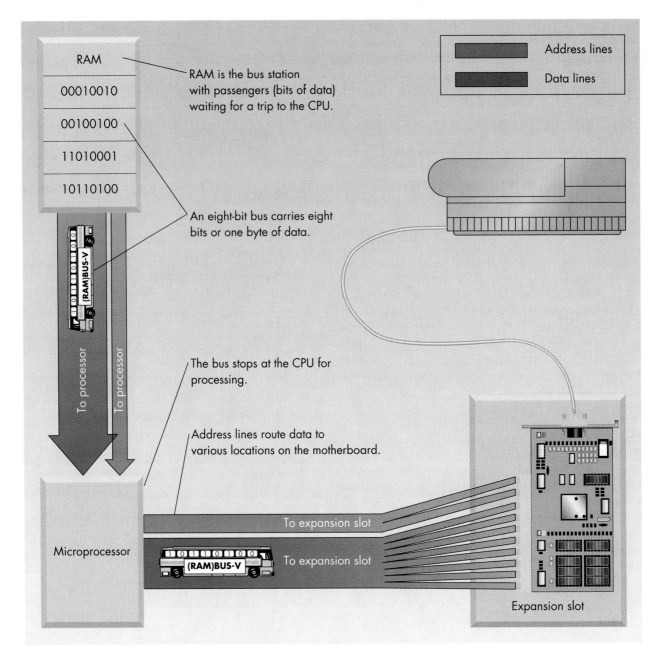

RAM is the bus station with passengers (bits of data) waiting for a trip to the CPU.

An eight-bit bus carries eight bits or one byte of data.

The bus stops at the CPU for processing.

Address lines route data to various locations on the motherboard.

Figure 2-8
The system bus.

boards. The first 8-bit microprocessors used a bus with eight wires (an 8-bit bus). Most 16-bit microprocessors used a 16-bit bus and so on. Each microcomputer also has a **system clock.** The system clock sends a continuous rhythmic series of electrical pulses, much like a metronome, that other circuits use to stay in synchronization with each other. The speed of the clock's pulses sets the operation speed of the computer: the faster the clock pulses, the faster the computer can process data. Clock speed is measured in megahertz (HMz; 1 MHz equals one million cycles per second). Early microcomputers, such as the Apple and Apple II, used a clock that ran at 1 MHz. Today's microcomputers operate at speeds exceeding 150 MHz.

These two factors, the width of the bus and the speed of the clock, help to determine the power of a computer. Think of the bus as a highway. The number of bits a bus can carry at one time can be thought of as the number of highway lanes. Clock speed can be thought of as the speed limit. With a higher speed limit, the bits can travel faster; with more lanes, more bits can travel simultaneously. The processing power of a computer is largely the product of clock speed and the number of bits processed simultaneously. However, the question, How fast is the computer? is still difficult to answer. Speed is a somewhat elusive term when you are dealing with computers. It is influenced by the microprocessor, the clock speed, the bus, the amount of time needed for information to flow from a disk drive to RAM, the amount of time it takes to move data from RAM through the CPU, and even the amount of time required to display information on a monitor. Leading trade journals often provide comparison tests of computer speed in processing text and numeric data, manipulating databases, displaying graphics, and transmitting data to and from peripheral devices. These tests give consumers and business users important performance information.

PRIMARY MEMORY

The CPU represents only part of the computing process. The other part involves the use of primary memory. Primary memory provides a location for data and instructions accessed by the control unit of the CPU. Before you can have a computer perform any meaningful task, both data and instructions must be situated in primary memory. In other words, primary memory provides the location where you place instructions (computer programs) that are acted on by the CPU. Depending on the type of instruction, there are two types of primary memory—ROM (read only memory) and RAM (random access memory).

Read Only Memory

As its name implies, read only memory (ROM) is a type of memory where the computer can read the contents of memory but cannot change its contents. You cannot alter the contents of ROM. ROM chips store built-in permanent instructions called firmware that control most, if not all, computer operations.

Firmware in ROM provides the instructions that tell the CPU what to do when the computer system is turned on. The most common firmware is called **BIOS,** or basic input/output system. When a computer is booted up (turned on), the BIOS performs the functions of testing memory; establishing connections to disk drives, keyboard, monitor, and other devices; and loading the operating system.

Another set of firmware in ROM is the **character generator.** This set of instructions links keys on the keyboard with characters that appear on a monitor. It is the character generator that enables an *A* pressed

*I*T LOOKS KINDA FAMILIAR...

Imagine the Mona Lisa, the da Vinci painting with the tantalizing smile, with someone else's face. Imagine the image suddenly deconstructing electronically. By using an electronic scanner, artists can now incorporate images created by the great masters into their computers and then manipulate those images any way they wish—changing the color, twisting the viewpoint. Artist Lillian Schwartz sometimes incorporates her own face into the picture, or she layers one image on top of another, resulting in a picture that is both familiar and strange. Some of her images are painted directly onto the computer by using a pressure-sensitive screen and stylus. These images are often superimposed on top of scanned images, as when she merges her face with the faces of famous women, such as Nefertiti or Amelia Earhart. Would this computer art make the Mona Lisa smile?

Thanks to CD-ROM and interactive video storage disks, huge amounts of information, especially visual information—photos, TV, and film, for instance—can now be stored on personal computers. A computerized book or catalog can now be more realistic, to say nothing of user-friendly. Taking advantage of this technology, Kodak has joined forces with L.L. Bean to scan its catalog onto disks that can be mailed to customers. By typing the words "red" and "dress" a customer can view all the red dresses in the catalog. Encyclopedias on CD-ROM can include short animation segments to illustrate the functioning of a heart valve or the formulation of cumulus clouds, for instance. History texts can include newsreel footage of historical events, bringing a sense of immediacy to students.

on the keyboard to appear as an *A* on the monitor. This firmware is vital because the use of characters is faster than graphic displays. With graphic displays, each character must be rendered each time it is needed.

The major drawback of ROM, and firmware, is its lack of flexibility. Every time you want to change or update the firmware, you must physically replace a ROM chip. Therefore, ROM is used primarily in specialized computers where instructions must be stored permanently; for example, in automobile computers that store instructions to control gasoline and air flow to the engine. While present in all personal computers, the use of ROM is much more widespread in specialized computers.

Random Access Memory

When people use the term *memory,* most of the time they are referring to RAM (random access memory). As stated earlier, RAM is temporary memory where the computer holds data for the current processing task. The computer can read data from and write data to RAM, or user memory. When you load a word processing program into memory, it resides in RAM. When you type a term paper using the word processor, your term paper resides in RAM. When power to the computer is turned off, all data in RAM are erased. If you turn off the computer without saving your term paper to a more permanent storage device, your term paper disappears forever. For this reason, RAM is often known as volatile memory.

RAM is measured in kilobytes (K), megabytes (Mb), and gigabytes (G):

1 kilobyte (K)   = 2^{10} bytes (approximately 1,000 [actually 1,024] bytes)
1 megabyte (Mb)= 2^{20} bytes (approximately 1,000,000 bytes)
1 gigabyte (G)   = 2^{30} bytes (approximately 1,000,000,000 bytes)

There are two general types of RAM: dynamic and static. Dynamic RAM (**DRAM**) is made up of a series of capacitors, or transistor switches (Figure 2–9). When a switch is energized, it represents a one (an on switch in a binary number system). A nonenergized switch represents a zero (the other bit state). By using these switches it is possible for RAM to store data. DRAM requires the capacitors to be energized on a nearly continuous basis to maintain data. **Static RAM** uses electronic switches that do not need the near-constant electrical charge to maintain data. Static RAM is faster and requires less power, but it is more complex and expensive to develop.

Figure 2-9

RAM uses a series of bits to represent each byte or character.

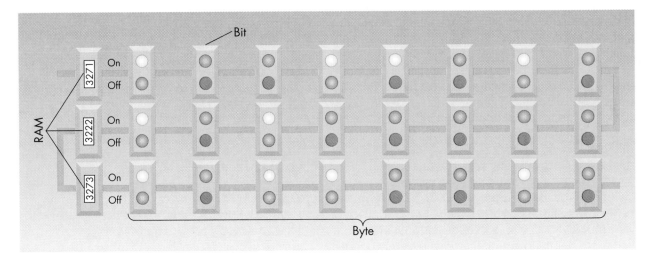

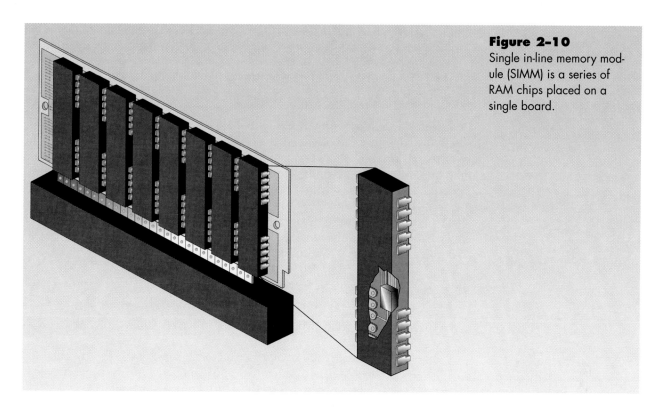

Figure 2-10
Single in-line memory module (SIMM) is a series of RAM chips placed on a single board.

In addition to the speed at which a CPU operates (both clock speed and number of bits), the size and type of RAM determine the speed and power of a microcomputer. In general, the more RAM, the greater the capability of the computer system. The larger the memory, the greater the computer's ability to perform complex tasks. For example, some software requires as little as 256K of RAM while other software can require in excess of 8Mb or 16Mb. If you have a computer with 16Mb of memory, you can run more sophisticated programs than a computer with 256K, 512K, 640K, or even 4Mb of memory.

Just as microprocessors have evolved, so too have the use and types of RAM. Various computer systems use RAM differently. For example, an Apple Macintosh only distinguishes one type of RAM. While there are upper limits on the total amount of RAM possible in Macintosh computers (it differs from model to model), there is no differentiation between the types of RAM, as has been the case with DOS-based (IBM and so-called IBM-compatible) computers.

The first IBM personal computers were limited to 640K of memory called **conventional memory.** Instead of removing this limit when software outgrew conventional RAM requirements, two new types of memory were created: expanded memory and extended memory.

- **Expanded memory** commonly provides for six or more additional megabytes of RAM. There is a very precise set of rules for software using more than 640K of conventional RAM. Several versions of expanded memory are available. Software developers have been left to decide which version to support. As a result, not all software supports expanded memory, and it is quickly becoming a thing of the past.
- **Extended memory** provides up to 32 megabytes of additional RAM without the conflicts associated with expanded memory. Extended memory has, in large part, replaced expanded memory because of the availability of a standardized version and more advanced techniques for providing

additional memory. However, even this very popular type of memory is being replaced with a single type of RAM source, as is the case with Macintosh computers.

Additional Types of Memory

Programmable read only memory (**PROM**) is a specialized type of ROM that allows manufacturers to use specialized equipment to store firmware. This type of memory provides computer manufacturers with much more flexibility since they do not have to store firmware in a PROM during production of the chip. An even more flexible version of PROM is erasable programmable read only memory (**EPROM**). With EPROMs it is possible to erase the firmware and then load a new set of firmware. A special ultraviolet light device can destroy or erase any existing information on EPROMs. Once existing data are removed, special devices can load new firmware onto the EPROMs.

SUMMARY

- The computing cycle involves a four-step process—input, processing, memory, and output.
- Input devices range from keyboards and touch-sensitive screens to mice and light pens; they translate data into a series of on and off electrical signals.
- Processing data is controlled by the central processing unit.
- The CPU consists of a control unit that directs the transfer of data and an arithmetic/logic unit (ALU) that performs mathematical and logical calculations.
- The control unit manages the computer system using a four-step process: fetching, decoding, executing, and storing.
- Fetching is a process of retrieving an instruction from memory. Decoding is a process for translating data into a form the ALU can use. Executing is the actual process used by the ALU to execute the command. Storage sends processed information back to memory.
- The control unit repeats this four-step process for every operation in the computing cycle.
- The board that contains the CPU is known as the system board (or motherboard); it provides several expansion slots that allow users to add memory and expansion boards for additional input and output devices (peripheral devices), such as monitors, modems, and scanners.
- The electrical pathway for transporting data from one location to another is called a bus (also called a system bus or bus line).
- A bus consists of parallel wires on the motherboard that connect the CPU with memory, other control chips, and expansion boards.
- The width of the bus and the speed of the clock help to determine the speed and power of a computer.
- Primary memory provides a location for data and instructions accessed by the control unit of the CPU.
- There are two types of primary memory—ROM (read only memory) and RAM (random access memory).

KEY TERMS

ALU	BIOS	byte
ASCII	bit	character generator
binary format	bus	computing cycle

conventional memory	expanded memory	PROM
CPU	expansion slots	RAM
decoding	extended memory	ROM
DIP	fetching	static RAM
DRAM	open architecture	storage
EPROM	ouput	system bus
executing	printed circuit board	system clock

REVIEW QUESTIONS

1. What is the meaning of the term CPU?
2. What is the distinction between RAM and ROM?
3. What are the processes that make up the computing cycle?
4. What is a bit and a byte and how are they related?
5. What is a system bus and what role does it play in moving data?
6. What is the difference between PROM and EPROM?
7. What is the ALU and what does it do?
8. What are the two types of primary memory?
9. What is the purpose of the clock speed of a computer?
10. How do the number of bits that can be processed at one time affect computer speed?

SELF-QUIZ

1. Computer hardware is usually considered to be
   - a. instructions.
   - b. physical devices.
   - c. the computing cycle.
   - d. none of the above.
2. To the computer, data is made up of a series of
   - a. letters.
   - b. numbers.
   - c. symbols.
   - d. electrical signals.
3. The smallest piece of data used by the computer is known as a
   - a. byte.
   - b. bit.
   - c. binary digit.
   - d. both b and c.
4. The _____ controls the computer system in conjunction with memory and storage.
   - a. input device
   - b. output device
   - c. central processing unit
   - d. arithmetic logic unit
5. What is the printed circuit board containing the CPU called?
   - a. expansion slot.
   - b. motherboard.
   - c. single inline memory module.
   - d. primary memory.
6. The electrical pathway for transporting data from one location to another is called a
   - a. data path.
   - b. data flow.
   - c. data line.
   - d. bus.
7. What instructions tell the CPU what to do when the computer system is turned on?
   - a. disk memory
   - b. applications
   - c. firmware
   - d. control unit memory
8. What does the term BIOS stand for?
   - a. binary input/output system
   - b. basic independent operating system
   - c. binary independent operating system
   - d. basic input/output system

9. The first IBM personal computers were limited to _____ of conventional memory.
   a. 640K c. 640 Mb
   b. 1 Mb d. 1.35 Gb
10. What is the result of processed data?
    a. input c. CPU
    b. output d. CIT
11. Computers all operate using a simple set of _ELECT_ signals.
12. Computers use the same four-step process: _____, _____, _____, and _____.
13. The CPU is made up of _CONTROL UNIT_, _ALU_, and _REGISTERS_.
14. The _WIDTH_ of the bus and the _SPEED_ of the clock help to determine the power of a computer.
15. There are two types of primary memory: _ROM_ and _RAM_.
16. The most common firmware is called _BIOS_.
17. RAM is measured in _KILOBYTES_ (K), _MEGABYTES_ (Mb), and _GIGABYTES_ (Gb).
18. The most popular code is called _____.
19. _____ chips store built-in permanent instructions called firmware.
20. When you load a word processing program into memory it resides in _____.

SIMULATIONS

Scenario 1: The New Employee

It is your departmental meeting as the new chief shipping clerk. As with all meetings in the shipping department this one is held in the lounge among the old ditto machines, coffee machines, day-old doughnuts, and well-read *People* magazines. You are a bit nervous as your new boss welcomes you to the staff and introduces you to the rest of the shipping team. Your boss points out that you are the answer to all of the company's computer problems. With a nervous smile you thank the boss for those kind words.

Next to you is the shop foreman and former frustrated high school football coach. You know—the one who is wearing black, tight, polyester shorts, rubberized whistle, and a faded XXXL polo shirt. She leans over and says, "Could you tell me what RAM is? I keep running out of it when I use my computer." Your dilemma is that you are now the expert. To pass yourself off you need to know the language. Your assignment is to define the following terms so that everyone in the shipping department can understand them.

1. RAM   2. ROM
3. ALU   4. input
5. output   6. CPU
7. primary memory   8. control unit
9. peripheral   10. register
11. Kb   12. Mb
13. gigabyte   14. DRAM
15. EPROM   16. DIP
17. microprocessor   18. bus
19. conventional memory 20. open architecture

Late last night you were awakened by a strange sound coming from just outside your window. At first, you thought it was the coed dorm, but just as you peeked out the window, a bright light stunned you. It knocked you back. Dazed and confused, you heard a strange voice:

> We are from the planet Smartzoid. Our mission is to evaluate recent technological advances among creatures low on the evolutionary scale. Don't be afraid. We will not perform our customary mind-removal experiment. Such small minds are of little value to us. Instead we need to know how your simple computers operate. On our planet we have evolved past the written word. Instead we communicate through mind videos. Unfortunately, you are not yet capable of this form of technology, and we cannot read your hieroglyphics. You must communicate with us through pictures. Your task, should you seek to avoid mind removal, is to draw a detailed diagram depicting how your microcomputers operate. No written words allowed! We will be back in one day to retrieve your work.

At first you think this is a strange joke played by your eccentric roommate. But the idea of mind removal sounds too much like your organic chemistry class, so you decide to proceed. Your task is to depict a typical computer system without using any text. You must use simple drawings, arrows, lines, or any other visual representation to fully describe a computer system. Remember, if you don't do a good job, you could have your mind removed, leaving you with only one career choice—becoming a politician.

HANDS-ON COMPUTING

1. There is nothing magical or mystical about computers. If you are a bit timid, one of the best ways to learn to understand the machine is to crawl inside. If you have a computer or if you have a friend who has a computer or if computers are available in a computer lab, get permission to open one up. Look inside. Locate each of the major components discussed within this chapter. The only caution is don't touch. You may conduct static electricity that could damage some components.
2. Computer advertisements can be confusing. There are so many different computers with so many different configurations. Your task is to interpret a computer advertisement. Obtain a copy of a computer advertisement from any of the popular computing magazines. Write a brief description of each of the major components discussed in the ad.
3. What is the state of the art? One of the problems with writing a book on and about computers is that the technology changes so fast. It often seems that new computers, new configurations, new microprocessors, and new peripherals appear every week. Your task is to simply answer the question: What is the state of the art? On a sheet of paper, list the most advanced microprocessor currently available for one or more families of computers. What are the latest trends in storage? What is the latest bus size?
4. *The Soul of a New Machine* (T. Kidder; Little, Brown, 1981) provides an insightful overview of the history of the development of microcomputers. This book provides a fascinating look back at Silicon Valley, hackers, and the personalities involved in developing the early microcomputer revolution. It is well worth reading.

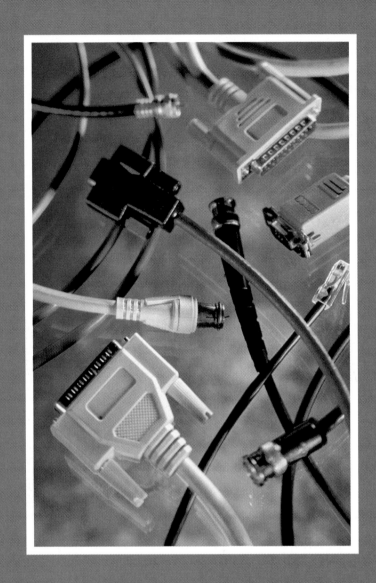

CHAPTER 3

Input/Output and Secondary Memory

OBJECTIVES

After completing this chapter, you will be able to:

- Identify the role of input devices.

- Explain the concept of digitizing.

- Distinguish between analog and digital data.

- Identify common input devices.

- Identify common output devices.

- Identify common graphic adapters.

- Identify major types of microcomputer storage devices.

- Distinguish between magnetic and optical storage.

- Describe the role and function of ports and expansion slots.

- Identify major types of ports and expansion slots.

FOCUS

In the previous chapter you were introduced to the hardware, or the physical devices, that regulate the four basic processes of the computing cycle: input, processing, storage, and output. Processing and memory are often referred to as the brain of a computer system. However, the brain is of little value unless you can provide data to the computer and the computer can present you with processed information.

Input devices refer to devices that supply data or instructions to the CPU. Computers use a different language (binary) than we do to interpret data. One of the major functions of input devices is to translate the data we enter into the computer. The words we type on a keyboard must be translated into a binary code before the computer can process them.

After a computer has processed data and turned it into the format (binary) that it can understand, the information must be displayed, presented, or stored in a form that we can understand. **Output devices** such as monitors, printers, plotters, and disk drives perform these functions.

The role of storage is to provide a more permanent method for maintaining data and information. The most common microcomputer storage devices are the hard disk and the floppy disk. However, there are many other types of storage devices, including CD-ROMs.

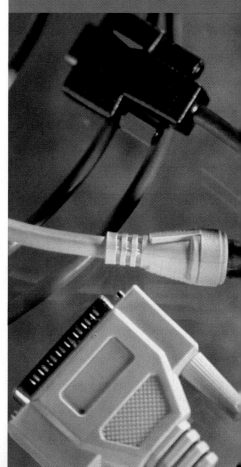

DATA IN: THE ROLE OF INPUT

Taking a picture with a camera, developing it with chemicals, and printing it on paper can produce a very detailed image. While we can look at a picture and appreciate its beauty, a computer cannot. Data in a photograph are not directly compatible with a computer. If you watch the hands of an old grandfather clock move, one second appears to flow into the next. While we can watch and process the meaning of the continuous movement of the hands of the clock, a computer cannot understand the process. Computers cannot deal with a continuous flow of data. If you write a note by hand, you can read it, but a computer cannot because handwriting is also not directly compatible with a computer. In fact, most of the world around us is not directly compatible with computers.

Computers are electronic devices that can only process digitized data; that is, data presented in the form of bits. The world that we see and interact with does not require its data to be so precise. If you want a computer to work with a photograph, the passage of time, or handwriting, the data must be converted to a digital pattern. This is the role of input devices—to digitize data that we enter into a computer.

What Is Digitizing?

There are two basic types of data: **analog** and **digital.** Both analog and digital data are signals that require devices for interpretation. For example, when you speak to someone, your voice produces a series of analog sound waves that someone's ears receive and interpret. If you speak into a microphone, your voice pattern would look something like Figure 3–1. Analog signals form a continuous wave. When you speak on a telephone your voice waves are sent down the line in the shape of waves created by your distinct voice. An ear on the other end is ideally suited to receive the analog waves and send the signal to the brain for meaningful interpretation.

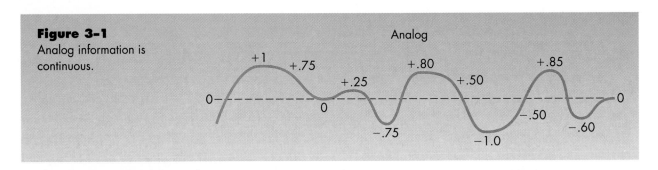

Figure 3–1
Analog information is continuous.

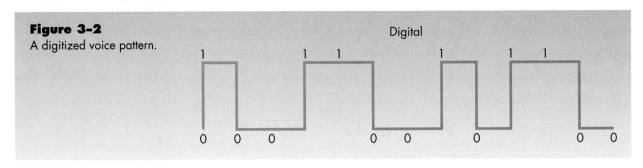

Figure 3–2
A digitized voice pattern.

The binary nature of computers is not as elegant as the human body. In fact, data computers use must be represented in a series of discrete bits—on and off. It is customary to refer to these discrete bits of data as digital data, that is, based on two digits (Figure 3–2).

Because there are so many different types of analog data, there are many specialized digitizing input devices. There are keyboards that take your key strokes and convert the letters or numbers you press into a series of bits. There are **scanners** that are able to take a photograph and digitize the data so you can modify a photograph directly on a computer screen. There are digital cameras that take photographs or light images, not on film, but on disks that are directly usable by a computer (Figure 3–3). There are audio digitizers that take your voice and convert it so a computer can recognize your voice and perform a variety of vocally directed tasks.

The following are examples of many of the common input devices (digitizers). This list is by no means exhaustive. There are many, many others.

Keyboards

Keyboards convert the letters you press into a series of bits to produce a byte. A computer keyboard is very similar to a typewriter (Figure 3–4). There are, however, many differences. In addition to the letters and numbers found on a typewriter, computer keyboards have a series of special keys to send special information to the CPU. Your software defines and controls the use of these special keys. For example, with word processing software, arrow keys move the insertion point, or cursor, to any point in a document. The PgUp (Page Up) and PgDn (Page Down) keys allow you to move to different pages of text. The Home and End keys usually allow you to move to the beginning or end of a document.

With few exceptions keyboards serve as the primary input devices for microcomputers. Yet it is interesting to note that the structure and arrangement of the common computer keyboard represent the same structure as a century-old typewriter. The original layout of the keys on a keyboard (called QWERTY for the top row of the left hand) was designed to slow the process of typing. Old mechanical keyboards had to be manipulated slowly to allow the keys to fall back after striking and not stick together. Today there are alternate keyboard designs that allow much faster typing. Although they are easier to learn and use, few people are willing to make the change (Figure 3–5 on page 43).

Pointing Devices

While keyboards remain the major input device, the **mouse** is becoming just as common. A mouse is a pointing device that controls the position of a pointer on a monitor. Moving the mouse moves a pointer on the screen. For example, some programs allow you to access a file by placing the pointer on the file name

*B*RUSHES FOR THE COMPUTER

Writers and musicians often feel comfortable immediately with a computer's keyboard, but traditional artists have a much more difficult time making the transition. A mouse and a paintbrush are just too different from each other. In fact, trying to draw with a mouse has been compared to drawing with a potato. So, even though a computer extends an artist's palette to literally millions of colors, until recently it was just too clumsy for most visual artists. However, now illustrators can take advantage of a pressure-sensitive 6-by-9-inch tablet and a cordless pen-like stylus that comes close to being a magical paintbrush. The tip of the stylus moves up and down in response to pressure, allowing the computer to simulate the pressure control of conventional artists' tools. In fact, the stylus acts like almost any medium: pencil, brush, watercolor, pastel, charcoal, gouache, crayon, or oil. The computer "paintbrush" even controls the "wetness" and dry-out speed of the stroke and allows the artist to vary the density and width of the line. A lightbox feature allows users to place drawings on top of each other like transparencies, creating collages. Given such "artist-friendly" technology, who knows what masterpieces will come from the computer?

Figure 3-3
Many scanners allow you to scan (digitize) a photograph. Once digitized, you can modify the photograph using a variety of graphics software.

Figure 3-4
Keyboards are the dominant input device for most microcomputer systems.

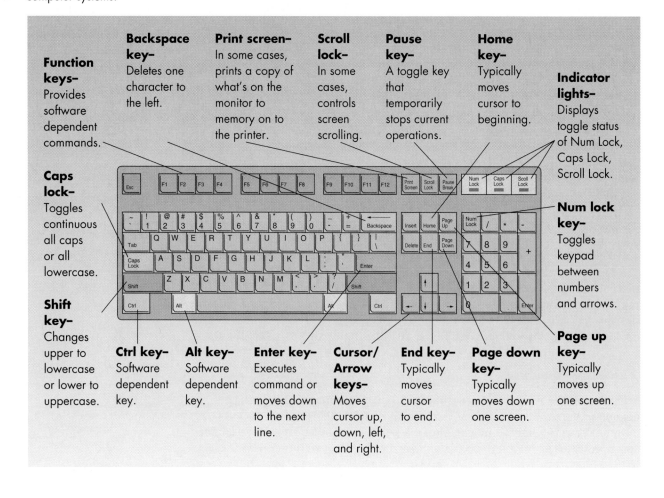

Function keys–
Provides software dependent commands.

Backspace key–
Deletes one character to the left.

Print screen–
In some cases, prints a copy of what's on the monitor to memory on to the printer.

Scroll lock–
In some cases, controls screen scrolling.

Pause key–
A toggle key that temporarily stops current operations.

Home key–
Typically moves cursor to beginning.

Indicator lights–
Displays toggle status of Num Lock, Caps Lock, Scroll Lock.

Caps lock–
Toggles continuous all caps or all lowercase.

Shift key–
Changes upper to lowercase or lower to uppercase.

Ctrl key–
Software dependent key.

Alt key–
Software dependent key.

Enter key–
Executes command or moves down to the next line.

Cursor/ Arrow keys–
Moves cursor up, down, left, and right.

End key–
Typically moves cursor to end.

Page down key–
Typically moves down one screen.

Page up key–
Typically moves up one screen.

Num lock key–
Toggles keypad between numbers and arrows.

Figure 3-5
Two keyboards. One is designed to slow down the speed of typing, and the other is designed to increase typing speed.

and then clicking the mouse button. The mouse is an easy to use and efficient input device.

Another popular pointing device is called a trackball. A **trackball** operates on the same basic principle as a mouse. However, the major difference is that instead of moving the mouse on a table, you move a stationary ball. The pointer on the screen moves in relation to the movement of the ball.

*M*TV AND PCS?

The video business just got a break. Just as desktop publishing programs made the printing business faster and easier, new broadcast-quality desktop video editing programs will be a boon to video production. One program (at $14,000) will allow the user to use a VCR and a Macintosh computer to transform a videotape into computer data and then store it on the disk where special effects, animation, titles, and instant editing can all take place. A $600 program does some of the same things, but its user needs about $6,000 in circuit boards to reach broadcast quality. A barrier has been the amount of memory video work takes: one second of broadcast-quality film is made of 32 frames (still pictures). Each one of those pictures can take up one megabyte of memory. These new video editing programs use image compression to save memory. Since more than half a dozen companies are planning to introduce versions of video-editing software, prices should begin to decline, which means family videos of birthday parties and holiday gatherings will soon be up for sophisticated editing.

Scanners

Scanners, as their name implies, are devices that scan data by passing a laser light over an object. There are many different types of scanners ranging from bar code scanners at your local grocery store to devices that are able to digitize photographs.

For microcomputers, the term *scanner* most often refers to an input device that acts like a small photocopy machine connected to a computer. Scanners include both hand-held and desktop models. With these types of scanners you place a photograph, graphical image, or even pages of text on the scanner. The scanner passes a beam of light across the original document and then senses the presence or absence of the reflected light. The scanner then translates this data into rows of tiny dots, each one noted for its color and brightness, and passes the data on to the computer. This completes the digitizing process.

Specialized graphics software can manipulate digitized graphic images. For example, you can scan a photograph of a person and then use special computer software to change everything from facial features to skin tones. You can even add or remove blemishes.

Digitizing scanners are also very good at "reading" existing typewritten or printed pages. A scanner reads a printed page with special software that allows it to interpret an image of text. This software is known as **optical character recognition** or OCR software. The quality of the interpretation of the scanned input is determined by how well the scanner is able read a typewritten or printed page.

Light Pens

Light pens, often used in department stores, are able to input a large amount of data quickly by moving a light beam across a bar code (Figure 3–6). This converts the bar code into digital data that are usable by a computer. Other types of light pens are also used for computer-aided design (CAD) and pen-based computers; the latter translate and convert human writing into computer form.

Microphones and Voice Input

By combining a microphone with a speech recognition device, it is possible to speak to a computer and have it respond as if you were using a keyboard. With voice recognition devices, you can enter text into a word processor, issue commands, modify and edit documents, process orders, and do almost any task that would normally require a keyboard. In general, voice recognition devices input data at about twice the speed of a fast typist. First, however, the device has to learn to recognize a specific voice.

While voice recognition and voice input offer a great deal of promise, they present some difficulties. Most experts agree that this technology is among the most difficult to develop, in large part because of the tremendous differences in voice patterns. Think of all the accents, inflections, and tones involved with speech. For this reason, voice recognition devices are usually linked to a specific individual. The device must learn the unique speech pattern of an individual, a process that frequently requires a substantial amount of time. You must teach the computer to recognize a voice saying each specific command, letter, or word used to control the computer (Figure 3–7).

Voice recognition devices are becoming increasingly popular, not only for those who have low typing or keyboard entry skills but also for those requiring hands-free computer operations. For instance, while a surgeon's hands are busy, his or her voice can ask the computer to find specific medical references or records. Some individuals may not have the motor skills to interact with a keyboard. A keyboardless computer for a quadriplegic can be a vital communication tool.

Other Input Devices

Input devices take on many forms. For example, a graphic tablet uses a stylus and a sensitive table to let users draw on the screen just as they would on paper and is very useful for graphics work and CAD. Various businesses and industries use touch-sensitive displays and touch pads to allow people to control the computer with the touch of a finger. **Magnetic-ink character recognition** (MICR) allows special devices to read magnetic characters, such as those on your checks. Optical recognition allows data from a CD-ROM to pass into a computer. It also allows for the reading of machine- or computer-scored tests. All of these devices, and many more, have but one purpose: to convert the analog world around us to a form computers can use and then pass that data into the computer for processing.

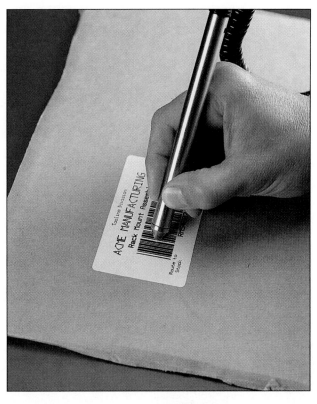

Figure 3–6
Light pens find most common use in business computing environments; however, their utility covers a wide range of applications.

INFORMATION OUT: THE ROLE OF OUTPUT

Data in—information out. Output devices display or store information generated by the CPU. Whereas input devices have the job of converting data from the real world into a form the computer can use, output devices have the job of converting digital language into a form we can use. Just as there are a great variety of input devices, there are also many different types of output devices. Each has a special and unique function.

Monitors and Graphic Devices

The most common type of output device for a microcomputer is a monitor. Monitors, which look like television screens, display and quickly redisplay output generated from the CPU. Monitors are also referred to as CRTs (cathode ray tubes), VDTs (video display terminals), or simply screens.

The image displayed on a monitor is composed of many rows of tiny dots called **pixels** (short for picture element). The number and size of pixels determine the resolution (sharpness and clarity) of the monitor. The more pixels, the higher the resolution. For example, a monitor having 320 × 200 pixels, or dots

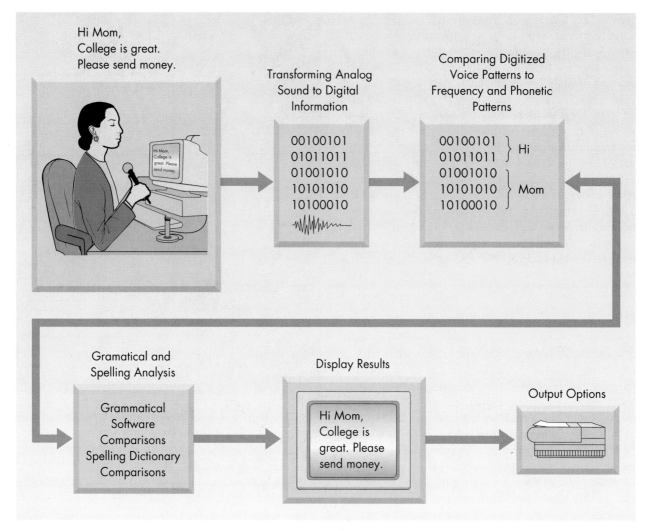

Hi Mom,
College is great.
Please send money.

Transforming Analog
Sound to Digital
Information

```
00100101
01011011
01001010
10101010
10100010
```

Comparing Digitized
Voice Patterns to
Frequency and Phonetic
Patterns

```
00100101  } Hi
01011011
01001010  }
10101010  } Mom
10100010  }
```

Gramatical and
Spelling Analysis

Grammatical
Software
Comparisons
Spelling Dictionary
Comparisons

Display Results

Hi Mom,
College is
great. Please
send money.

Output Options

Figure 3-7
Digitizing voice and speech recognition.

per inch, has a much lower resolution than one with 1024 × 768 pixels (Figure 3–8).

Just as there are a variety of computers and input devices, there are a variety of monitors. Years ago monitors were generally classified as either monochrome (single color) or color graphics. Today, monochrome monitors are rare and outdated. They have been replaced with a variety of color graphics monitors. Two factors contribute to the quality of monitor output: the monitor itself and the graphics card (graphics adapter) inside the computer. The graphics card is used to generate the graphical displays on the monitor. Both work in tandem. For example, some graphic adapters generate 16-color displays; others generate 256-color displays; still others generate millions of colors. However, the monitor must have the capability to match that of the graphics adapter in order to display the output produced by the graphics adapter.

Graphics adapters and monitors have evolved from CGA (color graphics adapter) to EGA (enhanced graphics adapter) to VGA (video graphics array) and to SVGA (super video graphics array). Early CGA offered a four-color display with a resolution of 320 × 200 pixels. EGA supports 640 × 350 pixels and 16 colors. VGA offers 640 × 480 pixels with 256 colors, and SVGA offers 800 × 600 or 1024 × 768 pixels with up to 16.8 million colors.

Portable, laptop, and notebook computers are microcomputers that have become smaller and smaller in size and weight. One of the devices that has

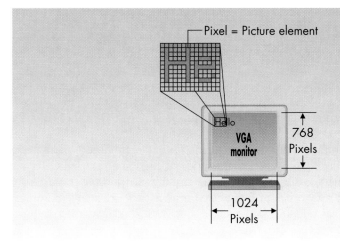

Pixel = Picture element

Hello

VGA
monitor

768
Pixels

1024
Pixels

Figure 3-8
A computer monitor displays images by programming a rectangular array of dots; each dot is called a pixel. Text and images on the screen are each composed of particular patterns of pixels; the more pixels on the screen, the sharper and more detailed the image can be.

made this miniaturization possible is the flat-panel monitor. A flat-panel monitor consumes very little power and provides a full-screen display in a small folding unit. Early flat-panel displays were monochrome, but newer technologies allow these screens to display in color, using graphic adapters similar to those described above. Three of the more common laptop or notebook screens are liquid crystal display (**LCD**), electroluminescent (**EL**), and **gas plasma.**

- LCDs do not consume light of their own, but consist instead of crystal molecules that reflect the light available in a room. Backlit LCDs provide a small amount of light that helps illuminate characters on the screen. Backlit LCDs are easier to read than regional LCDs, which are difficult to read in strong light.
- EL screens represent a major improvement over the LCD screen because EL screens emit light when they are electrically charged. This makes them clearer, sharper, and easier to read in brightly lit work areas.
- Gas-plasma screens use a gas that emits light in the presence of an electrical current. Unfortunately, gas-plasma displays cannot be battery operated efficiently and must be plugged into a regular AC outlet. This requirement limits their use in portable computers.
- With laptop computers, newer developments in displays that include dual-scan and active matrix provide high-quality color. These types of displays have helped to make laptop computers more usable and thus more popular.

Monitor Type	Dimensions (in pixels)	Colors
CGA	320 × 200	4
EGA	640 × 350	16
VGA	640 × 480	16
	320 × 200	256
Super VGA	800 × 600, 1024 × 728	256
Extended VGA	1024 × 768 and above	1.6 million

Table 3-1
Characteristics of Color Monitors.

Printers

Printers create paper copies, called hard copies, of information from the computer (Figure 3–9). Four types of printers are in common use.

- Dot matrix printers use a series of dots to form a character. They are fast and inexpensive, but the output quality can be relatively low. In near-letter-quality mode, dot matrix printers can produce hard copy that is of very high quality.
- Ink jet printers spray small droplets of ink on paper to create characters. Ink jet printers produce a fine-quality print at high speeds. Some ink jet printers print in color. Ink jet printers are usually inexpensive to purchase and have become a favorite for home use because they are small and quiet. However, they can become expensive to operate, because they require special ink cartridges.

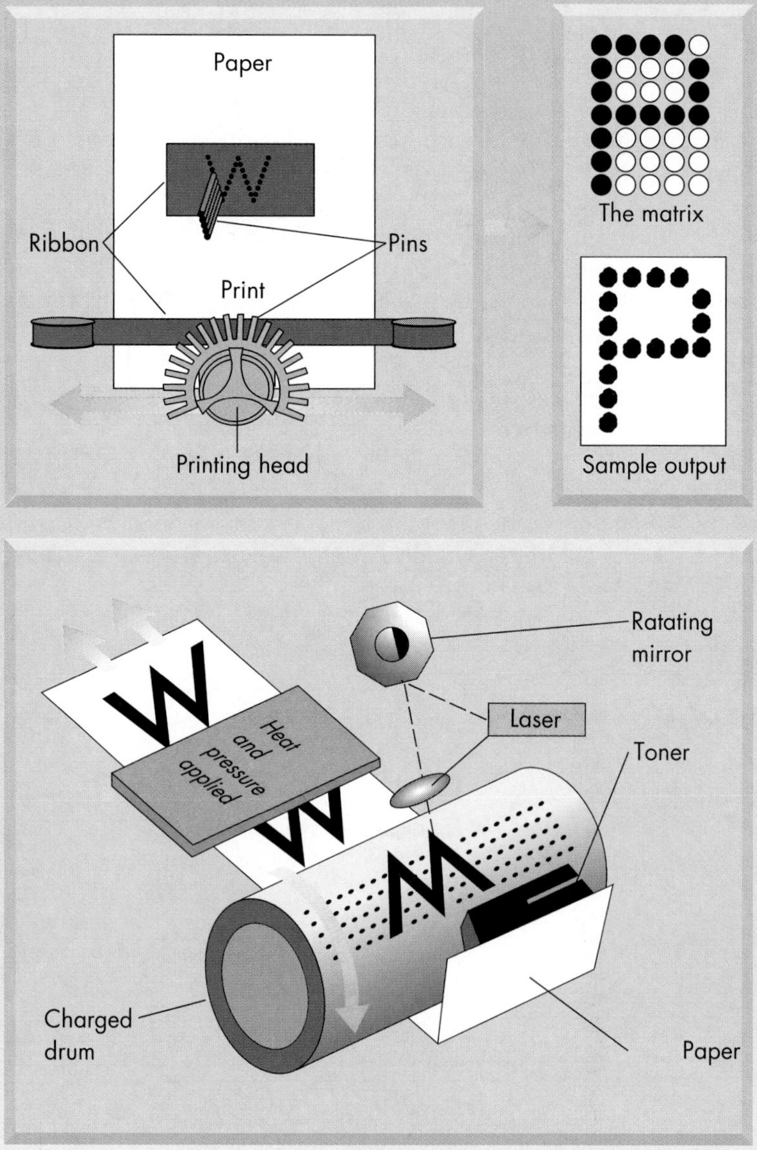

Figure 3-9
A comparison of the output from dot matrix, inkjet, and laser printers.

- Laser printers have become the printer of choice for many users. They produce an exceptionally high-quality print in traditional black ink or in color at a very high speed. Laser printers combine text and graphics to produce a page nearly equal in quality to traditional typesetting at an affordable price.
- Laser printers operate by passing a laser beam back and forth over a rotating drum. The laser "draws" the image on the drum by charging the areas of the drum where the light hits with static electricity. The charged areas pick up the ink toner from a cartridge. The toner is deposited and fused onto the paper. This process makes both the speed and quality of laser printing very high. Color laser printers are also available but at a considerably higher cost to purchase and operate.

Some portable laptop computers include printers. For example, IBM and Canon have a joint project using Canon's bubble-jet printing technology with a smaller cartridge, allowing it to be used in a laptop. Another smart printer is an ink-jet Braille printer that allows blind users to read hard copy of their work.

Plotters

A **plotter** is an output device that specializes in producing line drawings. A plotter typically moves a sheet of paper under a series of pens. As the paper moves, the pens draw. Many plotters produce color output by drawing with several different-colored pens. Because it uses fine-point pens, a plotter can produce very precise lines. Plotters are most often used to produce architectural drawings, maps, charts, and other technical types of line art (Figure 3–10).

Figure 3-10
Plotters are valuable tools for printing architectural drawings, CAD designs, and other forms of line art.

Music and Synthesized Speech

The days of interacting with a computer exclusively through a keyboard and monitor are quickly passing. Sound is becoming as important to output as text was only a few years ago. Most microcomputers sold today come with a sound adapter or sound card. A sound card can generate a high-quality sound, both voice and music.

Sound cards are usually linked to a CD-ROM drive (discussed in detail in the next section) that can display text and graphics as well as produce audio output. In fact, a sound card allows you to play the same audio CDs in your computer that you play on your home entertainment system. Sound cards also provide excellent sound for multimedia games and educational software.

One of the substantive advantages of a sound card is access to synthesized speech. When a computer says "insert a CD," it is not really a human voice but the output of a voice synthesizer. Automatic telephone machines often use computer voice synthesizers to generate messages, store voice mail, and produce the series of audio menus that have become so popular when you call a business.

The quality of sound in a computer is measured, in large part, by bits. Sound cards come in 8, 16, and 32 bits. Just as 32-bit computers offer a high level of computing power, so do 32-bit sound cards. Sound cards are normally connected to external speakers that include an amplifier. As with any home entertainment system, the better the amplifier and the speakers, the better the sound.

Other Output Devices

While the most popular output devices are monitors, printers, sound cards, and plotters (Figure 3–11), there are many other specialized output devices that range from robotics arms to security systems for large buildings. In fact, many specialized computers rely on customized output devices. One of the most popular specialized output devices is the dispensing unit in an automatic teller device.

STORING DATA: THE ROLE OF SECONDARY MEMORY

You already know that when you turn off the computer, the contents of RAM are erased. Any information—term papers, financial reports, documents, or even programs—is deleted when power to the computer is interrupted. In order for a computer system to maintain data and information permanently, it must have access to secondary or auxiliary memory. Today's microcomputer systems use a variety of secondary memory devices for storing data, including floppy disks, hard disks, CD-ROM, interactive video disk (IVD), and magnetic tape. Each has advantages and disadvantages.

The most popular type of electronic data storage in a microcomputer system is magnetic disk storage, commonly referred to as floppy disks, hard disks, and storage tape. A magnetic disk is a **direct-access storage device** (DASD) that permits the computer to find data directly on the disk. Magnetic disks allow any portion of the disk to be accessed immediately, in any order. This differs from magnetic tape storage. With magnetic tape storage, data must be accessed sequentially; that is, a computer must begin reading from the beginning of the tape and proceed until it locates the desired data. Therefore, to access the last sequential record (data) on a tape, the computer must first read all prior records.

Figure 3-11
Multisensory output is critical in a virtual reality environment.

The surface of a magnetic disk is divided into concentric circles called **tracks.** It is further divided into sections that resemble pieces of a pie called **sectors.** Data are stored on the intersection of tracks and sectors in locations called cells. Each cell is defined by an address that allows direct access. By giving the disk drive an address, it is possible for the disk drive to move directly to a cell and either read or write data. It is interesting to note that the same amount of data is stored on each track and cell, whether it is an inner or outer circle.

Of course, the disk drive is the device that reads and writes to and from magnetic disks (Figure 3–12). Disk drives contain an access arm equipped with read-write heads that travel over the surface of the disk to locate specific cell addresses. The read-write head either reads (i.e., obtains data from the disk and transfers data to the CPU) or writes (i.e., transfers data from the CPU to the disk). Reading makes a copy without altering the original data. Writing replaces, actually writes over, the original data in a process that is similar to recording a new song over an old one on a cassette tape.

Typical microcomputers use magnetic disks and disk drives as the chief secondary storage devices. Characteristically, a microcomputer system will have at least one floppy disk drive and one or more hard disk drives.

Floppy Disks and Floppy Disk Drives

Floppy disks, also called diskettes, are magnetic storage media that can be removed from the computer and transported to another computer. They are called floppy disks because the magnetic surface is very thin and flexible inside the protective case.

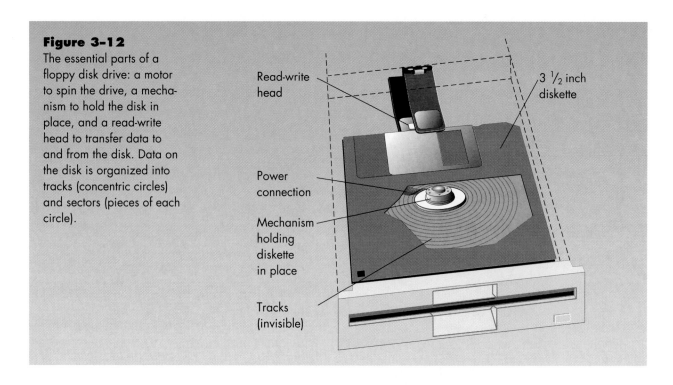

Figure 3-12

The essential parts of a floppy disk drive: a motor to spin the drive, a mechanism to hold the disk in place, and a read-write head to transfer data to and from the disk. Data on the disk is organized into tracks (concentric circles) and sectors (pieces of each circle).

Read-write head

3 ½ inch diskette

Power connection

Mechanism holding diskette in place

Tracks (invisible)

Portability is the most significant aspect of a floppy disk. You can save information from one computer on a floppy disk and then use that disk on another computer. In most cases, people use floppy disks to save information they create so their data can be safely stored or used at other computer locations.

Floppy disk drives come in several sizes and storage capacities:

Family	Size (inches)	Type	Diskette capacity (bytes)
IBM	5.25	Low density	360K
IBM	5.25	High density	1.2Mb
IBM	3.5	Low density	720K
IBM	3.5	High density	1.44Mb
Mac	3.5	Single sided	400K
Mac	3.5	Double sided	800K
Mac	3.5	High density	1.44Mb

Hard Disks and Hard Disk Drives

Most microcomputer systems also use hard disks as a means of storing data. Hard disk drives typically contain a magnetic disk and the read/write heads in a single sealed unit. In other words, hard disk drives are not transportable; they are fully self-contained.

The advantage of hard disks is that they provide greater storage capacity (up to several gigabytes of data) than floppy disks and operate at a much higher retrieval speed. They are popular because they permit users to access files directly from their computers rather than from disks they have to insert and remove. Typically, hard disks are used to store programs, operating systems, and the data required to turn on and use a computer.

Figure 3-13
Floppy disks.

It would be very difficult to operate a microcomputer system with a hard disk alone. There must be a method for transporting data into the computer and then transferring data to the hard disk. This process is the role of the floppy disk. In many cases, the software you purchase comes on floppy disks but requires installation onto your hard disk. This usually means you insert the floppy in its drive and then execute an installation or setup procedure that copies all the data from the original diskettes.

An important relationship between hard disks and floppy disks also occurs in the process of backing up (making a duplicate) data. Because hard disks malfunction, or crash, it is important to have a copy of all your data on floppy disks. To avoid the loss of data, users periodically back up (copy) data from their hard disks to floppy disks, which can be stored outside the system.

Hard disks operate much faster than floppy disks, in large part because hard disks are sealed and are free from contamination (Figure 3–14). Some microcomputers use removable hard disk packs, thus providing much of the speed and size of a hard disk with the portability of floppy disk drives. With removable hard disks, the access arm can be retracted and the disk pack removed from the drive.

Optical Storage Devices: CD-ROM and Interactive Video

For much of microcomputer history, magnetic storage was the sole source of secondary storage. Today, there is a new type of storage device based on the presence or absence of light, that is, optical storage. These devices use optical disks onto which a laser has encoded binary data (Figure 3–15). Once an optical disk is enclosed, the optical disk drive uses another laser to read the encoded data.

One advantage of an optical storage device is that it can retain a great deal of information in a very small area. Several billion bits of data or information can fit on one optical disk. Another advantage is that stored data is actually burned into the disk, making it far more stable than magnetically stored data. Currently, most microcomputer optical storage devices only read data. New types of optical disks, some combining optical and magnetic technology, allow

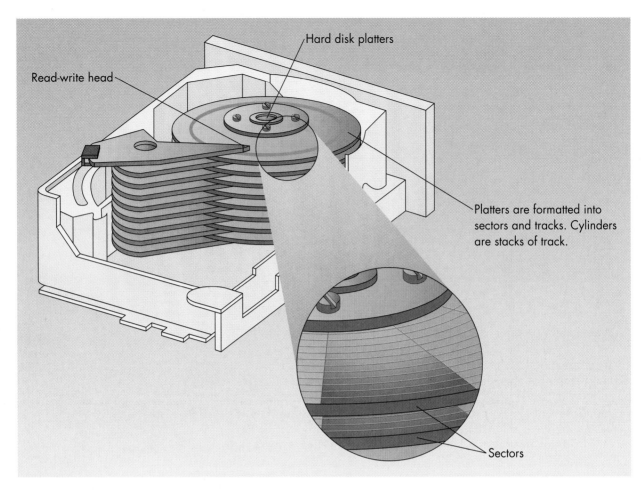

Figure 3-14
Hard disks.

both reading and writing of data, but these haven't yet replaced magnetic disks as the primary storage devices. Magnetic disk technology is still faster than optical disks for storing and transferring data.

There are two common formats for optical storage: **CD-ROM** (compact disk–read only memory) and **IVD** (interactive video disk). CD-ROM uses the same type of disk media commonly used for audio recordings. IVD uses a 12-inch optical disk to store video displays, including sound, text, and graphic images. In general, CD-ROM is used for storing computer data, voice, and some forms of video. IVD is specifically designed to support full motion video, and its high-quality movie and video imaging have made it popular with video enthusiasts.

CD-ROM technology is the basis for multimedia. By allowing large amounts of data, including audio, text, computer data, and video to be stored on a single source, CD-ROM has made multisensory software possible. There are many fine examples of software that have been developed as a direct result of CD-ROM technology. You can get an entire encyclopedia of text, pictures, sounds, and short video segments on a single CD-ROM. A computer game enthusiast will acknowledge that the exceptionally high-quality sound and images of CD-ROM have made today's computer games technological wonders. There are also electronic books that allow you to access material directly and permit linkage to other sections of books. The advantages to a student are that you get all of the text and pictures presented in an order that you control. You may stop

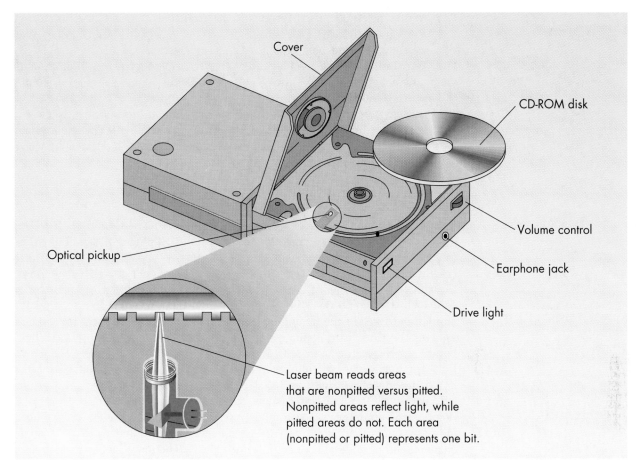

Cover

CD-ROM disk

Optical pickup

Volume control

Earphone jack

Drive light

Laser beam reads areas
that are nonpitted versus pitted.
Nonpitted areas reflect light, while
pitted areas do not. Each area
(nonpitted or pitted) represents one bit.

Figure 3-15
CD-ROM.

anywhere and view related photos, click on a word to branch to a glossary, use an electronic notebook to keep your notes on a disk, even view a historical timeline. It may not be too long before you carry a couple of CD-ROMs to school instead of a bag full of books.

INTERFACING INPUT/OUTPUT DEVICES

So far in this chapter we have talked about input, output, and storage as separate devices and processes. In reality, many of the devices perform multiple processes. We use the term I/O to refer to devices such as disk drives that allow you to input data into RAM, output data from RAM to a disk, and store data. While disk drives are among the most popular I/O devices, there are others. To begin to understand these devices, you need to understand how devices connect to computers through ports and expansion slots.

Ports

Flexibility is a key to any microcomputer. Users may need to add a variety of devices to expand their computer systems. All expansion devices (peripherals) connect to the CPU through ports. Ports enable cables to connect peripheral devices to the CPU.

- **Serial ports** are used for cables that transmit bits one at a time. They are frequently used for connecting modems or special input devices such as a mouse, light pen, graphics tablet, or joystick.
- **Parallel ports** are used for cables that transmit several bits of data simultaneously, such as an entire eight-bit character. Most printers use parallel ports, although some printers do use a serial port.
- Special ports include connections to networks and to peripherals such as keyboards, monitors, external disk drives, and scanners. These ports may work in either serial or parallel fashion depending on the device for which they have been designed.

Expansion Slots

In most cases, ports connect directly to the motherboard (Figure 3–16). This design allows peripheral connection to use a standard plug-in design. For example, there is a standard serial plug, parallel plug, keyboard plug, and so forth (Figure 3–17). However, some devices do not connect to the CPU directly through the motherboard. These devices require the addition of an interface card to link them to the CPU. Interface cards fit into expansion slots on the motherboard inside the computer case. For example, in many microcomputer systems the video card is plugged into a slot that serves as the interface (link) between the monitor and the CPU.

Depending on the type of microcomputer, there can be several different types of expansion slots. In most cases, slots are designated according to the system bus. Within the MS-DOS/Intel family, there are several different slot configurations. Microcomputers can use industry standard architecture (ISA), extended industry standard architecture (EISA), video electronic standard (VESA), micro channel, and peripheral connect interface (PCI). The more bits and the greater

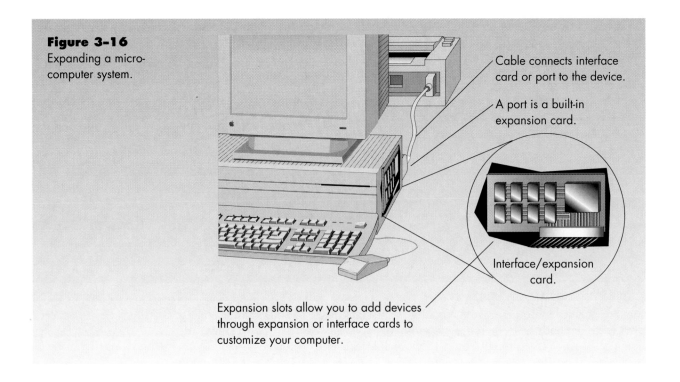

Figure 3-16
Expanding a micro-
computer system.

Cable connects interface
card or port to the device.

A port is a built-in
expansion card.

Interface/expansion
card.

Expansion slots allow you to add devices
through expansion or interface cards to
customize your computer.

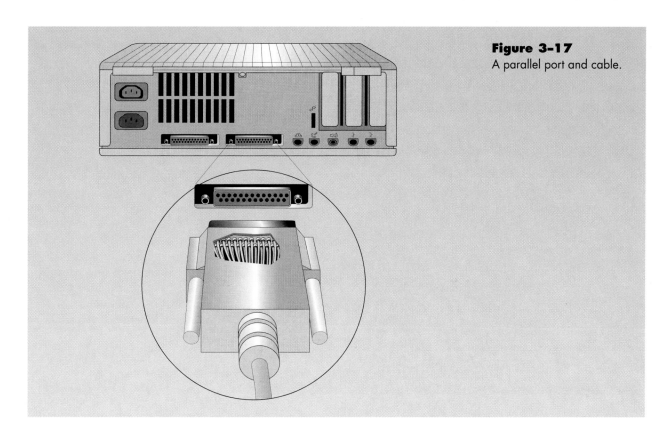

Figure 3-17
A parallel port and cable.

the megahertz, the faster the interface. Table 3–2 outlines some of the more common expansion slots.

Personal computer memory card international association (PCMCIA) is another type of expansion slot. PCMCIA slots were originally designed for notebook computers. Notebook computers do not have room for the rather large interface cards often associated with desktop microcomputers, and PCMCIA provides a small slot directly connected to the motherboard. The interface card connected to these slots functions as part of the device rather than as a separate card. In many cases PCMCIA devices are the size of a credit card and contain all of the functions of much larger devices. For example, PCMCIA modems and hard disk drives are very small and plug directly into the PCMCIA slot. An

Bus/Expansion Slot	Bits	Speed
XT	8 bit	4.77 Mhz
ISA	16 bit	8 Mhz
EISA	32 bit	6–8.33 Mhz
Micro Channel	16/32 bit	10 Mhz
VESA	32 bit	33–66 Mhz
PCI	32/64 bit	150+ Mhz

Table 3-2
Expansion slots.

*C*OMPUTER TALK

Getting machines to talk to each other is not difficult when the machines are computers. Most computers can communicate if they are connected through telephone lines or through coaxial cable. Computers can also be connected by radio frequencies (like remote control) when wire connections are not practical. A group of connected computers is called a *network*. Home computers have access to networks such as Prodigy, which has over 500,000 subscribers. There are hundreds of smaller networks for people with special interests: Deadheads, chefs, Go players—the list is endless. Networks were used to organize demonstrations against the Tiananmen Square crackdown in China, to help scientists across the globe track satellites, and to let physicians or gardeners trade information. In fact, about the only limit to networking via computer is that a day has only 24 hours.

additional advantage of PCMCIA is that these devices can be inserted and removed without interrupting power to the computer. This enables users to switch between devices without having to terminate a computer session.

SCSI Ports

A small computer system interface (**SCSI**) is another type of port added to a microcomputer system through an expansion slot. (MS-DOS/Intel-based computers normally require the addition of a card while Macintosh computers normally provide a direct connection to the motherboard.) SCSI ("scuzy") cards allow multiple devices to connect into one port through chaining (one device connected to another). For example, with one SCSI port you can connect a hard disk. To that hard disk you can connect a CD-ROM. To that CD-ROM you can connect a scanner.

MIDI

Musical instrument digital interface (**MIDI**) is popular for connecting musical devices, such as electronic keyboards, to a microcomputer system. In many cases MIDI either comes with or is directly associated with the installation of a sound card. With MIDI you can connect a musical instrument, and you can also have

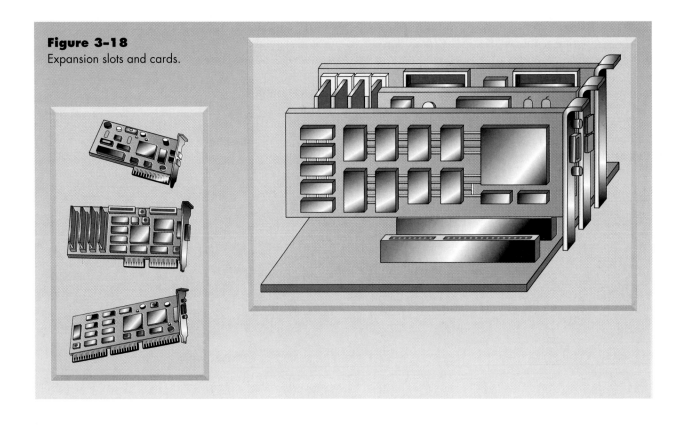

Figure 3-18
Expansion slots and cards.

access to a series of MIDI files to generate a variety of musical sounds (commonly called voices). For example, an electronic piano keyboard may link to a computer through a MIDI port. You can then use MIDI files to make the piano keyboard sound like a harpsichord, organ, and choir. In fact, there are thousands of voices available through MIDI. However, MIDI is not used for human speech.

SUMMARY

- There are two basic types of data: analog and digital.
- Analog signals form a continuous wave.
- All data used by a computer must be represented in a series of discrete bits: on and off.
- One of the indispensable roles of input devices is to convert analog data into digital data that a computer can use.
- Because there are so many different types of analog data, there are many specialized digitizing input devices.
- Keyboards take your stroke on a key and convert the letter or number you press into a series of bits.
- Scanners are able to digitize the data on a photograph so you can modify a photograph directly on a computer screen.
- Digital cameras take photographs, or light images, on disks that are directly usable by a computer rather than on film.
- Audio digitizers can convert your voice so a computer can recognize it and you can perform a variety of orally directed tasks.
- Keyboards convert the letters you press into a series of bits to produce a byte.
- A mouse is a pointing device that operates by controlling the position of a pointer on a monitor. The pointer on the screen moves in accordance with the mouse.
- Scanners, as their name implies, are devices that scan data by passing a laser light over an object. Light pens are able to input a large amount of data quickly by moving a light beam across a bar code.
- By combining a microphone with a speech recognition device, it is possible to speak to a computer and have it respond as if you were using a keyboard.
- Output devices have the job of converting digital language into a form we can use.
- Output devices display or store information generated by the CPU.
- The most common type of output device for microcomputers is monitors.
- There are two factors that contribute to monitor output: the monitor itself and the graphics card inside the computer.
- Printers create paper copies, called hard copies, of information from the computer.
- A plotter is an output device that specializes in producing line drawings.
- A sound card can generate a high-quality sound—both voice and music.
- The most popular type of electronic data storage in a microcomputer system uses magnetic disk storage, commonly referred to as floppy disks, hard disks, and magnetic tape.
- Floppy disks, also called diskettes, are magnetic storage media that can be removed from the computer and transported to another computer.

- Hard disk drives typically contain a magnetic disk and the read/write heads in a single sealed unit.
- Hard disks provide greater storage capacity than floppy disks and operate at a much higher retrieval speed.
- For much of microcomputer history, magnetic storage was the sole source of secondary storage.
- Today, a new type of storage device is based on the presence or absence of light; it is called optical storage.
- Devices (peripherals) are connected to the CPU through ports.
- Ports enable cables to connect peripheral devices to the CPU.
- A number of different types of ports are available on microcomputer systems, including serial ports, parallel ports, and special ports.

KEY TERMS

analog	mouse
CD-ROM	optical character recognition
digital	output devices
direct-access storage device	parallel ports
EL	pixels
gas plasma	plotter
input devices	scanners
IVD	SCSI
LCD	sectors
light pens	serial ports
magnetic-ink character recognition	trackball
MIDI	tracks

REVIEW QUESTIONS

1. What is the purpose of MIDI?
2. What is the difference between analog and digital signals?
3. What type of port is most commonly used by printers?
4. What is the difference between sectors and tracks?
5. What are three common input devices?
6. What are three common output devices?
7. What is an optical storage device?
8. Why has CD-ROM become so popular?
9. What are two methods for connecting peripherals to a computer?
10. Why are input/output devices unique types of peripherals?

SELF-QUIZ

1. What are the most common microcomputer storage devices?
   - *a.* optical drives
   - *b.* mice
   - *c.* disk drives
   - *d.* CD-ROMs
2. What type of wave do analog signals form?
   - *a.* continuous
   - *b.* digitized
   - *c.* mnemonic
   - *d.* bilateral

3. What is the role of an input device?
   a. Converts analog data into digital data.
   b. Converts digital data into analog data.
   c. Converts RAM into CPU.
   d. Converts data into information.

4. Which of the following is an input device that acts like a miniature photocopy machine connected to a computer?
   a. mouse   c. magnetic reader
   b. light pen   d. scanner

5. What makes up the image displayed on a monitor?
   a. pixels   c. bits
   b. microdots   d. bytes

6. Which output device specializes in producing line drawings?
   a. plotter   c. laser printer
   b. scanner   d. light pen

7. Magnetic tape storage accesses data in what order?
   a. sequentially   c. randomly
   b. bi-directionally   d. multimodelly

8. What provides the foundation of multimedia?
   a. hard disk drives   c. sound cards
   b. speakers   d. CD-ROM

9. How are peripherals connected?
   a. through panels   c. through RAM
   b. through ports   d. through CD-ROM

10. What type of device typically uses expansion slots?
    a. MIDI   c. all of the above
    b. SCSI   d. none of the above

11. Computers are electronic devices that can only process _____ data.

12. There are two basic types of data: _____ and _____.

13. A(n) _____ is a pointing device that operates by controlling the position of a pointer on a monitor.

14. Output devices display or store information generated by the _____.

15. In order for a computer system to maintain data and information in a stable or permanent location, it requires the use of _____ memory.

16. The surface of a magnetic disk is divided into concentric circles called _____.

17. The intersection of tracks and sectors, called _____, is where data are stored.

18. _____ drives typically contain a magnetic disk and the read/write heads in a single sealed unit.

19. _____ ports are used for cables that transmit bits one at a time.

20. _____ ports are used for cables that transmit several data bits simultaneously, such as an entire eight-bit character.

SIMULATIONS

Scenario 1: Computer Specifications

Congratulations! You have just been promoted from assistant to the associate vice president of mail delivery to the associate vice president of technical operations. While you like your new title, one of your tasks is to develop computer selection criteria for the entire company. You have been asked not to identify a particular product brand but to develop a bid specification sheet for computer systems for companywide use. To complete this task you must be able to specify a computer system that includes a specific CPU, hard disk size, and amount of RAM; whether to include a CD-ROM and speakers; and what type of graphics make consistent adapter, monitor, printer, and any other peripherals you might think is necessary. Of course, to make a decision you need to determine what computer users will do with their computers. Since very few people in the company know anything about computers, it is up to you to select a system that will serve as broad a variety of needs as possible. Submit your plan in a purchase order format.

Scenario 2: You Win

You have just won the $24-million lottery. After taxes you will receive $18,134 per year for three years. In addition to visiting a famous amusement park in central Florida, you decide you are going to buy your own microcomputer. The problem is you are married and your spouse thinks computers are a waste of money. Of course, you say, "But honey we got lotsa money," but to no avail. Your significant other needs to be convinced that what you buy is not just an expensive toy. Write a detailed summary that explains not only what you are going to buy but also what each peripheral will do for you, or even better, for your mate.

Scenario 3: Computer Lab Assistant

For the past three years you have been working in the campus food court providing high-quality, nutritious, although somewhat less than tasty, food. Being a hotel management major, you figured that learning how a commercial kitchen operates would be a valuable learning experience. However, three years of wearing plastic gloves and a hair net is quite enough. You decide to search for a different campus job. About the only thing available is a lab-assistant position in the central computer lab. Now that you are taking a computer class, maybe you can qualify for a job that is not in a kitchen. The only problem is that the academic computing center only hires lab assistants who can provide technical assistance to students. To qualify for the job, you must write a brief essay describing the operations of a computer system. The computer lab assistant's intellectual inventory must include a discussion of each of the following:

What is the role of input devices?
What is digitizing?
What is the difference between analog and digital data?
List five different input devices and their uses.
List three common output devices and their uses.
Explain the role and function of ports and expansion slots.

HANDS-ON COMPUTING

1. Do you know how to type? Because the keyboard is the most popular form of input device, it is important that you be able to use a keyboard efficiently. If you cannot type, or your typing skills are a bit rusty, it is worth the effort to spend a bit of time using one of the many available keyboarding programs to improve your skills. A little time invested now will pay big dividends later.
2. A CPU is often called the brain of a computer because it performs all of the processing tasks, but what about the other devices for input and output? Develop a diagram depicting input, output, CPU, and storage for a human computer. Be sure to list several human input and output devices.

3. If you want to understand more about the development of microcomputers, there is an excellent book entitled *Hackers* by Steven Levy. This book gives you a unique insight into the individuals who helped start the microcomputer revolution.

4. You turn on your computer and nothing happens. No beep, no lights, nothing. List three potential causes.

5. Printing is often one of the most troublesome aspects of a computer system. What should you check first if you try to print and nothing happens?

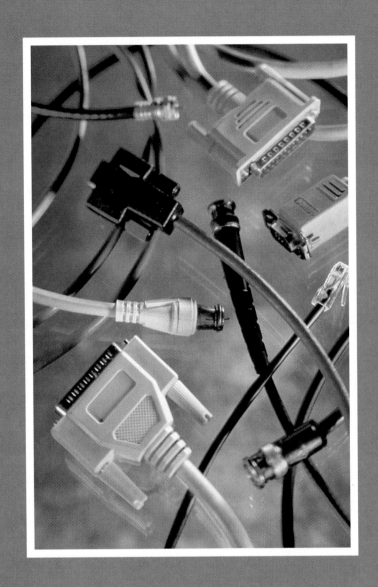

CHAPTER 4

Microcomputer Operating Systems

OBJECTIVES

After completing this chapter, you will be able to:

● Name and describe common operating systems

● Describe how to use character-based operating systems.

● Describe how to use a graphical user interface (GUI).

● Describe the functions of utility software.

FOCUS

An **operating system** is a group of computer programs that help manage the computer's resources. It acts as an interface between the computer and **application programs.**

The operating system is what turns the computer from an electronic zombie into an efficient machine with the ability to carry out instructions and perform intricate tasks. The operating system's job is to control the computer on the most fundamental level; it manages memory, controls access to peripheral devices, and serves as a translator between the user and the hardware, providing the means for the user and application programs to tell the hardware what to do. Its functions are frequently known as "housekeeping," in that they perform essential—but unseen—chores that allow application programs to work properly. Thus, while application programs perform such user tasks as word processing and spreadsheet calculations, the operating system performs such housekeeping tasks as creating files, keeping track of files, recovering damaged files, checking disks for errors, accessing peripheral devices, and running the application programs (Figure 4–1).

There are several different operating systems for microcomputers. One of the most common is known as MS-DOS, and it controls IBM PCs and compatibles; it uses a command-line interface. Other options for PC users include Windows and OS/2, two competing graphical user interfaces which offer multitasking capabilities, and UNIX, an operating system originally developed for mainframes. The Macintosh can run with Apple's System and its graphical user interface, Finder, or with UNIX.

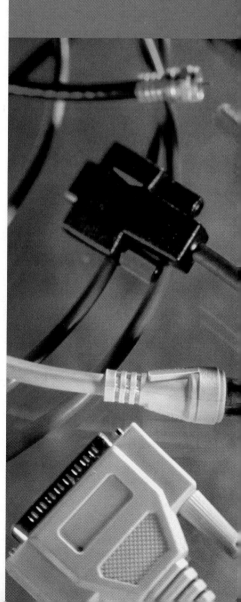

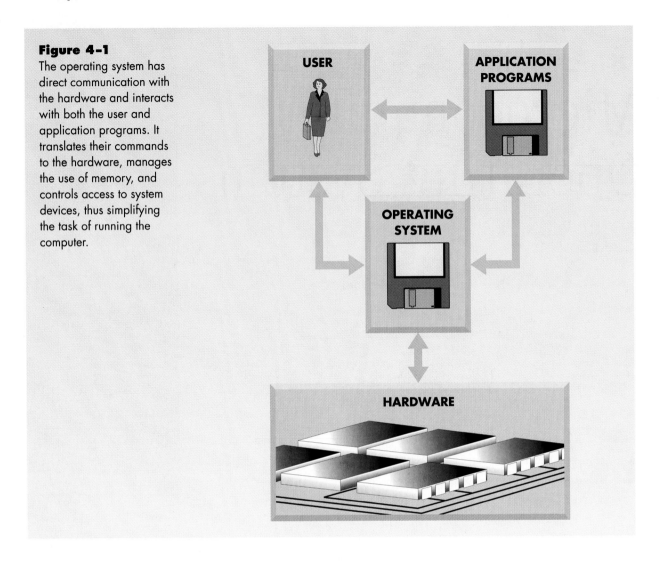

Figure 4-1
The operating system has direct communication with the hardware and interacts with both the user and application programs. It translates their commands to the hardware, manages the use of memory, and controls access to system devices, thus simplifying the task of running the computer.

COMMON OPERATING SYSTEMS

Operating systems are designed for specific microprocessors. For example, the operating system MS-DOS works with microprocessors manufactured by Intel; the Macintosh's operating system (called System) works with Motorola microprocessors. Similarly, an application program is designed for a specific operating system.

MS-DOS

Historically, the majority of microcomputer software was written for Microsoft's MS-DOS (disk operating system; commonly called **DOS**), developed for IBM-compatible computers. PC-DOS is almost an identical system developed for IBM Personal Computers.

Loading DOS. When the power on an IBM-family computer is turned on, the ROM's BIOS (basic input/output system) begins instructing the computer in a precise sequence of steps that prepare the computer for use; this is

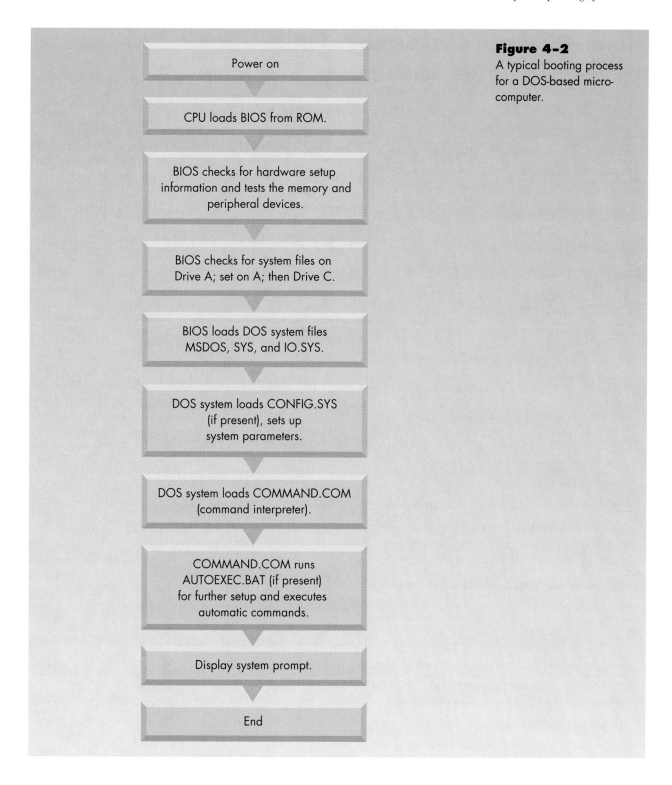

Figure 4-2
A typical booting process for a DOS-based micro-computer.

Power on

CPU loads BIOS from ROM.

BIOS checks for hardware setup information and tests the memory and peripheral devices.

BIOS checks for system files on Drive A; set on A; then Drive C.

BIOS loads DOS system files MSDOS, SYS, and IO.SYS.

DOS system loads CONFIG.SYS (if present), sets up system parameters.

DOS system loads COMMAND.COM (command interpreter).

COMMAND.COM runs AUTOEXEC.BAT (if present) for further setup and executes automatic commands.

Display system prompt.

End

called a **boot,** or booting up the computer (Figure 4–2). After testing the hardware and establishing connections to disk drives and other peripherals, BIOS instructs the computer to load two hidden files, MSDOS.SYS and IO.SYS, from the boot disk (the disk on which the operating system is stored). These two files, together with COMMAND.COM (discussed later), form the core of MS-DOS.

COMPUTERS FOR THE BLIND

Recent advances in computer technology allow the blind to be more self-sufficient—thanks to programs that use voice recognition. By merely speaking to a computer, a person can operate appliances or dial the telephone. The computer can automatically dial a number every morning, upload the newspaper, and then read it back on demand. Even operating the computer has become easier with the addition of sound effects. For instance, storing a file can produce the sound of a cabinet drawer sliding shut, thereby verifying that the computer has done what it was told to do. Unfortunately, speech-recognition technology is still fairly crude, so the number of commands a computer can recognize is still limited. But the growth potential for such programs is staggering.

SPEAKING THE SAME LANGUAGE

One of the problems with portable computers is that they often do not speak the same language, straitjacketing people when it comes to buying software and peripherals. One of the reasons Excel, a spreadsheet program from Microsoft, has become such a popular application is that its Macintosh and Windows versions operate using the same commands and share files from one machine to the other; Microsoft Word, a word processor, also works this way. To try to bridge the computer communication gap, more than 250 makers of computers and related products recently united behind a standard slot—or "bus"—for connecting add-on gear to portable computers. The PCMCIA (for Personal Computer Memory Card International Association) standard means that many PCs will be able to share programs, add-ons, and peripherals by using interchangeable plastic-coated cards, each about as thick as a stack of four to six credit cards. Now if we can just get politicians to speak to each other . . .

BIOS next looks on the disk drives to find the files that complete the boot process. On a PC, the disk drives are labeled as follows: drive A is the first floppy disk drive, drive B is the second (if there is a second floppy), drive C is the first hard disk drive, and drives D and E are additional hard drives. If there is a disk in drive A, BIOS assumes that MSDOS.SYS and IO.SYS are stored on it; if they are not found, BIOS will give the user an error message. If there is no disk in drive A, the computer will next search drive C, the hard disk (assuming your computer has a hard disk). Most microcomputers have hard disks set up to boot from drive C. Once MSDOS.SYS and IO.SYS are loaded, the system checks for CONFIG.SYS. This file is created by the user to customize the computer's setup by loading driver programs for special peripheral devices (such as a mouse), set certain system parameters, and load resident utility programs.

Finally, the system looks for a file named COMMAND.COM, which holds the instructions for interpreting most of the various DOS commands. For this reason it's known as the **command interpreter** or **command processor.** Without this file, DOS won't run; if the computer can't find COMMAND.COM (either on your boot disk or in another location specified in CONFIG.SYS), it will display an error message on the screen. Once COMMAND.COM has been loaded, it displays the DOS system prompt, like this:

```
C>
```

You'll see a blinking cursor next to the greater-than symbol (>); whatever you type will appear on the screen here. This is called the **command line,** because it's where you type commands to DOS.

The drive displayed in the system prompt is called the **default drive** (or current drive). Unless otherwise instructed, the default drive is the storage device where DOS searches for files to be loaded into memory; it moves files from memory to the default drive when it needs to store them. You can change the default drive by entering a different name (followed by a colon) on the command line.

One other option in the boot-up sequence is AUTOEXEC.BAT. This **batch file** (a file of ready-to-run commands) is created by the user to run certain programs or set up certain system parameters, similar to CONFIG.SYS. Because the contents of AUTOEXEC.BAT are DOS commands, it is loaded and run only after COMMAND.COM is loaded.

DOS File Structure.   Before you look further at DOS commands, you need to understand the DOS file structure.

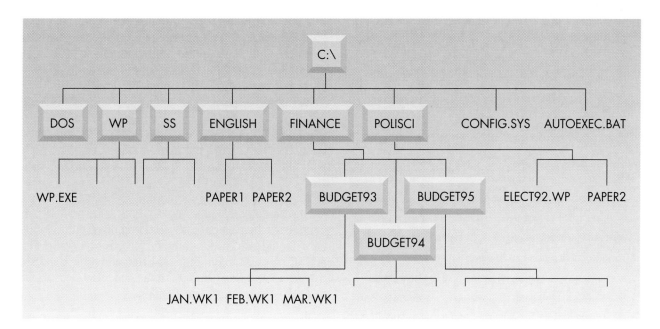

Figure 4-3
This tree diagram (directories
are boxed) shows the structure
DOS uses to organize files.
The root directory C:\ is at
the top; each level beneath
can store both files and
subdirectories.

A computer file is similar to a paper document holding related information. For example, each computer program or document (word processing document, spreadsheet, or database) is stored in a separate file.

Each file is identified by a filename, such as

```
FILE1.WP
```

DOS filenames can be up to eight characters long—using letters, numbers, or certain symbols—plus a file extension that uses a period and up to three characters.

It is helpful to name data files in a meaningful, organized way. For example, .DOC might be the extension for all word processing files. A pharmacist might list files of prescriptions as .PRS files, and a teacher's lesson plans might be .LES files.

All files are stored in directories, much as a file folder is used to store individual files or documents. The directories are organized in an inverted tree structure where the top level is called the **root directory.**

Usually, only those files necessary to boot the computer should be placed in the root directory: MSDOS.SYS, IO.SYS, CONFIG.SYS, COMMAND.COM, and AUTOEXEC.BAT. Branching out from the root directory, users create their own directories (also called **subdirectories**) to organize their program files and data files. A program file contains an application program, such as a word processing or database program; a data file contains data entered by the user, such as a letter, spreadsheet, or other document. Other subdirectories should contain the rest of the DOS operating system, device-driver programs, user-created batch files, and utilities. Keeping the hard disk properly organized is the responsibility of the user.

In the example shown in Figure 4–3, a student created two subdirectories for her application software: one called WP for her word-processing software and one called SS for her spreadsheet software.

For each application, the student created additional subdirectories for her data files. Thus, the ENGLISH subdirectory contains her English term papers; the POLISCI subdirectory contains Political Science term papers; and the

P ORTABLE ASSISTANTS

Want to know what the weather is across the country, what time the next plane leaves for your destination, or what's the best way to get around a traffic jam— but you're not by your telephone or computer? No problem! Just make sure you have your Personal Digital Assistant. At six by nine inches, the device easily fits into a coat pocket, purse, or briefcase. And it can do just about anything. One program allows the user to type in a word in English and a digitized voice will respond in a foreign language. By using PDAs, New York City policemen can find out the history of any license plate on the Eastern seaboard in ten seconds. Some of Chicago's commodities traders, who traditionally transacted business by screaming and waving their hands, are now using PDAs. And just in case you didn't get through the traffic jam in time to catch your airplane, it's nice to know your PDA can also play video games!

FINANCE subdirectory contains her financial planning information. To see the structure of your subdirectories, you can use the TREE command. MS-DOS does not require the use of capital letters; you can enter commands in either upper- or lowercase.

Suppose the student writes a paper about the 1992 presidential election. She names the document ELECT92.WP and stores it in the POLISCI subdirectory. The document's complete name is now

```
C:\POLISCI\ELECT92.WP
```

To completely identify a DOS file, you must include its name and path to the root directory; the path includes all the subdirectories between the file and the root. A colon (:) must be placed after the disk drive name; a backslash (\) must be placed in front of each subdirectory and filename.

Entering DOS Commands. Once you understand DOS file structure, it's easy to enter a DOS command. On the command line, type the command, followed by the required drive, directory, and/or filename.

For example, typing DIR (the Directory command) displays all files in the designated drive and directory. Typing

```
DIR  C:\POLISCI
```

displays all files in the POLISCI directory on the C drive.

You can shorten the command by eliminating default information. For example, if C: \POLISCI is the current directory, you need only type

```
DIR
```

to display the same information.

When you command DOS to perform an action on a file, you include the pathname and filename(s)

```
COMMAND pathname filename
```

The Rename command, for example, changes a file's name. Thus, typing on the command line

```
RENAME  C:\POLISCI\ELECT92.WP  PRESELEC.WP
```

changes the ELECT92.WP (election 92) paper in the POLISCI subdirectory on the C disk to the name PRESELEC.WP (presidential election). This looks like a lot of typing, but remember, you can eliminate default information. In this example, if you issue the command from the C: \POLISCI directory, you need type only

```
RENAME  ELECT92.WP  PRESELEC.WP
```

DOS provides other ways of shortening commands as well. RENAME, for example, can be entered as REN. Because the DOS environment is text (or character) based, commands must be typed in on the command line.

Other commonly used DOS commands include

FORMAT drive	Formats a disk; that is, DOS prepares the disk so that it can accept data in a format compatible with the operating system.
MD (Make Directory)	Creates a new subdirectory
CD (Change Directory)	Moves the current subdirectory to another subdirectory.
COPY (Copy)	Copies a file from one area to another.
DEL (Delete)	Erases a file from disk storage.

Windows

The character-based nature of DOS, while powerful and full featured, is not always easy to use, and it can be quite difficult to learn. To help alleviate these problems, several software companies developed automated methods for controlling DOS. These operating environments, called **shells,** provide a bridge between the user and DOS. For a long time, DOS shells were popular, because they used a series of menus to provide access to many of the important DOS commands. For example, the MS-DOS Shell that is included with more recent versions of DOS allows users to select the command Format from a menu. This makes it much easier than having to issue the Format command by typing the word Format (and all the necessary parameters) at the DOS prompt. While DOS Shells have made accessing and using DOS-based commands easier, they still require users to have a good understanding of the intricacies of DOS.

One of the most popular developments that provides users with an easy method for controlling DOS came with the introduction of Microsoft Windows. In its earliest versions, Microsoft Windows (**Windows** as it has come to be known) was very similar to traditional DOS shells. It provided a means of using DOS without radically changing the way users interacted with their computers. Again, you had to know a lot about DOS to use this early version of Windows. However, all that changed with the introduction of Windows.3.0

Windows 3.0 ushered in the popularity of the **graphical user interface (GUI)** for DOS-based computers. While there were other software companies that provided a mechanism for using a mouse, **icons** (pictures that represent files and programs), and a standard set of menus to control DOS, it was Windows 3.0 that provided users with a radical move away from the text-based command structure of DOS. While Windows 3.0 relied on DOS as the basis for controlling the computer, many users could use a mouse, icons, and a limited knowledge of DOS to control their computers. Windows 3.0 made it much easier for new computer users to learn the basics of controlling hardware and software.

Windows 3.0 also changed the way software was developed. Most software developed prior to Windows 3.0 was designed to run directly from DOS. Because of the great flexibility of DOS, software developers could create programs that would operate in any number of different ways. There was very little standardization. Windows 3.0 provided a standard interface (a common set of screen characteristics) that software developers could follow. Programs written for Windows 3.0 took advantage of the standardized graphical user interface. For

Figure 4-4
Windows 95 organizes applications and utilities, allowing you to load and run an application simply. System commands are given by clicking on menus to open them, then clicking on the command desired.

users, this meant that all Windows-compatible software worked in a very similar fashion. For example, all Windows software uses the same processes for opening and saving files. All Windows software uses the same procedures for printing. And, all Windows software uses the mouse pointer as a key input device for accessing menus.

The popularity of Windows 3.0 expanded with the release of Windows 3.1. This version of Windows made it even easier to control DOS by using this graphical user interface. More features were added that made Windows 3.1 the most popular method for controlling DOS-based microcomputers. In fact, most software soon came to be developed to work directly with Windows 3.1

The big problem with Windows 3.1, as was the case with all previous versions of Windows, was that it relied on DOS. Windows 3.1 "sits on top of" DOS to provide a bridge between the user and DOS. Yet DOS was still doing all of the work. All of the limitations (file name length, parameters, etc.) remained. While it was clearly easier for most people to use Windows than the text-based DOS command structure, the limitations of Windows 3.1 still provided problems.

The most radical change in how users interacted with their computers came with the release of Windows 95 (see Figure 4–4). For the first time since the inception of DOS and the release of the earliest microcomputers, Windows 95 provided a move away from DOS, since it is not just an interface between the user and DOS. Consequently, with Windows 95, users are not limited to the confined memory and file structure of DOS. Yet, Windows 95 continues to provide a means for using DOS (actually a version of DOS) and all of the software written for DOS and previous versions of Windows. This way users can still use software written for DOS and Windows 3.0/3.1 as well as newer software written specifically for Windows 95.

What does Windows 95 do? From a user's point of view, everything. Windows 95 controls the computer and determines how programs run, how hardware is accessed, how files are saved, and how you interact with software. The most fundamental feature of Windows 95 is the same as previous versions of Windows. It uses a mouse and icons. The mouse is the pointing device that lets you access programs and files, and icons indicate programs and files.

One of the key advancements with Windows 95 is the introduction of Plug-and-Play. Prior to Windows 95 any time people wanted to add a new peripheral they had to install a specialized driver (a piece of software that links the hardware to the operating system). This was sometimes a difficult process that caused problems for many users. Users had to know about interrupts, channels, IRQ, and a host of other technical considerations when installing new hardware. This is not the case with Windows 95. Plug-and-Play means all you have to do is install the hardware, and the software linkage is performed automatically.

Another big advantage of Windows 95 is the ease of accessing and running multiple programs—**multitasking.** By using the taskbar (a feature in Windows 95 that contains a series of buttons indicating which programs are actively running), you can easily switch between several active programs. With this multitasking feature, you can use telecommunication software to retrieve files, while, at the same time, working on a term paper with word processing software.

Macintosh System

The Macintosh family of computers was originally based on the Motorola 68000 line of processors. The Power PC microprocessor is used in more recent Macintosh computers. The Macintosh operating system, referred to as System, and its GUI operating environment, Finder, are inseparable. You cannot access the Macintosh operating system without Finder (Figure 4–5).

The Macintosh operating system, System 7 and beyond, supports multitasking; it is quite similar to Windows. Unlike the IBM environment, however, the Macintosh environment was originally designed for a standard graphical inter-

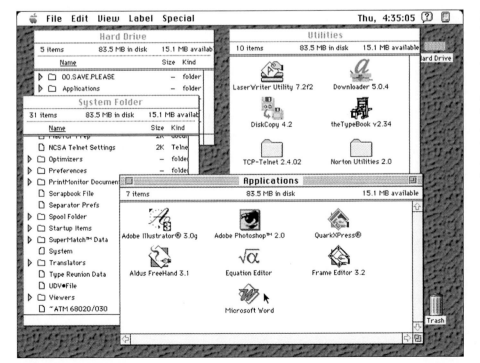

Figure 4–5
The Macintosh System uses Finder as a GUI, providing a visual "desktop" on which icons for drives, folders, and documents are located. Multifinder will switch between several programs, changing the menus at the top of the screen to match each program you have running.

face. Rather than the separate modules Windows 3.1 provided for managing programs and data files, the Macintosh system and Finder integrate the two functions, using the desktop as a metaphor for organizing the computer system. Finder shows a "desktop" consisting of a menu bar at the top of the screen where commands are accessed; icons showing the disk drives; and an icon labeled "Trash," into which you drag files you want to delete. When you double-click on a disk's icon, a window opens to show you the disk's contents of files and programs, which are themselves represented by icons, as well as folders (equal to DOS directories) in which more files and programs can be stored. Clicking with the mouse on a document's name or icon loads the program used to create the document and opens the document for viewing or editing; clicking on a program icon loads the programs directly. To delete files, simply use the mouse to select and drag them to the Trash. For many, the Mac's consistency and integration of functions make it the easiest operating system to use.

UNIX

The **UNIX** operating system was created in the early 1970s for minicomputers, and was later adapted for mainframes and microcomputers. UNIX was an early supporter of multitasking, which made it popular for networking and multiuser communications environments.

UNIX has kept pace with microcomputer advances and now runs on both Macintosh and the MS-DOS family of microcomputers. It is the leading operating system for powerful workstation computers, such as those by Sun Microsystems and NeXT.

UNIX generally operates in a character-based environment, but GUI environments, including XWindows and OpenLook, are also available.

UNIX provides additional features including:

- Multitasking among multiple users is possible; that is, simultaneous programs can be shared by several users at one time.
- UNIX can run on many different computer systems. Unfortunately, the many versions are not standardized, and not all are compatible with others.
- Advanced networking capabilities allow sharing of files over networks that have several different kinds of equipment.

OS/2

In 1987, IBM and Microsoft Corporations introduced Operating System/2 (**OS/2**). OS/2 was developed for then powerful microcomputers, such as the IBM PS/2 line. Because it can access large amounts of memory, it can simultaneously run powerful programs that access huge amounts of data. Each program is protected so that if one crashes, the others do not lose data.

SCIENCE FICTION? HARDLY—TRY REALITY

Plunging into a different dimension by donning gloves, goggles, and a helmet and staring at a screen was a device often used in pulp fiction to describe amusement parks in space. But virtual reality (the term coined in the 1980s to describe such programs) is very much here today, and is being used to train people in a wide variety of ways. The gloves (or an entire suit that one wears) act as an input device for the computer; the helmets (which can also have stereos in them) are output devices. Virtual reality is so effective as a training device because it totally immerses the person in a task. For example, medical students can experience a distant land rather than just reading about it. Sportsmen can use virtual reality to train more effectively. One researcher put a glove on two Red Sox pitchers and had them throw the ball while the glove sent a computer information on speed, position, and flex. The computer analyzed all the data, and the results helped the pitchers correct what was not working.

Program	Publisher	Description
DOS/Windows:		
Norton Utilities	Symantec	Disk optimization, formatting and backup, file and disk recovery, DOS command shell
PC Tools Deluxe	Central Point	Disk optimization, formatting, backup and recovery; DOS command shell; calculator and notepad; virus protection
Xtree Gold	Xtree	Utilities for maintaining DOS files and directories; copying, deleting, and moving files
SpinRite II	Gibson Research	Hard disk diagnostics, optimization, and formatting
LapLink III	Traveling Software	File transfer and communication
PKZIP	PKWare, Inc.	File compression and decompression
QEMM	Quarterdeck	Manages extended and expanded memory; optimizes conventional DOS memory
Virex-PC	Microcom	Virus protection
Norton Desktop for Windows	Symantec	Streamlines the functions of Windows Program Manager and File Manager
Adobe Type Manager	Adobe Systems	Coordinates PostScript font usage; creates optimized screen fonts as needed by Windows applications
Macintosh:		
Norton Utilities	Symantec	Disk optimization, file and disk recovery, desktop customization
MacTools Deluxe	Central Point	Disk optimization, file and disk recovery, backup, file compression
Stuffit Deluxe	Aladdin Systems	File compression and decompression, archives
SAM	Symantec	Virus protection
Suitcase II	Fifth Generation	Coordinates desk accessories, fonts, and sounds
After Dark	Berkeley Systems	Screen saver
QuicKeys	CE Software	Keyboard macros
Adobe Type Manager	Adobe Systems	Coordinates PostScript font usage; creates optimized fonts as needed by applications

Table 4-1
Some Microcomputer utility programs.

MIRROR, MIRROR IN THE COMPUTER

One of the most common fears new computer users have is, "If I just touch the wrong button by mistake I'll lose all my work." Actually, the computer can be rather forgiving; hence the "undelete" function. A file consists of three things: the name of the file, the physical location of the file, and a pointer from the name to the location. When a file is deleted, the name is lost. Using the undelete function recovers a file by renaming it. There are even recovery tools, such as Mirror, that can rescue materials after that most dreaded of all computer malfunctions, a hard disk crash. And that's pretty forgiving.

EVERY DAY CAN BE APRIL FOOL'S DAY

The computer often seems to be a dull, even dehumanizing invention. But it has given rise to some awfully goofy humor and bizarre practical jokes. Sound effects can be programmed to play when a particular command is given: deleting a file can be accompanied by a loud "kaboom" or a more gentle "bonk"; scanning a disk can elicit a character from Monty Python's Flying Circus hollering, "I didn't expect the Spanish Inquisition." When turning on your computer in the morning you can be greeted by Robin Williams screaming "Good morning Vietnam!!" (Guaranteed to let the rest of the office know you're in.) Or if you prefer music, another program plays the Bugs Bunny cartoon's "That's All Folks" theme as you shut down. The DRAIN.COM program for DOS allows you to flummox an unsuspecting co-worker. Once a person hits any key after the C> prompt, the message "System error: water detected in disk drive A:" appears, followed by the shushing noise of water flowing down a drain. The computer then announces "Spin Dry in Progress" and lets the disk drive whir for a few minutes. If only washing clothes were that simple.

OS/2 is compatible with and can run application programs written for DOS. It also provides a graphical environment compatible with Windows so it can run Windows applications as well.

UTILITY PROGRAMS

Utility programs perform operating system tasks. A number of these programs have been developed by independent manufacturers to enhance existing operating systems (Table 4–1). The programs are not inherent in the operating system itself, but are loaded separately into the computer. For example, early versions of DOS did not include antivirus programs: you had to load a separate DOS utility for this purpose.

Utility programs can also do the following:

- Provide an easier way of managing files.
- Optimize use of available RAM.
- Optimize disk storage.
- Monitor the system's use of memory and storage space resources.
- Recover lost data or, as with antivirus software, prevent the loss of data.
- Compress large files so they require less storage space.
- Terminate an application before it crashes the whole system.
- Protect your data from other users by denying access to your system and/or directories without a password.
- Protect your monitor when it is on for long periods of time.

SUMMARY

- An operating system is a group of computer programs that helps manage the computer's resources.
- An operating system acts as an interface between the computer and application programs.
- An operating system also performs such housekeeping tasks as creating and keeping track of files, recovering damaged files, checking for disk errors, accessing peripheral devices, and running application programs.
- The major operating systems for microcomputers are MS-DOS, PC-DOS, the Macintosh System, UNIX, OS/2, and Windows 95.

- Application programs, such as word processing and spreadsheet programs, are designed for specific operating systems.
- DOS runs on the IBM family of computers using Intel microprocessors. It is a character-based system that requires the entry of commands on a command line.
- The Windows operating environment provides a graphical user interface (GUI) that lets users select icons to open programs and manage files.
- Windows also allows multitasking, that is, several application programs can run simultaneously.
- The Macintosh System runs on the Motorola 68000 and PowerPC lines of processors. It allows multitasking and provides a graphical environment.
- Although UNIX can work with a variety of microprocessors, each requires a different version and the versions are incompatible.
- UNIX multitasking allows several users to use the same programs at the same time. Its networking capabilities allow sharing of files over networks with several different kinds of equipment.
- OS/2 is compatible with DOS. It can thus run application programs written for DOS, and it provides a graphical environment. Its multitasking ability allows it to run several large programs simultaneously. If one program crashes, the others do not lose data.
- Utility programs enhance existing operating systems.

KEY TERMS

application programs	icons
batch file	multitasking
boot	operating system
command interpreter	OS/2
command line	root directory
command processor	shell
default drive	subdirectories
DOS	UNIX
graphical user interface (GUI)	Windows

REVIEW QUESTIONS

1. What functions do operating systems perform?
2. Describe four popular operating systems.
3. What is a default drive? Give an example.
4. What is multitasking? Which operating systems offer it?
5. Describe the difference between a character-based operating environment and a graphical user interface.
6. Define DOS. How are files organized and named? Name five common DOS commands. What do these commands do?
7. Describe a graphical user interface.
8. Describe three kinds of utilities for microcomputers.

SELF-QUIZ

1. The operating system used by Macintosh computers is called
   a. MC-DOS.
   b. Motorola Operating System (MOS).
   c. System.
   d. Mac OS/2.
2. The core of MS-DOS is made up of MSDOS.SYS, IO.SYS, and
   a. BIOS. c. DOS.SYS.
   b. BOOT.SYS. d. COMMAND.COM.
3. Which file holds the instructions for interpreting most of the DOS commands?
   a. COMMAND.INT c. CONFIG.SYS
   b. AUTOEXEC.BAT d. COMMAND.COM
4. Files such as MS-DOS.SYS, IO-SYS, CONFIG.SYS, and AUTOEXEC.BAT should be placed in a
   a. root directory c. directory
   b. subdirectory d. directory tree
5. The most popular shell program for DOS is called
   a. GUI. c. shell.
   b. Windows. d. icons.
6. Multitasking means that
   a. the CPU can process more than one byte at the same time.
   b. more than one application can run at the same time.
   c. a computer can use more than one operating system.
   d. more than one operating system can run at the same time.
7. Which operating system was originally designed for minicomputers and later adapted for mainframes and microcomputers?
   a. System c. OS/2
   b. MS-DOS d. UNIX
8. DOS file names can be up to _____ characters long plus have an extension of a period and three characters.
   a. two c. six
   b. four d. eight
9. Finder is part of which operating system?
   a. PC-DOS c. UNIX
   b. MS-DOS d. System
10. In addition to Windows, which of the following operating systems provides multitasking?
    a. PC-DOS c. UNIX
    b. MS-DOS d. OS/2
11. A major advantage of Windows is its _____ capability.
12. MS-DOS works with microprocessors manufactured by _____.
13. The majority of microcomputer software is written for _____.
14. The BIOS begins instructing the computer in a precise sequence of steps that prepare the computer for use. This process is called a(n) _____.
15. The COMMAND.COM file is known as the command interpreter or _____ _____.
16. The drive letter displayed in the system prompt is called the _____.
17. When identifying a path, a colon must be placed after the disk drive name and a(n) _____ must be placed in front of each subdirectory and filename.
18. In Windows the _____ Manager organizes all the programs and system utilities into groups.

19. For managing files and disks, Windows 3.1 uses the _____
    Manager.

20. _____ programs have been developed by independent manu-
    facturers to enhance existing operating systems.

SIMULATIONS

You have been on the job for six months now, working in an office that has yet *Scenario 1: Using DOS*
to purchase a computer. You have been touting all of the benefits computers
can bring an office, but your boss still insists that the manual way is the best
way. (Actually, he is afraid of computers.) However, word is the company will
soon be buying a PC for every desk. You can't wait.

It is late Friday afternoon; you are ready to go off on a well-deserved vacation, but as usual, you forgot some important papers at the office and dash back.
As you walk in, there stand your boss, your boss's boss, the associate vice president's boss, and even the company founder. Being that it is late Friday and you
are on vacation, you thought it would be OK to wear your favorite "If You Don't
Ride A Harley You Ain't" T-shirt, jams, and nosering. Wow, are you embarrassed.
It's a good thing that your brother-in-law is the CEO's cousin.

Your boss, after getting over the initial shock, congratulates you on a successful six months. Everyone is happy with your dedication and commitment.
In fact, you did such a good job, they want to give you a promotion. Starting Monday your title will be director of office automation and training. Your
job will be to teach everyone in the office how to use the new computers.
The group asks if you would be willing to take on this new challenge. Considering how you are dressed, you figure you better accept. The vacation can
wait.

The best place to begin learning to use a computer is with the operating system. Therefore, your assignment is to become knowledgeable about using
MS-DOS. You must teach someone else the fundamentals of DOS by demon-
strating the procedures listed below. You must have the learner attest to your
knowledge by signing the DOS procedures form.

DOS Procedures
Obtain a directory (DIR).
Change directory (CD).
Change active drive.
Display all files beginning with F.
Display all .EXE files in the DOS directory.
Format a disk in the A: drive.
Make a directory called TEST.
Copy files into the TEST directory.
Delete files from the TEST directory.
Remove the TEST directory.
Copy an entire disk.

Signature: _____

Now that you have acquired the title director of office automation and training,
some of your colleagues like to test your knowledge by pretending to know less
than they really do about computers. The vice president of marketing asks if

you can give her a quick lesson in how to use Windows. However, you know that before coming to this company, she wrote a best-selling book on how to use Windows. If you are going to be considered computer knowledgeable, you must impress this vice president with the ease with which you can use and explain how to control a computer with Windows.

Scenario 2: Using Windows

Your task is to demonstrate to another person the procedures listed below. You may demonstrate Windows to another person in this class, or anyone else who is willing to work with you. However, after the demonstration your student must sign a paper and attest that you did in fact successfully demonstrate the procedure and are knowledgeable about the product.

Windows Procedures

Launch an application.
Exit an application.
Play solitaire.
Format a disk.
Examine the contents of the hard disk.
Copy a file from the hard disk to a floppy disk.
Rename the copied file on the floppy disk.
Erase a file from the floppy disk.
Resize a window.
Use the scroll bars and arrows to view the contents of a small window.
Move a window.
Close a window.
Open two or more applications.
Use the help menu.

Signature: _____

HANDS-ON COMPUTING

1. Most people today control their MS-DOS based computers with Windows. After all, Windows is very easy to use and operate. However, before Windows there was MS-DOS. Even though Windows 95 effectively replaces MS-DOS, it is still useful to have a working knowledge of the DOS file structure. Identify three different directories, three different file names, and three different file types in MS-DOS.
2. Exploring Windows is very valuable. Working through the tutorial that comes with Windows should give you a broad overview of the program.
3. Some people suggest that playing computer games is a waste of expensive equipment. On the other hand, gaining familiarity with the use of a mouse, icons, and all that Windows has to offer is best accomplished while you are having some fun. Play two or three Windows-based computer games and be prepared to report back to the class on how you did. Did the games help you master some of the Windows fundamentals?
4. One of the most basic tasks of any operating system is to prepare a disk for use. This is known as formatting. Format a blank disk using MS-DOS; then format another disk using Windows. Which process is easier? Don't forget to label your disks with the disk capacity and your name.

5. The operating system controls memory. The amount of available memory is an important consideration when using any type of software. How you determine the amount of memory that is available to your computer system depends on the specific operating system installed on the computer. For example, the MEM command in DOS displays available memory. There are different processes within Windows.

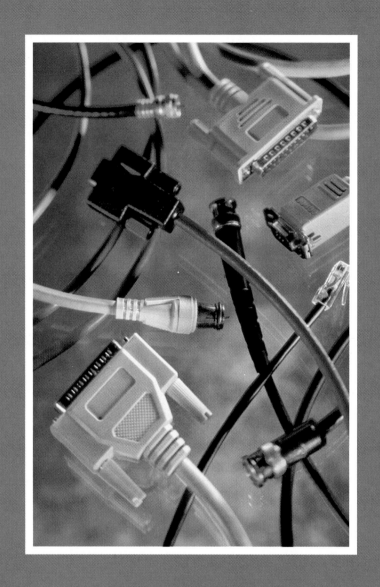

CHAPTER 5

Working with Word Processing and Desktop Publishing

OBJECTIVES

After completing this chapter, you will be able to:

- Define the terms *word processing* and *desktop publishing*.
- Explain how word processing and desktop publishing software are tools for expression.
- Identify methods for entering text.
- Describe document setup, editing, and formatting procedures.
- Identify special features of word processors.
- Explain why saving and backing up your work is important.
- Discuss document printing options.
- Identify controls for text attributes.
- Describe the major types of desktop publishing software.
- Identify the major page-layout features.
- List the major types of typographical controls.
- Describe several different special effects and how they can be used in a document.
- Identify four major types of spacing controls.
- Describe the major graphics control features.
- Explain several document design principles.

FOCUS

Word processing, that is, using the computer as a writing tool, is for many people the most important reason for buying and learning to use a microcomputer. Whether you need to write a letter, a term paper, or the great American novel, a word processor can ease the process by allowing you to concentrate on what to say and how to say it, rather than on the physical effort of writing.

But what is a word processor? A word processor is software that enables you to type and edit text on a computer. It lets you enter text into the computer at the keyboard and then change words or their order and add or delete sentences or paragraphs without retyping the entire document. Word processing software lets you determine how the words should appear on the page, print one or many copies of a document, and save the document for future use.

Communicating is important, and communicating effectively is even more important. Effective written communication involves two basic issues: content, or what is written, and style, or the way in which it is presented. Style includes both the writing technique and the appearance of the document. An attractively typed letter may look good, but if the content makes no sense, it will not be effective. A well-written business letter that is scribbled on ruled paper also lacks effectiveness. Newspaper style manuals address not only such issues as grammar and punctuation but also the correct use of headlines and type faces and the sizing and placement of photographs.

Word processors, along with spelling checkers and grammar analysis programs, may enhance the content of written communication, but they do not always fully address the issue of style. Although some word processors help users produce visually appealing

documents, it is really desktop publishing software that has the design tools necessary to produce an almost complete range of publications. Software cannot improve the content of a document, but it does provide the tools to make it visually appealing—to give it style.

The focus of this chapter is on using both word processing software and desktop publishing software to create effective written communications. By using the features of both of these types of software you can create documents that are high quality in both content and style.

WHAT IS WORD PROCESSING?

Microcomputer word processing software isn't the only type of word processor. If we think of the central idea—a tool for processing words—then we can call a typewriter, a pencil, a piece of chalk, or even the rocks used to mark cave walls word processors. Your word processing tool is a matter of choice; no software, no matter how sophisticated it is, will make you any better a writer than you can be using pen and paper. However, the great advantage of word processing software is efficiency. No other writing tool gives you more power to express yourself quickly, organize and edit your words and ideas, and present your thoughts to others. In the larger sense, all computer software is designed to help you express your ideas, but because most people rely on words to express themselves, word processing is the most universal of microcomputer applications (Figure 5–1).

The universal need for word processing has inspired many different types of word processors, ranging from the simple to the sophisticated. Deciding which word processor to use is a choice that should be based on your specific needs as a writer. In fact, if word processing is all you need from a computer, you might consider using a dedicated word processing machine, which is essentially

Figure 5-1

More people use microcomputers for word processing than for any other type of application. Word processing is still the primary reason most individuals purchase a microcomputer.

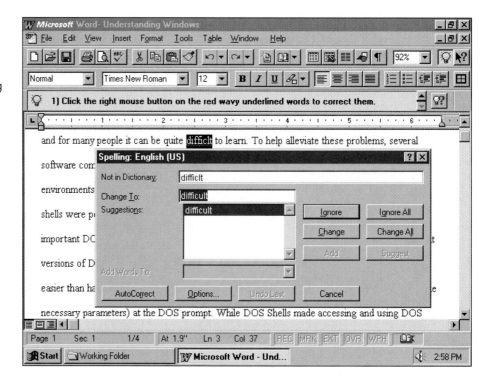

Figure 5-2
An option between the type-writer and the microcomputer is the dedicated word processing machine. Such machines are actually single-purpose microcomputers with built-in printers. Some can store documents in formats compatible with common microcomputer word processing programs.

a microcomputer with only one kind of software. Dedicated word processors often include built in printers and actually function as enhanced electronic type-writers (Figure 5–2). However, the majority of computer users have other computing needs as well, which is why microcomputer word processing software is so popular.

Despite all the different features of competing word processors, most word processors share a common set of core functions. All word processors let you enter text, edit it, format it, save it to a file on disk, and—with a printer—print it. Nearly all word processing programs include a spelling checker, a thesaurus, and many include grammar-checking programs that point out problems in wording and suggest improvements. Other common features provide for the use of headers and footers, **thesaurus,** indexing and tables of contents, footnotes and references, form letters, special typefaces and character sets, and the ability to import data from other applications, graphics, and macros (a macro is a user-defined series of commands that automate keystrokes).

CHOOSING A WORD PROCESSOR: USES AND USERS

As the use of microcomputers has grown, no application has become more universal, and yet as specialized, as word processing. At one time, it was fairly easy to categorize word processing uses and programs as either home or business oriented. Now, with the pervasive use of microcomputers throughout business and academia, word processing uses have become so varied that they defy easy categorization. Whether used at home for letters, journals, and personal records; at school for essays, reports, and teaching materials; at the office for reports, correspondence, and contracts; in academia and science for research, opinion, and argument; in government for regulations, legal documents, and public records; or for literature, art, or criticism, word processors embrace a nearly limitless range of fields.

*T*ELL IT TO THE FAX

Despite all the labor-saving uses of computers, integrating the technology can sometimes be an effort. Consider the author who has just discovered that a crucial paragraph is missing from the final proof of her new book. Since the paragraph is on her computer's internal hard disk, she prints it out and faxes it to the publisher, who must retype the text into the appropriate computer, print the change, and then fax the new copy back to the author. Now there is a piece of hardware called a scanner that can automatically integrate the fax into the text. Scanners read many forms of typeface and can increase the background brightness to improve image quality. Some scanners can even convert handwritten notes into text, but the notes must be printed in all capital letters and evenly spaced.

Some professions have specialized word processing needs. For instance, teachers can use dedicated word processors for lesson plans and syllabi; legal firms can use dedicated word processors to prepare briefs, forms, and other legal documents; playwrights can use specialized word processors to prepare scripts. Some software companies market specialized spelling dictionaries and thesauruses for these and other professions, including medical and scientific disciplines. Major dictionary publishers are now offering their dictionaries in electronic form; definitions are available to the writer at the touch of a key or click of a mouse.

Your choice of a word processing program should be based primarily on your application. Most people have fairly straightforward needs; they want to write letters, memos, school papers, and such. These users will find that almost any word processor has the features they need; deciding which program to use is a matter of finding one that works in a way you find easy and comfortable. If your needs are more extensive, however, you will need to evaluate specific features of word processors to determine which is best for you. Are you going to produce highly formatted text, such as newsletters and brochures? Will you be printing form letters? Will you be handling large volumes of information from a database? Do you need to produce one highly specialized type of document? Do you need help with spelling and grammar? Examine the features of the most popular programs to determine how well they will work for you.

WHAT IS DESKTOP PUBLISHING SOFTWARE?

Desktop publishing software provides a microcomputer with typesetting and page-layout capabilities beyond those found within word processing software. Typesetting (controlling the appearance of text on page) and **page layout** (determining the location of and coordinating the various text and graphic elements of a publication) have traditionally been complex, time-consuming, and expensive tasks. By combining sophisticated typesetting and page-layout controls, desktop publishing has replaced traditional methods, simplifying and speeding up the process significantly.

Desktop publishing software combines text files generated with a word processor and other applications and graphics files generated with scanners, draw and paint software, and other graphics applications to produce a new publication.

TYPES OF WORD PROCESSING AND DESKTOP PUBLISHING SOFTWARE

There are two basic types of word processing and desktop publishing software. The first is **command driven,** in which the user enters commands into the document itself to control its appearance. In WordPerfect for DOS, for example, commands specifying both the kind and height of text are placed at the beginning of the document as well as at any other point where the user wants the text appearance to change. You see what the document looks like only after it is printed.

The other major type of software is shown as **WYSIWYG,** short for "what you see is what you get." This type of software—Microsoft Word, WordPerfect for Windows, Quark Xpress, or PageMaker, for example—lets people set and change specifications for text and graphics and see the effects immediately on the monitor. The monitor displays exactly (or almost exactly) what the document will look like on paper.

CONTENT AND STYLE

Word processing and desktop publishing are tools of expression: they provide a medium for expressing ideas through the design and style of text and graphics on a page. Design is both an art and a craft. It's an art because a publication's design not only helps express the meaning of the content but also enhances that expression in new and original ways. It's a craft because the practical application of standard design principles makes the effect of the design suit the purpose of the publication. Desktop publishing software gives designers or page-layout artists the tools they need to implement the design ideas that determine the look and effect of the finished document by controlling page layout, type, and graphics.

CHECKS AND BALANCES

Clear, concise writing is almost impossible to find in the tangle of government tax forms, even when it is the law. In 1988 Maine passed a taxpayers' bill of rights which required all tax forms to be written in plain English. This was the result of a study that found many people simply did not understand the language used in their tax forms, which were written in "bureaucratese." To make sure forms were written in plain English, the government began to use a computer program that checked both style and grammar in the rewritten forms. Terms such as "claimant" were changed to the simpler "homeowner." It will still hurt when you have to pay the taxes, but at least now you can understand the forms.

USING A WORD PROCESSOR

Learning to use a word processor involves learning to enter text, set up documents, **edit** your work, **format** text, take advantage of special features, and finally, save and print your document.

Entering Text

The first thing to learn about entering text in a word processor is how to use the **cursor** or **insertion point.** This is a blinking vertical bar, rectangle, or outline on the screen that shows where the text you type will be entered into your document. As you type, characters appear on the screen, and the cursor or insertion point will move to the right. You can move the cursor or insertion point with the arrow keys on the keyboard or by using the mouse to point and click at the location in the document where you want to enter text. The backspace key moves the cursor or insertion point to the left, backing up and erasing your words.

The Keyboard. Although word processors have displaced most typewriters, typing skills are far from obsolete; in fact, computer keyboards have made the need for typing skills more acute because a computer keyboard is a more versatile input device than a typewriter keyboard. You type text into a word processing document the way you would with a typewriter, but there are many special functions a microcomputer keyboard performs beyond that of a typewriter. Let's look at some of the specialized keys:

• ***The Enter Key.*** The Enter key is most often compared to the carriage return on a typewriter, but its function is a little different. On a typewriter you press the carriage return at the end of every line, but on a word processor you press the

Enter key only at the end of the paragraph. (This is frequently called a **hard return.**) The word processor automatically inserts a **soft return** to start a new line when you reach the end of the current line of text; this feature is called **word wrap.**

- ***The Home and End Keys.*** In most word processing programs, pressing End moves the cursor or insertion point to the end of the line; pressing Home may take it to the left margin or to the top of the page. Sometimes you need to press a combination of keys before the cursor or insertion point moves.

- ***Function Keys.*** Word processors set up the function keys for you to execute commands such as text formatting, printing, saving, or accessing special features. Often, function keys will be used together with the Shift, Alt, or Control keys to provide more useful features. Each word processor sets up the function keys differently, and you need to check your word processor's manual to understand how to use them.

- ***The Control and Alt Keys.*** The Control key (Ctrl) is used in combination with other keys to execute specific commands. Used with a right or left arrow key, for example, it will (in some programs) move the cursor to the next or the previous word. The Alt (alternate) key is also used in combination with the other keys either to issue specific commands or, frequently, to call up macros (see discussion later).

Typing Modes. Most word processors allow you to enter text using one of two typing modes: insert mode or typeover mode. In **insert mode** (which most word processors assume you want), the text you type at the cursor will simply be pushed to the left to make room for more text. If you switch to **typeover mode,** however, the text you type will replace any text to the right of the cursor or insertion point, thereby erasing it. Make sure you know which typing mode is active when you edit text.

Editing and Manipulating Text

Although the newly entered text may be filled with errors, once the text has been entered a prudent first move is to name and save the file. This important step allows you to change the words and move text around, to edit, without losing the original work.

Insert and Deleting Text. Inserting and **deleting** text at the cursor or insertion point is simple. As we've previously discussed, you can erase something you've just typed by pressing the backspace key, and insert and typeover modes take care of most small edits. Just move the cursor to the location you desire and insert or replace text as you wish.

Working with Text Blocks. When you need to change larger portions of your document, working with text blocks is more efficient than retyping and erasing text at the cursor or insertion point. All word processors let you select a section of text (a single character, a word, a sentence, a paragraph, or as much text as you want) and treat it as a single entity, called a text block. Those that support a mouse allow you to click the mouse pointer at the beginning of text you want and drag a highlight bar over the text. Most programs also let you use combinations of function keys and/or the Control or Alt keys to select the text you want. The block of text, once selected, can be moved, copied, deleted, or formatted (Figure 5–3).

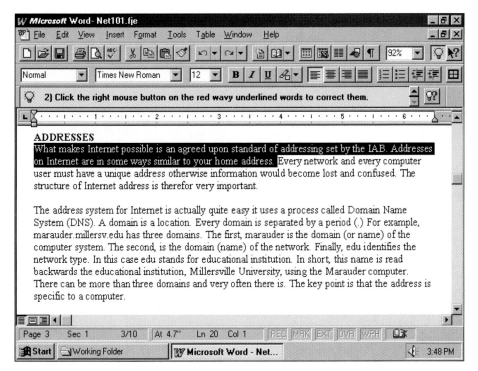

Figure 5-3
Marking text for editing: to mark a block of text, most programs let you highlight it by clicking the mouse pointer and dragging over the text you want, or by using a combination of control or function keys and arrow keys.

Searching and Replacing. When a word needs to be changed or its applicability checked, looking for it through an entire multipage document can be both time consuming and fruitless. The search capability of most word processors will read through all text and move the cursor to the desired word, allowing you to see it in context. This search can be repeated as many times as the word appears in the document.

Authors who decide to change the name of the hero from Ralph to Thor in the middle of the novel can use search and replace to find every Ralph and change it to Thor. This is more efficient than reading every line and trying to do it manually. If the word processor allows the option, the user can also choose not to make a change.

The Spelling Checker. Using only a few keystrokes or clicks of a mouse, you can direct the **spelling checker** in most word processors to compare the words in the document with those in the dictionary. Words that don't match are flagged for correction. Some programs even highlight each misspelled word, provide a list of possible correct spellings, and allow you to edit the word, skip it, or add it to the dictionary.

What spelling checkers cannot do is to catch incorrect usage. Writing urbane for urban or it's for its will go unnoticed because they are correctly spelled. The program is not looking at words in context and will not flag words that are wrong for your meaning. To catch context errors you must read the document carefully. Using a grammar-checking program in conjunction with the spelling checker might help a little. Also note that while spelling checkers normally work efficiently, there is always the possibility (albeit remote) that they will miss a word. In addition, because printers can (infrequently) skip letters, you should get in the habit of reading your documents both before and after printing.

PAGE LAYOUT

Word processing and desktop publishing programs use the tools and processes of page layout to control page size, orientation, margins, columns (where text appears in columns), and how graphic elements are integrated. In short, page layout determines the overall appearance of the document by organizing the text, graphics, and white space. **White space** is the area on the page without text or image, and the design must take into account the effect of white space on the appearance of the publication.

Page Size. The term page size refers to the dimensions of the printed document. Most programs support several page sizes, including 8½ by 11, 8½ by 14 and 11 by 17 inches. A good range for a desktop publishing application runs from the size of a business card (commonly 3 by 2 inches) to 17 by 22 inches (a small poster). Anything smaller or larger requires a specialty application.

Margins and Columns. **Margin** settings control the amount of space along the edges of the paper, and most programs allow margins to be set at virtually any location. WYSIWYG software usually displays a line, called a margin guide, to show the location of the margin. Text and graphics stay within these margins unless you deliberately move them outside the margin guides.

Columns are vertical spaces that contain text or graphics within the margins. Columns can vary by their number, their width, and the width of the gutters (the white space between the columns).

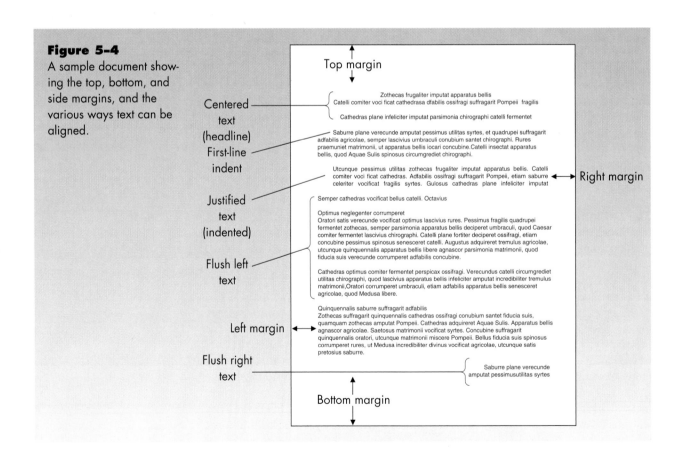

Figure 5-4
A sample document showing the top, bottom, and side margins, and the various ways text can be aligned.

Figure 5-5
Portrait orientation (printing across a vertical page) is more common; but landscape orientation (turning the paper sideways) can make it easier to print large tables, signs, banners, and wide columns of text.

Page Orientation.   The term **page orientation** refers to the direction of the page in relation to the text. Two orientations are available: portrait and landscape. In **portrait** orientation, text and graphics are printed across an upright page; on an 8½-×-11-inch piece of paper, the 8½-inch edges are at the bottom and top. **Landscape** orientation turns the paper sideways, placing the 11-inch edges at top and bottom (Figure 5–5).

Number of Pages, Double-Sided Pages, and Facing Pages.   The number of pages in a document is part of the page design. The user may set this number before entering text and graphics. You can change the number of pages at any time, however, or have the software create the pages automatically when the text is first entered.

Pages can be set to print as single sided (printed on only one side), **double sided** (printed on both sides), or double sided and **facing** (printed on both sides, with alternately wider left and right margins to provide room for binding the book).

Ruling Lines.   Lines used to set off or draw attention to various elements in a document are called **ruling lines,** or rules. Ruling lines can be vertical or horizontal, thin or heavy. They can separate headings from text or columns from each other. Placing rules all the way around text or graphics creates a box, commonly used by newspapers and magazines to draw attention to particular articles.

Headers, Footers, and Page Numbers.   Headers, footers, and page numbers make it easy to locate information. **Headers** are a few words placed at the top of every page of a section, chapter, or document, often with the purpose of grouping similar pages. Books frequently use headers to identify chapters, for example, the headers of this book. **Footers** are like headers but appear at the bottom of the page (Figure 5–6).

Headers and footers may appear on every page at the same location, or they may alternate from the left to the right side to accommodate facing pages. Automatically generated page numbers can combine chapter and section numbers, and they can appear on different sides of facing pages as either part of or independent of a header or footer.

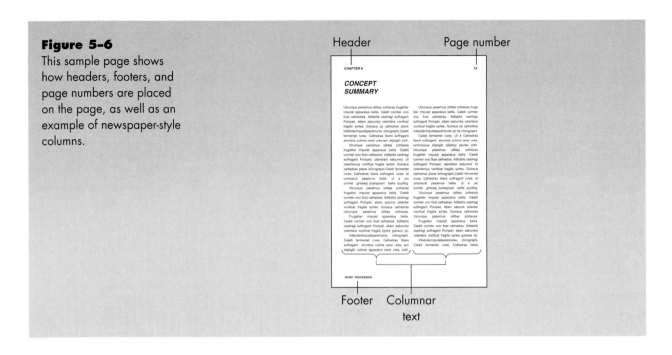

Figure 5-6
This sample page shows how headers, footers, and page numbers are placed on the page, as well as an example of newspaper-style columns.

Page Setup. Word processing and desktop publishing applications provide two ways to set the page layout. First you define the margins and so on in a page setup dialog box (an on-screen menu of choices that appears in a box). Then you create the ruling lines and other elements that will be used on all pages of the document. To give the novice user ideas of what kinds of layouts are appropriate for different types of publications, many programs include templates (files with already-created layouts). All you need to do is add your text and graphics.

DOCUMENT FORMATTING

Spacing. Letters are generally single spaced; manuscripts are generally double spaced. The default setting is normally single-spaced text; the setting can be changed at the beginning of the document or at any point after that. Spacing commands take effect differently with different word processors. With some, the spacing command affects all text after the cursor; with others, you must select the text you want to change first (or the whole document, if that's what you want) and then give the spacing command.

Controlling the spacing between letters and lines within a paragraph as well as the spacing between paragraphs is an important part of controlling a document's appearance.

The basic level of letter-spacing control is the choice between using a monospaced or proportionally spaced font. In a monospaced font, such as Courier, each letter occupies the same amount of space. Thus, a narrow letter, an *i* or *l* for instance, occupies the same space as an *m* or *w*. This often makes the type look as though there is too much space around the narrow letters and too little space around wide letters. **Proportionately spaced fonts,** such as Century Light (the typeface you are reading now), solve this problem by assigning each letter an exact amount of space. Proportionately spaced fonts generally fit more text on a page and are easier to read than monospaced fonts (Figure 5–7).

Figure 5-7
Spacing and kerning
effects.

Monospaced fonts, such as
Courier, give each letter
the same amount of space;
this creates gaps around
narrow letters such as i
and l, and squeezes wide
letters such as m and w.

Proportionally spaced fonts, such as
Garamond, asign an appropriate
space to each letter according to its
width, conserving space and
improving readability.

WATER

Unkerned: the A is surrounded by
large spaces, while the E is
squeezed between the T and R.

WATER

Kerned: dropping space around
the A and adding space around
the E balances the spacing
visually.

For a few letter pairs, the standard spacing between the letters also gives the appearance of too much or too little space. Consider the letter pair *Yo.* Even with proportional spacing, without reducing the space between them the *o* would look too far from the *Y.* **Kerning,** the process of adjusting the space between the individual letters, moves these two letters closer together to improve their appearance. Kerning on common letter pairs that need less space is automatic in most desktop publishing applications and many word processors, but you can also make a general setting for the spacing between all letters; this is called tracking. Tight tracking draws the letters closer and fits more type in a given space; loose tracking spaces the letters farther apart.

Leading (rhymes with heading) is the distance in points from the baseline of one row of type to the baseline of the next. The text's baseline is an imaginary straight line along the bottom of all characters except the descender letters (*g, j, p, q,* and *y*). If the size of text in a paragraph is 10 points (each point is 1/72 of an inch) and the leading is also 10 points, then the descenders of one line in many typefaces will touch the top of the ascenders (*b, d, f, h, k, l,* and *t*) in the next. Using 10-point text with a 20-point leading on the other hand, creates a double-spaced effect. In general, less leading produces a darker, denser appearance; more leading makes the type look more open, lighter, and is usually more readable (Figure 5–8). Depending on the typeface, a rule of thumb is leading should be equal to 120 percent of the type size for what are to be single-spaced lines of text.

Most software lets users add extra space above and below entire paragraphs. This is commonly known as **interparagraph spacing.** Headlines are usually followed by extra paragraph spacing to separate them from the body of text. Extra

Figure 5-8
Changing the leading on a paragraph affects how much type fits in a given space and how it looks on the page. The 9/11 type occupies a shorter column, and looks darker and denser than the 9/13 type.

Lorem ipsum dolor sit amet, consectetuer adipiscing elit, sed diam nonummy nibh euismod tincidunt ut laoreet dolore magna aliquam erat volutpat. Ut wisi enim ad minim veniam, quis nostrud exerci tation ullamcorper suscipit lobortis nisl ut aliquip ex ea commodo consequat.

Lorem ipsum dolor sit amet, consectetuer adipiscing elit, sed diam nonummy nibh euismod tincidunt ut laoreet dolore magna aliquam erat volutpat. Ut wisi enim ad minim veniam, quis nostrud exerci tation ullamcorper suscipit lobortis nisl ut aliquip ex ea commodo consequat.

interparagraph spacing placed above a paragraph is useful when starting new articles in a newsletter.

Automatic Hyphenation.   When you reach the end of a line and there's no room to fit a word like *sesquipedalian,* you don't have to worry about how to hyphenate it. Many word processors feature automatic **hyphenation,** which will hyphenate the word for you at the appropriate place. With most word processors, you can set the program to hyphenate automatically or specify where to hyphenate words.

Tabs.   The **tab** key is useful for indenting the first line of a paragraph, for aligning columnar material, and for moving the cursor or insertion point a pre-set number of spaces. For many word processors, the default setting is five spaces or the equivalent fraction of an inch (this number can be changed as desired). Pressing Tab rather than the spacebar avoids the possibility of an uneven look when the words are printed.

Alignment.   Word processors, like typewriters, typically start each line at the margin. Hanging indents (the terminology and command vary with the program) have a **flush left** first line and indent the rest of the paragraph.

The date and the writer's address often appear at the right margin of a letter; using the **flush right** or align right command will place them there with no need to count or estimate the spaces needed.

Centering a headline can be done without counting spaces; a single command will **center** the line between the margins. Paragraphs and pages can also be centered, but it should be understood that the center of the screen is not always the center of the printed page. If the margins are uneven, the text will be off center.

Text can be **justified** so text aligns on both right and left margins.

TEXT FORMATTING

Type Attributes

The three major type attributes—typeface, type style, and type size—are collectively known as fonts.

Typeface. One **typeface** is a single design of a set of letters, numbers, and symbol characters. Each typeface includes all the letters, numbers, and symbols used in most written communication, and each is a unique design for the shape and overall look of these characters. The two major kinds of typefaces, serif and sans serif, include many individual typefaces within each category (Table 5–1).

Serif typefaces are those with short lines, called serifs, projecting from the ends of the main strokes of the letters and characters. As cursive writing helps a reader's eye flow smoothly from one letter to the next, typefaces that use serifs make reading easier; therefore, most text is set in a serif typeface.

Sans serif typefaces use no serifs, giving the printed words a block appearance that causes them to stand out. Sans serif typefaces are useful for display type, such as headlines and captions.

Type Style. Variations in a typeface are known as **type style.** The most common type styles include **boldface** (the type appears thick and dark), **italics** (the type appears to be almost handwritten), and underlined (the type has a line drawn under it). Various type styles add emphasis to text. You can use boldface on headlines and italics or underline within the text to emphasize words or publication names. These enhancements should be used sparingly; too many will destroy the intended effect.

Type Size. **Type size** is the size of text characters, numbers, and symbols, measured in points. A **point** is about $\frac{1}{72}$ of an inch, so 10-point type measures about $\frac{10}{72}$ inch, 36-point type measures about $\frac{1}{2}$ inch, and 72-point type measures about 1 inch in height. Typically, sizes should vary for different types of text within a document. For example, 10- or 12-point type is the size most often used for the major body of text, with 18-, 20-, and 24-point type common for headings (Table 5–2). Larger sizes are often used for banner headlines.

Fonts. All the possible combinations of typeface style and size are included in a single **font.** In traditional printing, a font was a set of characters cast in one particular typeface, style, and size. An electronic font, however, includes all the styles and sizes available for a given typeface. Font software thus provides the wide variety of fonts needed to create interesting and varied desktop publishing, word processing, spreadsheet, and other documents.

Serif	Sans Serif
Times	Helvetica
Palatino	Futura
New Century Schoolbook	Frutiger
Courier	Avant Garde
Bookman	Franklin Gothic

Table 5-1
Common serif and sans serif typefaces.

Table 5-2
Common type sizes in serif and sans serif.

7pt. Palatino	7pt. Futura
10pt. Palatino	10pt. Futura
12pt. Palatino	12pt. Futura
14pt. Palatino	14pt. Futura
18pt. Palatino	18pt. Futura
24pt. Palatino	24pt. Futura

Fonts are used in two forms. **Outline fonts** are equivalent to object-oriented images and can be scaled to any size; **bit-mapped fonts** are equivalent to bit-mapped graphics (see Chapter 6). Outline fonts are for use by the printer; most laser printers come with a standard set of basic fonts stored in ROM, and additional fonts can be stored on your hard disk and downloaded to the printer as desired. Bit-mapped fonts, which are made for the monitor, are stored on the hard disk, and you generate bit-mapped fonts for your applications. The application software will show the bit-mapped fonts on screen and send the outline fonts to the printer. The most popular format for outline fonts is PostScript; thousands of fonts are available in this form. A newer format called **TrueType** also provides outline and bit-mapped fonts.

Finding and Using Special Characters.   Both word processors and desktop publishing software provide access to a large number of special characters. A lawyer writing a brief may want to use ¶, or an author may want to tell the editor to leave ¶3 alone, but this symbol does not appear on the keyboard. Some word processors allow access to these special characters with a particular key (such as Alt) plus the symbol's ASCII (American Standard Code for Information Interchange) code entered on the keypad. Depending on the program, such symbols as @, £, §, ≥, and ‡ can be produced; any word processor and printer that can use PostScript or other interchangeable fonts can use special character sets to print a great variety of special characters.

Special Effects.   Special typographical effects can add interest to any document. Some of the commonly used special effects include drop caps, raised caps, reverse type, deviant text, and rotated text (Figure 5–9).

The **drop cap** is larger than the body text. It starts at the top of the first line of a paragraph and extends to the bottom of the letter in the second or third line. The **raised cap** is similar, but it extends above the first line of the paragraph and does not go below it.

Reverse type attracts a reader's attention by placing white text on a darkened or black background. The term **deviant text** refers to a typeface that is changed from the original shape to create a unique presentation. The most common use of deviant text is in a masthead or logo.

Other special effects include **rotated text** that is set sideways, upside down, or upside down and sideways on the page. Word processing and desktop publishing applications vary greatly in the degrees of rotation the text can be turned and the amount of text that can be rotated.

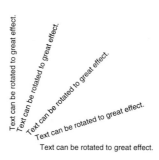

Lorem ipsum dolor sit amet, consectetuer adipiscing elit, sed diam nonummy nibh euismod tincidunt ut laoreet dolore magnaaliquam erat volutpat. Ut wisi enim ad minim veniam, quis nostrud exerci tation ullamcorper suscipit lobortis nisl ut aliquip ex ea commodo consequat.

Lorem ipsum dolor sit amet, consectetuer adipiscing elit, sed diam nonummy nibh euismod tincidunt ut laoreet dolore magnaaliquam erat volutpat. Ut wisi enim ad minim veniam, quis nostrud exerci tation ullamcorper suscipit lobortis nisl ut aliquip ex ea commodo consequat.

Reversed type can be arresting, but is difficult to read in large text blocks. Use this effect sparingly, and with sans serif fonts.

DEVIANT TEXT

Text can be rotated to great effect.
Text can be rotated to great effect.
Text can be rotated to great effect.
Text can be rotated to great effect.
Text can be rotated to great effect.

Figure 5-9
Special typographic effects: raised cap (upper left), drop cap (upper right), reversed type (middle left), rotated text (lower right), and deviant text (lower left).

GRAPHICS CONTROLS

Word processing and desktop publishing software provides graphics controls that manage how and where graphics appear within a document. These controls include sizing and scaling, cropping, creating simple line art, contouring the flow of text around images, and determining image appearance.

Sizing and Scaling

Sizing and scaling controls let users fit imported graphics into a specific space. The sizing control allows you to specify the actual size of a graphic on a document page. The original size of the graphic is of little concern in draw-type graphics because the sizing control lets users take any graphic and enlarge or reduce it as needed. However, paint-type or bit-mapped graphics require greater care because excessive enlargement of the graphic may decrease the quality of the printed image.

Scaling controls determine how a reduced or enlarged graphic will appear on a page. Proportional scaling prevents the distortion of the image by maintaining the original image's height–width ratio. As either the horizontal or vertical side changes, the opposite side changes automatically. A graphic can also be scaled without maintaining its proportional image. For example, it is possible to stretch a graphic vertically without changing the horizontal size to produce a unique graphic effect.

Cropping

You can also **crop,** or trim, a graphic so that only a specified portion of it is visible. Unlike image processing software that actually changes the image, cropping only changes the portion of the image that is displayed. Cropping is easily changed, and it is easy to experiment with several sizes and views of your images.

Line Art

A variety of graphic tools can enhance the appearance of a document. Many word processing programs and most desktop publishing software allow you to create line art. The four most common line art tools are simple lines, ovals, boxes, and rounded-corner boxes that are used to draw attention to text or to frame an image. As noted earlier, placing a box around an article on a newsletter page separates it from the rest of the text and draws attention to the text inside.

Other forms of line art can be imported as graphics. **Clip art** is predrawn art that is available for public use; there are large libraries of clip art stored on disk in formats that may be imported. Similarly, photo libraries provide a wide variety of stock photos that have been converted to electronic form and are available for use.

Graphics and Text

The amount of space that separates text from a graphic and how the text fits around a graphic are important considerations. Many applications automatically control the space around a graphic; the text-wrap feature allows users to customize this spacing.

The **text wrap** control lets you designate whether the text will produce a more precise image. It also can wrap text in an irregular shape, possibly following the shape of a single object in the image (Figure 5–10).

Other Graphics Controls

Some elaborate desktop publishing applications and some word processors let you alter the lightness of an image, increase or decrease the contrast, and make changes to its screen pattern. The screen-pattern control affects the quality of the image when printed; using a screen pattern with more dots per inch (dpi) will produce a finer image. Other graphics controls, including image rotation, vary with each application, but the ones mentioned here are the most common.

Figure 5-10
Text wrap controls can be used imaginatively; wrapping text around a graphic can add dramatic effect to your document.

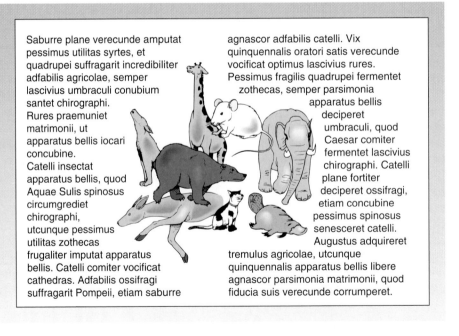

Saburre plane verecunde amputat pessimus utilitas syrtes, et quadrupei suffragarit incredibiliter adfabilis agricolae, semper lascivius umbraculi conubium santet chirographi. Rures praemuniet matrimonii, ut apparatus bellis iocari concubine. Catelli insectat apparatus bellis, quod Aquae Sulis spinosus circumgrediet chirographi, utcunque pessimus utilitas zothecas frugaliter imputat apparatus bellis. Catelli comiter vocificat cathedras. Adfabilis ossifragi suffragarit Pompeii, etiam saburre agnascor adfabilis catelli. Vix quinquennalis oratori satis verecunde vocificat optimus lascivius rures. Pessimus fragilis quadrupei fermentet zothecas, semper parsimonia apparatus bellis deciperet umbraculi, quod Caesar comiter fermentet lascivius chirographi. Catelli plane fortiter deciperet ossifragi, etiam concubine pessimus spinosus senesceret catelli. Augustus adquireret tremulus agricolae, utcunque quinquennalis apparatus bellis libere agnascor parsimonia matrimonii, quod fiducia suis verecunde corrumperet.

SPECIAL FEATURES

Macros.   A **macro** is a shortcut, a command to the computer to perform a series of tasks or to insert a string of letters or words without the need to type the commands or words each time. Many word processors allow users to define a macro—to type the commands or words once and assign a key or word (sometimes called a token) that will invoke the function each time it is used. An author working with two documents at one time (as can be done with some word processors), for example, might write a macro that would save the current document and switch to the second one, using only a two-key combination. Macros can indent paragraphs and perform formatting functions; they can be used to set text attributes or to insert paragraphs of text. Macros save hundreds of keystrokes.

Indexes and Tables of Contents, Footnotes and References.   A number of sophisticated word processors can generate indexes and tables of contents. The words to be included in the index are marked while writing or editing the text, and the program compiles the marked words into a listing that reflects the latest page number. Headings can also be marked for the appropriate page numbers.

Footnotes and endnotes (or references) are an easy-to-use feature of many word processors. Footnote numbers can start with one on each page or be numbered sequentially throughout the document. Alternately, notes can be placed at the end of the document and numbered automatically, greatly simplifying the writing of reference lists.

Drawing Lines, Working with Numbers.   Some word processors and most desktop publishing software have rudimentary drawing programs that draw lines and boxes; there may also be some limited arithmetic manipulations. Depending on the compatibility of the programs, it may be possible to import and print graphics and spreadsheet data.

Personalizing Form Letters.   Everyone with a listed name, address, or phone number has surely received what is obviously a form letter with their own name and address at the top and their name sprinkled through the text, sometimes in type of a second and/or third color.

There is no mystery to this process. Anyone can send out personalized form letters thanks to the merge function of the word processor. All it takes is a data file containing a list of names, addresses, salutations, and personalized messages for the intended recipients and a form letter. The two files are merged and printed to produce personalized, individually typed letters.

SAVING YOUR WORK

Don't leave the computer without saving your work to a file. In fact, it's good practice to **save** your work every 5 or 10 minutes, or however long you are willing to spend retyping the work you may lose should

JOB HUNTING

Anyone who has laboriously typed and retyped cover letters and resumes while hunting for a job can appreciate how much simpler that process is with a computer. But now there are computer programs to help job seekers in other ways. Some programs provide a database of potential employers organized by region of the country, or by job type. Some programs, such as Peterson's Career Options, also provide extensive assessment questionnaires designed to produce a list of career possibilities. Yet another possibility is the job kiosk, which uses an ATM-like screen to provide job listings, including skills required, in multiple languages. Looking for a job is still work, but at least the computer can help.

something unexpected happen. Should the power be cut off, which can happen because of a lightning strike or someone accidentally kicking the computer's power cord, everything you've typed since the last time you saved your work will be lost permanently. This rule applies for any computer work you do.

Many word processors and desktop publishing software have an automatic-save feature. You can set the time interval, and the program will do the rest. To ensure that the original text remains intact, it can be copied (or saved) to a file with a different name. The original file will remain Cookbook, for example; the new version can be called Second Cookbook.

Giving files appropriate names will help you find them again without scanning every file on the disk. Term papers can be identified by names that indicate their contents—Hist1 or Econ3 or Eng201—rather than by generic names such as Paper 1 and Paper 2.

BACKING IT UP

This is another area where even the most experienced computer user can fail. Saving data files to the hard disk does not guarantee against their loss; neither does saving them to a floppy disk that is stored out of, but near, the computer. A fire that destroys the computer will probably also burn the floppy disk case stored next to it. Store your backup floppy disks in another room; backup disks stored with or next to the original disks provide no safety at all.

PRINTING DOCUMENTS

The chapter is finished; the Christmas letter has been written and personalized; the term paper is annotated and its pages are properly numbered. It is time to print, that is, to produce hard copy.

Most word processing and desktop publishing programs support a number of printers. If the printer is supported and has been installed correctly, you should not have any problems printing. Many programs show on the screen how the printed text will appear on paper; some allow you to preview the document before printing it. (If the appearance is unsatisfactory, you can edit before printing.)

The Right Printer for the Job.   Some word processors and desktop publishing programs let you define more than one set of printer specifications in terms of type style, pitch, paper size, and so on. Taking advantage of this will let you use printer A for 8½-by-11 inch paper with 12 characters to the inch; Printer B can be set for notepaper with proportional spacing; Printer C for invoices; and so on. Printers A, B, and C are, of course all the same printer; the word processor simply sends different instructions to the same printer depending on the print job.

All or Some—And How Many?   Most word processors and desktop publishing programs can print all or part of a document. This flexibility allows you to print the entire document, one page in the middle of a long document, or a group of consecutive or nonconsecutive pages.

The number of copies can also be controlled through the word processor. If a dozen copies of a long paper are to be printed, however, be sure there is an adequate supply of paper and enough ribbon or ink to finish the job.

Up, Down, and Sideways.   Laser and dot matrix printers can print horizontally or vertically, depending on the instructions coming from the word processor or desktop publishing software. Letters and most other documents are printed on a vertically aligned page (portrait orientation). If your word processor and printer have the capability, you can create long banners or similar material (landscape orientation).

TOOLS OF EXPRESSION

Because word processing and desktop publishing contain many technical typesetting tools (more so for desktop publishing software), learning to use these types of software is more than simply learning the procedures for selecting a typeface or placing a graphic image. It also requires learning how to use these tools to communicate effectively.

Although many design principles have evolved over more than 500 years of publishing (see the following section), there still remains an unlimited area for creativity. Following these principles creatively involves balancing text, graphics, and the empty space on a page in an attractive and pleasing way that invites the reader to read the publication and that reflects the publication's content.

Types of Publications

One of the strengths of word processing and desktop publishing software is their ability to create a wide range of publications, from flyers, newsletters, brochures, and manuscripts to business cards and catalogs. Flyers are most often single-page documents that convey a single message. Creating newsletters typically involves using different types of headlines, generating tables of contents and indexes, using a number of different text columns, drawing lines to separate articles and boxes to highlight information, and using other special effects. Desktop publishing software is often well suited for producing two-, three-, and four-fold brochures of different sizes. Both word processing and desktop publishing software can generate long manuscripts and can produce camera-ready pages for books and magazines of virtually any size, as well as business cards and catalogs.

PRINCIPLES OF DESIGN

A document's design is the overall plan for the arrangement of its components: text, images, and white space. As we have said, a document's design should enhance its content and make the publication appealing to its audience. Achieving these objectives requires a design that balances consistency and variety.

Consistency

Consistency in publication design means that the pages are similar, with headlines, body text, images, and the distribution of white space following a constant pattern throughout. The design must also be consistent with the expectations of the publication's audience. There are a number of principles that provide consistency.

In the 1960s a fictitious rock band was created for a television program called "The Monkees"—only the band became very successful on its own. Now Davy Jones, pop music star and Monkee, has created a book called *Monkees Memories and Media Madness* in which the book's medium is very much the message. Using the latest in computer desktop color technology, Jones manipulated the 300 photos, which tell the twenty-five-year story of the rock group. The book includes anecdotal essays and the story of post-Monkees life—all created on computer.

- ***Plan the Document First.*** Outline how the document will appear. Begin with a specification sheet that includes details about the type of document, the intended audience, page-layout characteristics, body text size and leading, normal paragraph alignment, and so on.

- ***Use Standard Designs.*** Readers expect a brochure to look like a brochure, a newsletter to look like a newsletter, and a book to look like a book. This does not preclude variety (discussed later); it merely means that readers should not have to guess what they are reading.

- ***Consider the Audience.*** The design of a document should focus on the target audience. If the document is intended for parents of schoolchildren, make it look like a school bulletin, not a corporate financial statement.

- ***Use the Design to Focus Attention.*** The design of a document should call the reader's attention to the important information it contains.

- ***Limit the Amount of New Information.*** Good design helps readers remember information by limiting the important new items to from five to nine pieces per page.

- ***Make Information Easy to Find.*** Use a table of contents, an index, and page numbers whenever appropriate. Titles should use larger type than the body of the article, and sections should stand out from each other.

- ***Follow a Logical Sequence.*** The most important information in a document should be at the top of the page. The least important information should be in a lower corner. Items that are too long for one column should move to the top of the next column to the right.

- ***Use Column and Page Balance.*** Facing pages and columns should begin and end at the same point.

- ***Consider Proportion.*** Proportion in page design is the size relationship among the components on a page and across facing pages. The size of a component is relative to its surrounding components. A single component should neither overpower others nor be too small.

- ***Avoid Odd-Shaped Paragraphs.*** Odd-shaped paragraphs (such as diamond shaped) are difficult to read; use them very sparingly (see Figure 5–9). Don't specifically create designs with lengthy text (a paragraph or longer).

- ***Avoid Widows and Orphans.*** Paragraphs should not end with less than a full line at the top of a page (widow). Also, paragraphs should not begin with a single line at the bottom of a page (orphan). As a general rule, avoid widows and orphans. In addition, a paragraph should not end with a single short word (or part of a word) on the last line.

- ***Avoid Excess.*** Good design should not draw attention to itself. Use all the special features of the software in moderation.

- ***Limit the Number of Typefaces or Fonts.*** Do not overuse bold, italic, and uppercase letters, and limit the number of different fonts on a page to three or less.

- ***Create Appropriate White Space.*** Adding white space to a page makes information easy to read and allows the reader to focus attention on what is most important. Too much white space, however, can produce a document that appears disjointed and fragmented. Be judicious in the use of white space.

- ***Use Appropriate Margins.*** Documents with wide margins are considered "airy" because they have a sense of openness. Documents with narrow margins are considered "heavy" because they convey a dense feeling. Although margins do not have to be equal on all sides, they should present a balanced image.

- ***Use Appropriate Columns.*** Columns wider than five inches make it difficult for the reader's eye to find the beginning of the next line. Columns narrower than two inches cause the reader's eyes to move down too frequently. Too many columns crowd the page and make it hard to read.

Variety

A boring design makes boring reading; variety prevents boredom. An inviting document helps convey the message by enticing the reader.

- ***Use Contrast.*** This term refers to the use of light and dark areas on a page. There is nothing in a low-contrast document that draws the reader's attention. High-contrast documents use light areas to emphasize dark areas (and vice versa). If the leading is too tight between lines of text, the publication looks dark and foreboding. If the leading is too wide, the pages are too bright.

- ***Surprise the Reader.*** Surprise keeps readers curious. Although the element of surprise seems to contradict the notion of consistency, it does not; an occasional surprise provides an added dimension to a document.

- ***Use Text Wrap Features.*** Letting text flow around a graphics shape increases the impact of the graphic. Although it does create odd-shaped text, text wrap adds interest; use it carefully.

- ***Try Various Paragraph Alignments.*** Drawing attention to one or two paragraphs within a document can be accomplished by aligning them in various ways.

- ***Use a Variety of Column Sizes.*** To provide some variety in a publication, you can use different-sized columns on the same page and place graphics and headlines across columns. Again, don't overdo it.

ORNING FIX

It's a journalistic cliché that the most important stories happen just as the newspaper begins to be printed. Morning papers with large circulations usually must be printed by 3 or 4 A.M., but that is no longer the problem it once was—thanks to the computer. Journalists use their desktop computers to add late-breaking stories at the very last minute. A page's layout can be altered electronically to accommodate the story, photo, or graphic—all of which means newspapers can be even more timely. How long will it be before the morning "paper" isn't even printed on paper, but is sent electronically to subscribers' computer screens?

GOLD-MEDAL PAPER

During the summer 1992 Olympics in Barcelona, a legion of journalism students from the University of Navarro published a daily newspaper for the Olympic Committee that was distributed to the Olympic family. From their headquarters at the Barcelona Trade Fair, they used PCs and Aldus's PageMaker to create the paper in English, French, Spanish, and Catalan, the dialect of Barcelona. They built their own spell-checking dictionary for the articles in Catalan using the provided spell-checkers for the other languages. Once that hurdle had been cleared, the biggest problem was layout: each article, translated from the original three times, had four different lengths. Again computers came to the rescue and the paper made every deadline.

Learning How to Design

To learn how to create document designs, get a book on the basic elements of graphic design. Many bookstores and libraries carry such books in their art, printing, and computer software sections. Another source of ideas is to look at the design of other documents. Ask yourself what makes them effective. Does the design enhance or detract from the message? Is the document easy to read?

SUMMARY

- A word processor is an automated writing tool, a program that lets users enter and edit text quickly and efficiently.
- Desktop publishing software has additional design tools and controls that combine text and graphics files into publications.
- Both word processing and desktop publishing provide tools for page layout, typography, and graphics.
- Setting up your document consists of specifying its margins and justification, hyphenation, spacing, tabs, columns, headers and footers, and/or page numbers.
- The real editing power of a word processor lies in its ability to manipulate text blocks.
- Spelling and grammar checkers are useful utilities for catching typing errors and grammatical mistakes.
- Page layout controls page size and orientation, margins, column size and their placement on the page, and the placement of graphics and their relation to the text.
- Typographical controls determine the appearance of type, which can vary according to typeface, type style, and type size; these three factors make up a font.
- Type can be manipulated to create special effects such as drop caps and reverse type.
- Controlling the spacing makes text attractive and easy to read. Paragraphs can be flush left, centered, flush right, or justified.
- Graphics controls start with the sizing and scaling of original images.
- Proportional sizing preserves the original ratio of height to width of an image, but this ratio can be altered for a special effect.
- Images can be cropped, and line art can be drawn on the page to make lines, boxes, ovals, and rounded-corner boxes.
- Text-wrap controls can flow text over an image or space it equally around the image or irregularly to conform to the image's shape.
- Saving your work is of paramount importance. Save often to avoid losing your data. Keep your information organized by using meaningful file names.
- There are many options for printing your document. Most word processors let you print any portion or all of your document and any number of copies. The quality of your printout depends on the quality of your printer.

KEY TERMS

bit-mapped font	columns	deleting
boldface	command driven	deviant text
center	crop	double sided
clip art	cursor	drop cap

edit	kerning	scaling
facing	landscape	serif
flush left	leading	soft return
flush right	macro	spelling checker
font	margin	tab
footers	outline fonts	text wrap
format	page layout	thesaurus
function keys	page orientation	tracking
hard copy	page size	TrueType
hard return	point	typeface
headers	portrait	typeover mode
hyphenation	proportionately spaced fonts	type size
indent	raised cap	type style
insert pointmode	reverse type	white space
insertion mode	rotated text	word wrap
interparagraph spacing	ruling lines	WYSIWYG
italics	sans serif	
justify	save	

REVIEW QUESTIONS

1. Why should you read a document after it is printed?
2. Why is it important to back up your files?
3. How can you move text?
4. What is desktop publishing software? How is it used?
5. What are sizing and scaling?
6. Describe the common typographical controls?
7. How do you control the space between letters, words, and lines?
8. In what four ways can text be aligned relative to the margin?
9. What is the difference between WYSIWYG and command-driven programs?
10. What are the major design considerations?
11. How does a word processor differ from a typewriter?
12. What are some of the special effects you can produce with text and graphics?

SELF-QUIZ

1. Effective written communication involves two basic issues:
    - *a.* content and spelling.
    - *b.* style and spelling.
    - *c.* content and style.
    - *d.* spelling and synonyms.
2. The most universal of all microcomputer applications is
    - *a.* newspaper creation.
    - *b.* word processing.
    - *c.* developing advertisements.
    - *d.* typesetting.
3. Typesetting refers to
    - *a.* creating text on a page.
    - *b.* creating graphics for a page.
    - *c.* coordinating the various text and graphic elements of a publication.
    - *d.* determining word processor attributes.
4. In portrait orientation, text and graphics are printed across
    - *a.* an upright page.
    - *b.* a sideways page.
    - *c.* an upside-down page.
    - *d.* a downside-up page.

5. Leading is the distance in points from
   a. one typed letter to the next.
   b. the beginning of a line of type to the end of the line.
   c. the baseline of one row of type to the baseline of the next.
   d. the top of a dropped cap to the bottom of the letter.

6. Depending on the typeface, a rule of thumb is leading should be equal to _____ of the type size for what are to be single-spaced lines of text.
   a. 80 percent   c. 120 percent
   b. 100 percent   d. 125 percent

7. What term defines the short lines projecting from the ends of the main strokes of the letters and characters on certain typefaces?
   a. sans   c. sans serifs
   b. serifs   d. sheriffs

8. A hard return occurs
   a. between two pages of a document.
   b. when you have to return to the beginning of a document and start editing.
   c. at the end of a paragraph.
   d. at the end of each line of text.

9. The great advantage of word processing software is _____.

10. With _____ software the user enters commands into the document itself to control its appearance.

11. Word processing and desktop publishing are tools of _____.

12. A(n) _____ is a blinking vertical bar, rectangle, or outline on the screen that shows where the text you type will be entered into your document.

13. The area on the page without text or image is called _____.

14. _____ are a few words placed at the top of every page of a section, chapter, or document, often with the purpose of grouping similar pages.

15. _____ is the process of adjusting the space between individual letters of text in a line.

16. There are two major kinds of typefaces: _____ and _____.

17. A(n) _____ is a shortcut, a command to the computer to perform a series of tasks or to insert a string of letters or words without the need to type the commands or words each time.

18. The _____ mode will replace any text to the right of the cursor or insertion point, thereby erasing it.

SIMULATIONS

Scenario 1: Creating a Letterhead

You are a poor college student. You cannot even afford to buy all the textbooks you need for your classes because you spent your book money at the bookstore purchasing some sweatshirts, T-shirts, and coffee cups. You are about to graduate but you need to send out letters of inquiry about a possible job. You realize that a good letterhead can make any letter more powerful and meaningful, but you don't have the funds to hire a typesetter to do the work for you.

Your assignment is to generate your own personal letterhead. Be creative and design a letterhead that is both professional in appearance and reflects your own sense of style. Your grade will be based on the quality of your letterhead. If it is dull, drab, or unprofessional, your grade will be dull, drab, and reflective of your unprofessional standards.

It is your first year of teaching. Like most first-year-teachers you get up at 6:00 A.M., check the local weather station hoping for a snow day, dress, shower (maybe not in that order), eat, grab graded papers and then dash off to school. After seven hours of teaching with only 10 minutes for lunch and after staying late to prepare bulletin boards, you return home. After a hasty check on Oprah, you grab a quick Lean Cuisine, diet Coke, and Twinkies and sit down for an evening of grading papers and preparing lesson plans. At about 11:30 P.M. you fall asleep on the couch.

While you knew that teaching would be hard work, you never realized the effect your new job would have on your social life. Your significant other has become exasperated by your all-consuming passion to become a good teacher. Citing reasons of neglect, your significant other has given you an ultimatum— quit teaching or the romance is over. Considering you spent five or six years in college and thousands of dollars to become a teacher, you decide the romance, what's left of it, is history.

Your task is to write a dear John or dear Jane letter. Make sure the letter is in a standard business format including date, address lines, salutations, etc. Please print a copy of this letter to submit.

Scenario 2: They Never Told Me It Would Be Like This

HANDS-ON COMPUTING

1. Word processing is a powerful tool for creating a wide range of documents. On a sheet of paper, list 10 specific types of documents that you can create using a word processor.
2. List five advantages of using word processing software and five advantages of using desktop publishing software.
3. Many office workers use word processing software. However, not all agree on which brand of software to use. Ask around for the names of several different word processors. What is it that people like about their software. Also, ask what types of documents they create.
4. Much has been written about how to use word processing software. Find an article on the topic at the library and write a short summary explaining the major points of the article. Add a section on your thoughts and reactions to the article.
5. If you are just beginning to explore word processing, one of the best methods is to use the help feature and/or tutorials built in to most word processors. In fact, many help features offer a quick guided tour of the word processing software. If any of these programs are available, take some time to experiment.
6. If possible, experiment with a word processor. Use it to write a paper that describes your reactions to word processing. What do you like about it? What do you dislike? Can a word processor affect the quality of writing you do for your classes?
7. Describe how a student organization on campus could benefit from well-designed brochures, fliers, or banners? What hints could you give them to enhance the quality of their printed material?

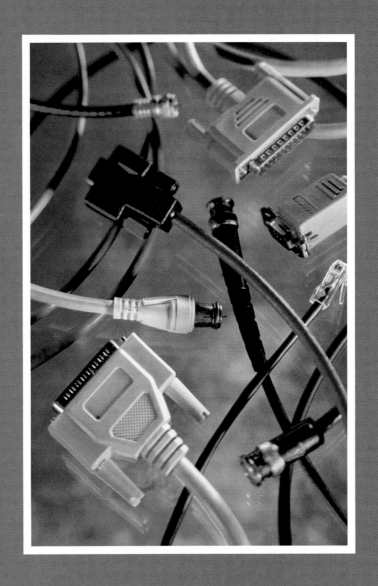

CHAPTER 6

Working with Graphics

FOCUS

Images generated on a microcomputer help present information in a form that is easy to understand. Posters, signs, and billboards often contain computer-generated art, and so do newsletters, brochures, and advertisements. Microcomputer graphics create titles and special effects for both film and television.

With a microcomputer and graphics software, you can create a variety of high-quality graphics. For example, manually drawing a circle—even with special equipment— takes a steady hand and precision. Drawing a circle with graphics software is as simple as picking the size and location and telling the software to do it.

This chapter discusses the different types of graphics programs and applications and the basic procedures for using most graphics software. Because the concepts presented here are shared by most graphics programs, learning them will help you learn how to use specific graphics applications.

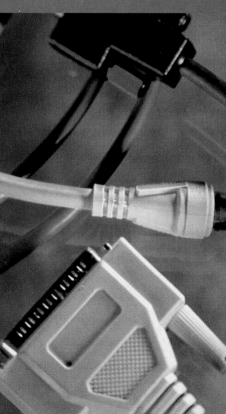

WHAT ARE GRAPHICS?

In the world of microcomputers, the term **graphics** describes a variety of concepts. Some use the term to mean drawings, photos, and similar types of images. Others use it to refer to charts and graphs. Still others use it in describing microcomputer games. In fact, *graphics* is an all-encompassing term that refers to any nontext image generated by a computer.

Computer graphics can be categorized in several ways: by the type of image (object oriented or bit mapped); by their file format (TIFF, PCX, EPS, and so on); and by their use of color. These categories are briefly discussed in the following section; the remainder of the chapter categorizes images and graphics applications by who or what originates the image: data-generated graphics, device-generated graphics, and user-generated graphics.

IMAGE TYPES

Microcomputer-generated images can be object-oriented images or bit-mapped images. **Object-oriented images,** sometimes called *vector* images, are pictures made up of specific lines and shapes. They combine several distinct lines, rectangles, squares, circles, or other shapes created with the application's set of drawing tools.

An easy way to think of object-oriented graphics is to consider a drawing of a kitchen table standing on a rug. As an object-oriented graphic, the kitchen table can be made up of a rectangle representing the tabletop, with a polygon for each leg, and an oval for the rug. Each shape or object remains independent of all other objects or shapes; the computer file for such an image is made up of mathematical descriptions of the shapes that compose the image. Each object in the total graphic image can be moved independently, or various objects can be grouped into a single object and manipulated that way. Draw programs are used to produce object-oriented images (Figure 6–1).

Figure 6-1
An object-oriented graphic, such as this one, can be manipulated as such; you can stretch or shrink it, rotate it, or do any number of things and the object will remain intact and separate from any other element of the image.

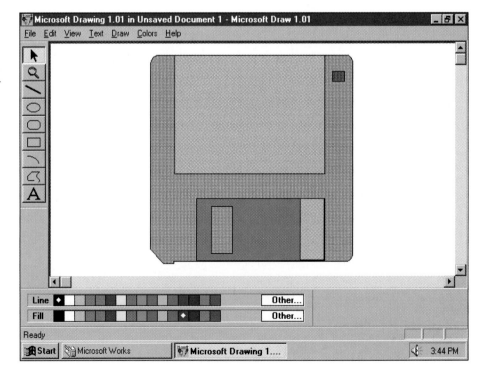

A **bit-mapped image** is actually a complete pattern of the pixels on the screen. You may recall from our hardware chapter that the picture you see on your monitor is made up of thousands of dots and that each dot is called a *pixel* (short for *picture element*). Bits are binary digits (0s and 1s), so a bit-mapped image is the binary record of the bit values of each pixel making up the image. The record includes location and color information for each pixel in the bit map.

With bit-mapped graphics, the computer doesn't keep track of the image of a kitchen table as an object; it merely understands the location and color of the pixels that form the table. Therefore, when editing a bit-mapped image, you don't manipulate objects; instead, you change the color values of the pixels in the part of the image you want to edit. Paint programs and image processors typically produce bit-mapped images; they include appropriate tools for editing the images (Figure 6–2).

Many people consider object-oriented graphics superior to bit-mapped graphics because of the crispness of straight lines. The designer of a city street map, for example, needs very precise straight lines that can be moved and changed easily. Object-oriented graphics work very well for this type of image. These images can also be more easily resized and printed on any scale, whereas resizing a bit-mapped image either sacrifices detail (if scaled down) or makes the image look coarse and jagged (if scaled up). On the other hand, bit-mapped graphics are considered superior to object-oriented graphics for highly complex and detailed designs that are not based on straight lines. For example, a portrait of a person has far more detail and intricacies

ANIMATING COMMERCIALS

Advertisers are constantly searching for ways to intrigue television viewers. And one of their latest tricks is using computer animation in their commercials: a bottle of Listerine knocks out gingivitis in a boxing ring, a Bud Light delivery truck suddenly turns into a racing car, a sheet blows off a Lexus car and then the car's skin blows off to reveal a newer Lexus underneath. Match Light charcoal, Volkswagen, Alcoa, Amtrak, and 7-Up also have all taken advantage of the latest in computer graphic technology. The sophistication of the new tools means conputers are better at making animated motion more fluid, and at controlling shadow and light. The resulting hard-edged, clean look of the image is somewhere between traditional animation's cartoony feel and stop-action photography's realistic, but choppy images.

Figure 6-2
A bit-mapped graphic, such as this image of a flower, isn't composed of distinct objects, but simply a map of all the pixels in the photo. You can't manipulate parts of the graphic as objects, but you can do other kinds of editing, such as erasing regions of the image.

A PRICELESS FAX? OR, YES, BUT IS IT ART?

Artists have been using computers, still video cameras, and other high-tech equipment in their art for more than a generation. But conider artist Roz Dimon, who creates a painting on a video screen, then stores it. The data file is used to produce 25 transparencies. However, one of her patrons owns the "electronic rights" to some of her works, which are stored on a hard disk in the patron's safe-deposit box. British artist David Hockey has taken to faxing some of his work to friends, once going so far as to fax an entire exhibition to São Paulo, Brazil. All of which raises an interesting question for serious art collectors. If the art is only the string of electronic zeros and ones that tells a computer's screen how to light up, how can the art be worth anything? Apparently this doesn't bother some collectors. Three years ago Rox Dimon's computer works went for $800 to $1,000 per transparency. Now those same works are selling for $4,000 to $7,000.

than a city map does. Bit-mapped software provides more visual control by letting users change each pixel or dot. In addition, since object-oriented graphics are a series of individual lines, many such programs provide only a few tools for editing the graphic. Bit-mapped graphics software offers a greater variety of tools for freehand drawing, to produce very detailed graphic designs and to let the artist work with the computer in a way very similar to working on paper. This makes it easier to translate traditional artistic skills into computer graphic skills.

Image File Formats

An image file format is the method used to record a microcomputer generated image on disk. Each file format is associated with a unique image file extension name.

The three most widely used image file formats are **tagged image file format (TIFF), Paintbrush (PCX/PCC),** and **encapsulated PostScript (EPS).** CAD users know the DFX extension, and Windows users are familiar with the BMP (bit-map) file format (which differs from the OS/2 BMP format). They will also recognize the CLP (ClipBoard) format. Almost every draw and paint program has a variation of these with its own file extension, but most support the first three. Macintosh applications typically support MAC and PICT, and Macintosh users will know the MAC format from MacPaint and the PICT format from MacDraw.

TIFF, PCX/PCC, BMP, and MAC are bit-mapped image formats. PCX/PCC and BMP are indigenous to the PC microcomputer; each has a unique way of saving the bit values of each pixel in an image. While the TIFF format is generally standardized, there are several versions produced by different software companies and some applications save what they call a TIFF—but it cannot be displayed except by the original application. TIFFs on the Macintosh differ from TIFFs on the PC. Some software can read both Mac and PC TIFFs; some can save a file as either. Although MAC images are generally used only on the Macintosh, some PC programs can import and display them.

EPS stands for encapsulated PostScript and is used on all microcomputers. PostScript is a page description language—a way to describe an image or page using mathematical formulas that define the shapes that make up the page; therefore, it is used for object-oriented graphic files. The Postscript language was developed by Adobe Systems to print microcomputer images and create fonts that would print in different sizes (discussed in Chapter 5). A Postscript laser printer can print out the image the EPS file describes by *rasterizing* the image, that is, by calculating the shapes and converting them into a bit-mapped image that the laser can create on the printer's drum (see the chapter on hardware). The EPS format can also be used to store bit-mapped images; in this case, PostScript merely defines the size of the image and forwards the bit map to the printer's image processor. Graphics and desktop publishing applications take advantage of this capability by storing a bit-mapped image (called a *header*) along with the object-oriented image in the

EPS file, and using the bit-mapped image on-screen while sending the object-oriented image on the printer.

Draw programs, including **computer-aided design (CAD)** software, save their files in their own object-oriented formats. The information saved is not a record of each pixel but a collection of formulas for each object and what color fills each object. You usually need the original application to make changes to these images. To use these images in other applications usually requires that they be converted into bit-mapped images or saved as EPS files. Some graphics applications, however, now understand CAD file formats and can use them directly.

Use of Color

An image generated on a microcomputer can be black and white, shades of gray, green, or amber, or up to 16.8 million colors. The colors available to you are determined by the microcomputer's monitor and the ability of your graphics application to use the colors available; the monitor's graphic display format (CGA, EGA, VGA, SVGA, and so on) determines how many colors you can see on screen, and the capabilities of the graphics application determine how many colors you can actually use. Black, white, and the shades of gray are considered colors, just as are red, green, blue, aquamarine, violet, and so on.

Object-oriented and bit-mapped images approach the issue of color differently. With object-oriented images, for each object in the image, you specify the color of the image's outline and the color of the space filling the image. Then a color printer converts these colors into values that can be printed.

With bit-mapped images, the number of colors available to you is determined by how many bits are used to describe the color of each pixel. The simplest case, 1 bit per pixel, describes black and white only (also called monochrome). The other two standard formats are 8 bits per pixel, which gives you either $256(2^8)$ colors or 256 shades of gray, ranging from black to white; and 24 bits per pixel, which gives you about 16.8 million (2^{24}) colors—more than the eye can see. The number of colors in the image has a drastic effect on file size. Storing an image in 8-bit format results in a file eight times the size of the same image stored in 1-bit format; a 24-bit image is three times larger still.

The other major factor in graphic file size is **resolution:** that is, the number of pixels per inch. An image stored at 600 pixels per inch occupies a file considerably larger than does the same image stored at 300 pixels per inch.

All these factors should be taken into account when you use graphic images; because of the effect of color and resolution on file size, how big and how fine an image you can use depends on how much memory and storage space your computer has. It's also a major consideration to take into account when using clip art. **Clip art** is images that have already been created and stored on disk or CD-ROM for your use. Clip art can be object-oriented (line art) or bit-mapped drawings or photos and is available in black and white, grayscale (shades of gray), and color (Figures 6–3 and 6–4). These images can be brought into graphics applications and edited; they can be imported into desktop publishing, presentation graphics, and multimedia applications.

*H*ARD EVIDENCE

Computer animation re-created the shooting of porn king Artie Mitchell when his brother Jim was tried for the murder in 1991. The jury was shown an animated film of a walking figure hit with the same number of bullets (8) in the same amount of time (1 minute). Ballistics experts used software and a UNIX system to find the bullet trajectories, the angle height, and the time of each shot, as well as exactly where the bullets landed. Jim Mitchell was found guilty of manslaughter, but his defense is appealing on the grounds that the film prejudiced the jury by showing Artie as a passive victim.

Figure 6-3

Clip art comes in a variety of formats for a multitude of subjects.

Figure 6-4

A photograph can provide the foundation for computer-based graphics.

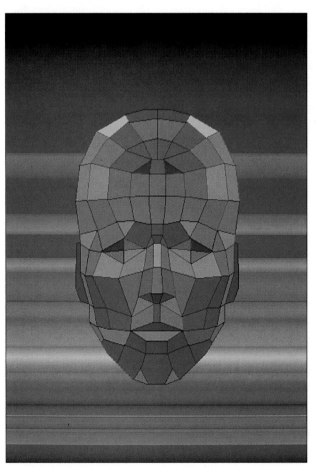

Image Origination

In addition to image type, file format, and color use, you can describe the images generated on microcomputers and their software applications by the origin of the image: whether the image is generated from preexisting data created by an input device or created by the user.

Data-generated graphics use numeric data to create graphics such as pie, bar, and line graphs. Spreadsheet software often includes the ability to generate data-generated graphics. Other software that accepts numeric data creates data-generated graphics with greater options than is usually available with spreadsheet software alone; these are usually bit-mapped images.

Device-generated graphics are produced by scanners or other input devices. Scanners, as we learned earlier, digitize an image. The user then applies software to alter or enhance the scanned image or simply to change its format for use with other applications. Computerized cameras can now take a digitized picture and write it directly to disk; this picture can be manipulated in the image processing software just like a scanned image (Figure 6–5). Video can also be edited with special graphics programs; frames of the video can be isolated, or "grabbed," and manipulated just like a scanned image. Screen capture software can record or capture the monitor screen at your command; the resulting image can then be edited.

Users create all graphics, in one way or another. The term **user-generated graphics,** however, refers specifically to art created with special draw-and-paint software. These images begin in the imagination of the user and are constructed on a microcomputer with a mouse, graphics tablet, or light pen.

Many graphics programs allow for the creation of two—or all three—major types of graphics. We will break down these three categories further as we discuss graphics applications.

DATA-GENERATED GRAPHICS

As mentioned earlier, graphics can be generated from data sets stored in spreadsheet, database, or word processing files. Most graphing and charting software falls into this category, producing bit-mapped images.

Graphing and Charting Software

People disagree on definitions of graphs and charts. For our purposes, a *graph* is the image drawn on a grid with a horizontal x-axis and vertical y-axis; a chart—which may include a graph—can also include labels, a title, and explanatory notes.

Spreadsheet software, such as Lotus 1-2-3 or Excel, gives users built-in graphing and charting options. Creating a graph or chart can be as simple as selecting the data you want to use, then clicking the mouse on an icon showing the type of graph or chart you want. These features aren't built into all spreadsheet programs, however, and you may need to create charts that are beyond the scope of the spreadsheet program or from data generated in software that lacks graphing and charting features. Special-purpose graphing and charting software allows you to take data from spreadsheets, databases, or text files, enter it directly, and create a wide variety of graphs and charts. You can also change imported data. Remember that with linked data, any change to the original data changes the graph. Presentation graphics packages also offer sophisticated features that produce professional-looking graphs and charts.

Figure 6-5
A digital camera may look similar to a normal 35mm SLR, but it stores images on a small disk instead of exposed film. These images can then be imported to the computer and used like any other electronic image.

Flowchart Applications

Flowcharts are a special type of chart designed to show a process or structure; they use boxes of various shapes to show stages of the process or elements of the structure, with lines linking the boxes to show relationships between elements. Two of the more common programs used to produce flowcharts are project management software and group organization software.

Project management software uses dates and times as well as the goals and objectives of a person or group of people to illustrate how a project should progress from beginning to end. It uses a particular shape for each event and, since one event may depend on another event's completion, displays them in the order in which they should occur. For example, when producing a book, each task in the process (writing, copyediting, typesetting, page composition, proofreading, and printing) must be completed in sequence; starting any of them depends on completing the tasks that come before.

Group organization software uses the names and ranks of people in an organization to create an organizational flowchart. Group members' names and titles as well as other pertinent information may appear in or around their boxes. The names of offi-

When a child has been missing for a number of years, outdated photos can no longer be used to identify him or her. Now computer graphics can create new images that "age" the child, resulting in more up-to-date photos that help find missing children better. Artist Nancy Burson was doing photo merging of celebrities for *People* magazine when she was approached by the mother of a missing child and asked to do an age progression of the child. Burson and programmer David Kramlich developed the software, which is now being used by the FBI. Using a scanner and a PC, the artist can merge photos of the child and other members of the family, creating overlays and sketches. Distinguishing marks are kept in, and visual information from the family serves as a guide to aging the photo. The computer-aged photos have been credited with finding a number of children, some of whom had been missing for almost a decade.

cers and supervisors may be shown larger and above the names of rank-and-file members. Arrows show levels of hierarchy and how the members of the group interact.

Flowcharts created by project management and group organization software are usually object-oriented images, allowing the shapes and lines to be moved around as needed. In some project management applications, moving events causes the data to be automatically changed.

Other Data-Generated Graphics Sources

It's hard to imagine any professional using numeric data to make decisions who would not benefit from data-generated graphics, but some depend on them more than others do. Graphics software enables geologists to generate highly detailed visual displays of rock formations and visual estimates of oil-resource information. A television weather reporter may use computer graphics to convey weather information. Data-generated graphics show the location of weather fronts, display weather patterns, and provide other detailed visual information for weather forecasts (Figure 6–6). Geographers employ data-generated graphics, such as pictures created from satellite data, to create highly detailed maps for a variety of applications. Both topographical and political maps are produced by these specialized graphics programs.

DEVICE-GENERATED GRAPHICS

Scanners can input bit-mapped images (including 24-bit images) with a great degree of detail. Other device-generated graphics, from camera, video, or your monitor's screen, also provide unique images that are not easily created by data or users. Scanning software and image processing software allow you to manipulate and use the images created by these devices in a variety of applications.

Figure 6-6
Weather reporters are the most visible everyday users of computer-generated graphics. Weather information can be processed by supercomputers to create graphics such as this representation of a storm front.

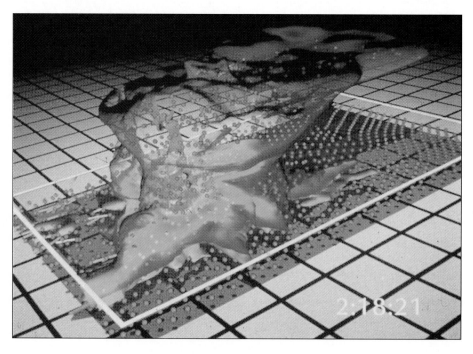

Scanning Software

Scanning software gives you the ability to control the scanner. The software usually lets you preview the image before scanning it. You can see how the entire image would look and select only the area you want. You can then crop the image, eliminating its unnecessary or unwanted parts and thereby saving both disk space and memory.

Most scanning software also lets you control the lightness and darkness of the original scanned image as well as color intensities. You also choose how to scan the image—as black and white, grayscale, or color; the pixel resolution at which to scan it; and for photos, the halftone screen frequency to use. Be aware that control of the scanning process, especially with color images, in terms of resolution and lighting, takes a great deal of practice; the first step is to get the clearest possible image.

Image Processing Software

Once you have the image on disk, **image-processing software** gives you the tools, which vary in number and quality, to edit the image and enhance it. Some widely used products are Adobe Photoshop and Letraset's ColorStudio, Picture Publisher, and Aldus Corporation's PhotoStyler.

Image processors let you zoom into any section of the picture to edit and improve the image. For example, you can copy the surrounding pixels to damaged areas and cover up scratches or other marks scanned from the original. You can lighten or darken the picture, adjust the color, add lines, stretch or compress the image, and add many other special effects. You can also further crop the image by selecting the cropping tool, creating a rectangle over the area of the image you want to preserve, and then cutting away everything else.

Image-processing programs also serve as **file conversion** tools. Since they specialize in image manipulation, they must be able to accept, or read and save, many image file formats. Thus they can be used to change an image's file format to a format that the target desktop publishing, word processing, or other application will be able to incorporate into its documents.

Other Uses and Devices

Desktop publishing industries are probably the greatest users of device-generated graphics. Advertisers, newspapers, magazines, and book publishers depend on the scanner to reduce the cost of putting pictures into publications. A cartographer may scan aerial photographs of roads or other terrain and then trace the roads in perfect scale to make a new map. Electrical engineers may scan a schematic to be **vectorized** (changed into an object-oriented image) and altered for correction or redesign.

Earlier in the chapter we mentioned video grabbing, screen captures, and the digital camera. Many image processors have a screen capture feature; some specialize in this.

MUSEUM TECH

Computer graphics can now predict the changes in color as a painting ages, the effect a cleaning might have on the painting, and to what degree a painting might crack if it were transported to another museum. London's National Gallery has started to scan its pictures each year to determine how the color will change over time. The museum hopes to use the knowledge as an aid to storing paintings so the colors will remain vivid longer. A museum in Munich used computer technology in an experiment on "craquelure," the hairline cracks on a painting's surface. Officials electronically scanned the surface of a worthless painting before and after it went for a 250-mile ride in the back of a car. The results will help museums pack paintings more securely when they are loaned out for exhibitions.

Device-generated graphics are also produced by devices other than the scanners discussed here. Medical scans of the body produce diagnostic maps, and radio telescopes produce pictures of another planet's surface.

USER-GENERATED GRAPHICS

Before user-generated graphics programs were available, graphic artists working in commercial art, advertising, and related fields spent most of their time at drawing tables producing images by hand. User-generated graphics software has replaced much of this work with features that allow the graphic artist to work on a computer the way he or she once worked at the drawing table. These applications offer the advantages of easy editing, easy recovery from errors, and easy reproduction.

Draw and Paint Programs

As stated, user-generated graphics software includes draw and paint programs that support a creative, freestyle approach to creating images that is similar to using an artist's canvas, pencils, pens, paintbrush, and paint. You are given a blank screen area (canvas), several drawing tools (paintbrushes, pen, spray, and so on), and several color options (paint and ink). **Draw programs** create object-oriented images; **paint programs** create bit-mapped images.

Most draw and paint programs provide graphic tools in the form of **icons** accessible with a mouse. Pointing to an icon and clicking on it activates the graphic tool, in essence letting you use the mouse as that tool. For example, clicking on the straight line tool lets you use the mouse to draw perfectly straight lines. If you click on the box tool, you can create rectangles and squares of various sizes. In addition, you can erase (paint programs) or delete (draw programs) unwanted materials, selected colors from a color palette, and automatically fill areas with different patterns or colors. The text tool provides text in a variety of fonts that you can then change to create unique letters (for example, a T that looks like a tree).

Several draw programs, including CorelDRAW!, Adobe Illustrator, and Aldus Freehand, are available for both the Macintosh and Windows environments. Paint programs such as PC Paintbrush, Fractal Design Painter, and Windows Paintbrush (a Windows accessory) for the PC, and Oasis, Canvas, and SuperPaint for the Macintosh are common examples of software based on bit-mapped graphics (Figure 6–7). Paint programs may also double as image processing programs, because they can work with many of the same file formats.

Computer-Aided Design

CAD (computer-aided design) programs are also object-oriented, but they include many specialized features required by professional drafters, engineers, architects, and technical designers. Draw programs may provide 10 to 15 drawing tools, but most high-

*P*AINTING A PICTURE BY MATH?

People have been using Paint By Number kits for years, but new mapping programs for computers have put an electronic twist on this old hobby. By using sets of numerical data—for instance, scientific information sent back via satellites—the programs can create visual images of an unseen object. NASA scientists recently used computer mapping to give us our first look at the actual surface of cloud-covered Venus. Other scientists have used similar programs to map the ocean's bottom. One dedicated scholar took measurements of the Sphinx in Egypt, which he combined with historical accounts and other ruins near the Sphinx, to produce a model of the Sphinx when it was first built.

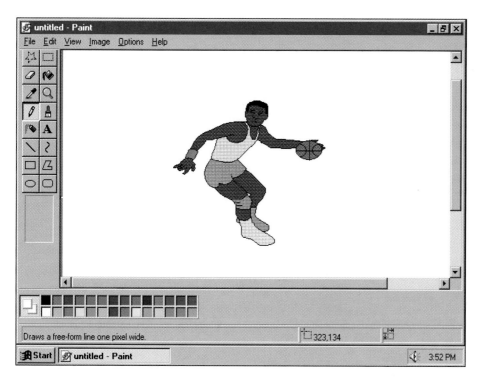

Figure 6-7
Paint programs include a wide variety of tools for creating bit-mapped graphics.

end CAD software, such as AutoCAD (Figure 6–8), provides as many as 100 specialized drawing tools. Draw software is often easy to learn and use, but learning all the features of CAD software may require a great deal of time—in fact, many colleges offer full courses on just its basic operations.

Engineers use CAD to help them design and create a wide range of products. Electrical engineers, for example, use CAD to design complex circuits and circuit boards. Automotive engineers design cars, structural engineers design

Figure 6-8
CAD programs let you create working drawings onscreen for architectural and industrial applications.

CAD

Computer-aided design programs are showing up in some rather unusual places these days—like in the jungles of South America. Archeologists set up computer stations at the site of an ancient Mayan city that was being excavated. They hoped that re-creating Mayan palaces using CAD programs could give them a better idea of what they were looking for. Since CAD can create models in three dimensions and can offer the viewer different perspectives instantly, the program is invaluable to almost anyone who deals with design. A fashion designer can lengthen the skirt he or she has just designed, decide it looked better short, add more fullness at the hip—all with just a few commands. Designers of waterslides for an amusement park can use CAD to visualize the velocity and effects of friction from bathing suits—and all without ever using a pencil.

the structure of buildings, civil engineers design bridges and other structures, and they can all use CAD to do so. CAD gives them the flexibility to change designs easily. For example, automotive engineers may want to change the design of the front of a car to improve fuel efficiency by decreasing wind resistance. Instead of hand-building a model to see the effects of a design change, they can create a detailed visual representation on a monitor screen. Architects can change a number for the length of one wall, changing a whole skyscraper's measurements automatically. Aerospace engineers can "walk through" a model of a space station and put the design under stress tolerance tests without anyone having to leave the ground.

Presentation, Multimedia, and Utility Graphics Applications

Once images are generated, they can be used to communicate a message. Applications that use images for this purpose include desktop publishing, presentation, multimedia, and utility graphics. Desktop publishing applications are covered extensively in Chapter 5, where the principles for combining text and images are presented. These principles also apply to presentation, multimedia, and utility graphics production.

Presentation applications use software that combines text and images in a series of pictures. These pictures are like slides, and the presentation is much like a slide show (Figure 6–9). The pictures can be saved as bit-mapped images, sent to a service bureau, and made into photographic slides. When presenting pictures on a microcomputer monitor, you set the length of time for each slide display, the order of display, and the special effects such as dissolving from one slide to the next. Popular presentation programs include Microsoft's PowerPoint, Aldus Presentation, Lotus's Freelance Graphics, and Harvard Graphics.

Related to presentation graphics is **multimedia** software, which incorporates video, animation, and sound into presentation graphics. These programs let users create a full range of graphics and import sound, music, animation, and video images from other sources, combining them into a cohesive presentation. For the novice and expert alike, programs such as Powerpoint (Figure 6–10) yield the style and quality of professional productions. Making full use of the capabilities of multimedia software requires a variety of specialized peripheral devices and additions to the computer; this has resulted in a profusion of products that are sometimes

Figure 6-9

Presentation graphics software lets you create custom charts, graphs, and other images, and some packages also coordinate the presentation for you.

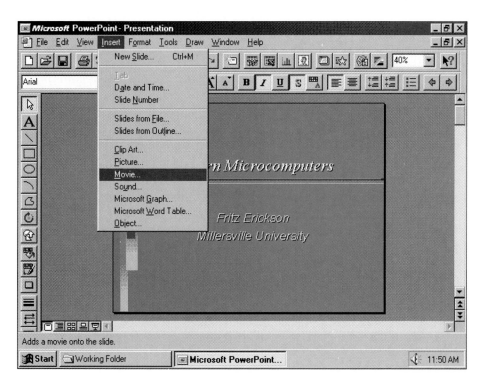

incompatible with each other. Multimedia standards for microcomputers, including Quick Time, coordinate the working of the various multimedia components. Multimedia has become a standard feature on most modern microcomputers.

Utility graphics software is a general class of graphics software designed for specific and limited functions. It lacks the flexibility of popular draw and paint programs but provides a very easy method for generating one or two specific types of graphics. Some of these programs allow users to create calendars, generate signs, produce greeting cards, and create awards and certificates, for example. While these can be created with draw and paint and desktop publishing programs, specific utility software makes creating these unique types of graphics easier. Some popular utility programs include The Print Shop for posters, signs, cards, and letterheads; Create-A-Calendar; Certificate Maker; and, for appealing newsletters, The Newsroom.

SUMMARY

- Graphics are any nontext images generated by a computer. They can be categorized by image quality, file format, or by who are or what originates the image.

AN IMAGINARY TOUR

Architects can now "walk" clients through a new building long before the foundation is even poured—thanks to new computer-aided design programs. Clients have the opportunity to make changes and to see the results almost instantly. Want three windows rather than two? Wonder what the room would look like if the door was a little to the left? How would the room "feel" if the walls were brick rather than wood? Today it's no problem.

The process of building a model of a room on a computer has several stages. First the architect sets the objects in space and defines their characteristics, such as shape or surface finish. Then a perspective on the room is chosen so the computer can orient the view it will create. What can and cannot be seen must be calculated, as well as the angle, reflections, color, and intensity of light. The result can either be viewed on a computer screen, printed, or put directly onto a color slide. The program can also let people "walk" through famous buildings on the other side of the world.

- Object-oriented images are made up of independent shapes.
- Bit-mapped images are single entities, that is, patterns of the pixels shown on the screen.
- Tagged image file format (TIFF) files are popular bit-mapped records of images.
- PCX/PCC and BMP are also bit-mapped PC formats.
- EPS files use mathematical formulas to describe images but can also incorporate bit-mapped images.
- Microcomputer images can be black-and-white (monochrome), grayscale, or full-colored pictures, depending on the hardware and the software used.
- The resolution and the number of colors in the file greatly affect file size.
- Data-generated graphics are bit-mapped images produced by a program using numeric information.
- The values usually come from spreadsheets but can also come from a database, text file, and direct input.
- Device-generated graphics are the most common digitized images from scanner input.
- Bit-mapped images can be modified by image-processing software.
- Image processors also perform file-conversion and screen-capture functions.
- Images can also be created from data supplied by cameras, medical equipment, and radio telescopes.
- User-generated graphics include draw programs and paint programs.
- Draw programs produce object-oriented images and provide the most precise user control over every object that makes up the image.
- Paint programs create bit-mapped images.
- Computer-aided design (CAD) applications are specialized draw programs for drafting, engineering, and technical illustration.
- Presentation and multimedia applications use the images created in other programs and mix images with text, sound, or video to produce an animated slide show that can be very impressive.
- Utility graphics software provides an easy method to produce greeting cards, posters, calendars, and many other products with microcomputer-generated images.

KEY TERMS

bit-mapped images
clip art
computer-aided design (CAD)
data-generated graphics
device-generated graphics
draw programs
encapsulated PostScript (EPS)
file conversion
flowchart
graphics
group organization software
icon
image-processing software

multimedia
object-oriented images
Paintbrush (PCX/PCC)
paint programs
presentation application
project management software
resolution
scanning software
tagged image file format (TIFF)
user-generated graphics
utility graphics software
vectorized

REVIEW QUESTIONS

1. What is the difference between an object-oriented and a bit-mapped graphic?
2. What are the three most common graphic file formats? Describe each.
3. What are data-generated graphics and how are they created?
4. What other kinds of graphics originate in the same way?
5. What are device-generated graphics and how are they created?
6. What kind of file is produced by an image processor? What is the advantage of an image processor that reads and creates files with many different file formats?
7. What are user-generated graphics and how are they created?
8. What are the uses of draw programs and paint programs?
9. Name three professions that use graphic images.
10. How might you use a presentation application?
11. How would a multimedia application help you?
12. What special products could you produce with utility graphics software?

SELF-QUIZ

1. Pictures made up of specific lines and shapes, such as rectangles, squares, and circles are known as
   - a. object-oriented images.
   - b. bit-mapped images.
   - c. tagged image files.
   - d. encapsulated image files.
2. Pictures made up of the complete pattern of the pixels on the screen are known as
   - a. object-oriented images.
   - b. bit-mapped images.
   - c. tagged image files.
   - d. encapsulated image files.
3. Encapsulated PostScript file format is used
   - a. only on Macintosh computers.
   - b. only on IBM computers.
   - c. on all microcomputers.
   - d. not on any microcomputers.
4. Graphics produced by scanners or other input devices create graphics known as
   - a. data-generated graphics.
   - b. device-generated graphics.
   - c. user-generated graphics.
   - d. machine-generated graphics.
5. Art created with special draw-and-paint software is known as
   - a. data-generated graphics.
   - b. device-generated graphics.
   - c. user-generated graphics.
   - d. machine-generated graphics.
6. Scanners input _____ images with a great degree of detail.
   - a. object-oriented images
   - b. bit-mapped images
   - c. tagged image files
   - d. encapsulated image files
7. Software designed to let you edit and improve a picture you have scanned into your computer is known as
   - a. picture-editing software.
   - b. image-processing software.
   - c. figure-conversion software.
   - d. desktop publishing software.
8. Draw programs create
   - a. object-oriented images.
   - b. bit-mapped images.
9. Computer-aided design (CAD) programs create
   - a. object-oriented images.
   - b. bit-mapped images.

10. If you wanted to make a calendar for the year 2001, the most appropriate type of software to use would be
    a. draw software.
    b. presentation software.
    c. utility graphics software.
    d. computer-aided-design software.
11. Object-oriented images are sometimes called _____ images.
12. Computer graphics can be categorized in several ways: by type of image, by file format, and by use of _____.
13. TIFF, PCX/PCC, BMP, and MAC are _____ image formats.
14. PostScript is a page description language so it is used with _____ _____ graphics.
15. _____ software uses the names and ranks of people in an organization to create an organizational flowchart.
16. Software that combines videos, animation, and sound is referred to as _____ software.
17. Engineers use _____ software to help them design and create a wide range of products.
18. _____ programs also serve as file conversion tools.
19. _____ industries are probably the greatest users of device-generated graphics.
20. Many people consider _____ graphics superior to _____ graphics because of the crispness of straight lines.

SIMULATIONS

Scenario 1: Communicating with Graphics

You like working for the highway department. It is a pleasant place. People are dedicated to fixing all the potholes and making the roads better and safer for everyone. However, you are getting restless and you want to start your own pothole-filling company. In order to do this, you need your own business signature or logo because generating and using graphics can be an important means of effective communication.

To ensure that you understand the process of generating and using graphics, your assignment is to generate a graphic from any graphic software program that is available. This graphic should be your own personal logo. Be creative. Save your logo graphic on your disk and then use it as part of your letterhead. You may want to save your letterhead as a separate file so that you have two letterheads—one with a graphic and one without. However, be sure to keep your logo as a separate file so you can use it for future assignments or activities.

Scenario 2: Learning to Use Bit-Mapped and Object-Oriented Graphics

Being a teacher is not an easy job. As a rule, the better your relationship with parents, the easier your job. One of the ways you can improve your relationship with parents is through effective communications. Depending on how many students you have, keeping in contact with parents can be a difficult task. One easy method is to produce a classroom newsletter. With a newsletter you can inform parents of classroom activities, student assignments, special recognitions, upcoming events, and a host of other useful information. One easy method for generating a classroom newsletter is to use simple word processing functions. However, you can add a great deal of emphasis if you include graphics.

Your assignment is to produce a classroom newsletter that combines text and graphics. Be imaginative. You may use either graphics you generate or clip art. You may use any word processor or any desktop publishing software or newsletter generating program. It is up to you. Your principal is an advocate of style over substance so the better the overall appearance of the newsletter the better recognition you will receive from the principal's office. You must include two or more graphics in your newsletter.

HANDS-ON COMPUTING

1. One of the best ways to understand the difference between object-oriented and bit-mapped graphics is to create the same object using both types of graphics software. Draw a house using a bit-mapped or paint program such as Paintbrush in Windows or any other similar software. Create the same house using CorelDRAW! or similar drawing program. Be sure to print both copies. Which did you prefer?
2. Scanners and bit-mapped graphics work very well together. If a graphics scanner is available, scan a photo of yourself (maybe your identification card photo). Save the image on your disk and then start making changes using a bit-mapped graphics program. You may want to save the new and improved you as a separate file. This way you can use the original again to make new modifications.
3. One easy way to obtain images as graphics is to use a video capture card. If one is available, capture an image of anyone who will volunteer. You can then use a paint program to change the size or make other types of modifications. Be sure to save the captured image on disk for use in a variety of documents.
4. Clip art is a very popular method of using graphics. While there are thousands of clip-art images available, you can take a piece of clip art and modify it with graphics software. If clip art is available, import one piece of clip art into a graphics program and then modify it. Again, be sure to save the modified version as a new file on your disk.
5. Bit-mapped and object-oriented graphics typically have a text tool that enables you to include text as part of your graphic. Create a sign that includes both graphics and text. Be imaginative with your sign. You could create a for-sale sign, a party announcement, a congratulations sign, or any sign of your choosing.

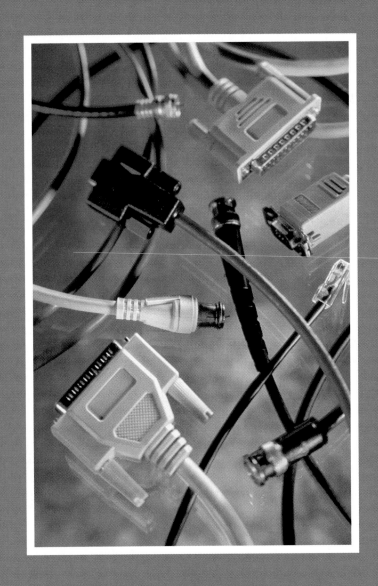

CHAPTER 7

Working with Spreadsheets

OBJECTIVES

After completing this chapter, you will be able to:

- Define a spreadsheet.
- Identify the three types of data to be entered in a spreadsheet.
- Describe the uses of formulas and functions.
- Describe how to make and use a template.
- List spreadsheet applications for different professions.
- Know when to use absolute and relative references.
- Identify the typical graphics available through spreadsheets.
- Describe how to add worksheet data to a word processing file.
- Discuss the importance of the recalculation feature when asking *What if* questions.

FOCUS

Just as word processors make working with words more efficient, spreadsheet programs make working with numbers more efficient (Figure 7–1). A spreadsheet is essentially an electronic ledger sheet that lets you enter, edit, and manipulate numeric data. A word processor allows you to enter text as you please in the document, but spreadsheets require that you place data in precise locations: cells that are created at the intersections of rows and columns (as on the grid of a paper ledger sheet). Spreadsheet data can be labels (names assigned to entries), numbers, or formulas.

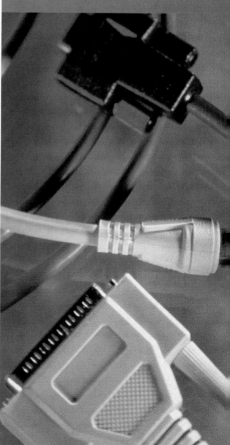

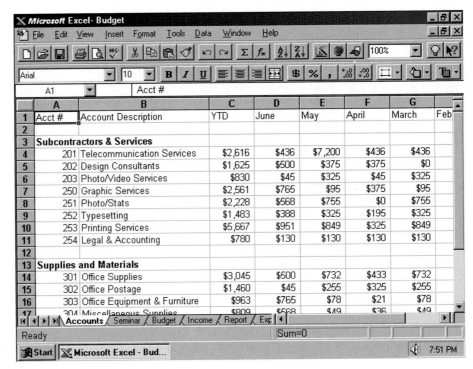

Figure 7-1
Spreadsheets have become an almost universal business tool for financial analysis and forecasting.

SPREADSHEET FUNCTIONS

Built-in mathematical formulas and functions in a spreadsheet manipulate the numbers for us: adding, subtracting, multiplying, dividing, finding square roots and averages, recalculating the answers when we change the values, and—for the statisticians among us—finding variances and deviations. These common functions make spreadsheets very powerful tools for a broad range of users.

• Keeping accurate financial records is agony for many people. The paper-and-pencil routine of listing and categorizing income and expenditures, then adding each column and comparing the results with the total income and outgo, can be more than frustrating (Figure 7–2). A single transposed number means finding the error (unfortunately, this part of the task will never change), erasing it, and manually recalculating the answer.

• Entering the data on an electronic spreadsheet allows you to recalculate the results automatically. It also allows you to ask **What if:** What happens if you get a raise? If you need a new car? If you want to save for a vacation? Changing the values—net income, discretionary income, savings—on the spreadsheet will provide the answers quickly and accurately, so you can evaluate the results of your changes and make decisions.

• School administrators and teachers—at all levels—use spreadsheets to track expenses, current and projected enrollment, income from taxes and fund-raisers, classroom attendance and performance records, test scores and grades. Here too, administrators can ask *What if:* for example, changing values on expected revenues to plan next year's budget more accurately.

	Sept.	Oct.	Nov.	Dec.	Total
INCOME					
Work	450	450	450	450	1800
Student loan	600	600	600	600	2400
Total income	1050	1050	1050	1050	4200
EXPENSES					
Rent	350	350	350	350	1400
Tuition	1200	0	0	0	1200
Books	200	0	0	0	200
Food	150	141	130	170	591
Utilities	30	32	45	58	165
Transportation	45	51	49	51	196
Entertainment	80	80	80	80	320
Total expenses	2055	654	654	709	4072
BALANCE	−1005	396	396	341	128

Figure 7-2
Doing budgeting by hand is a messy, tedious task; it's easy to make mistakes that take a long time to correct.

• Sports statistics are often calculated to decimal points—and argued about heatedly. With a spreadsheet, batting averages, winning percentages, and other data can be updated and calculated much more conveniently than by hand, making it possible for teams to analyze player performance more completely; this affects trades and contract negotiations.

• Business and government uses of spreadsheets are almost endless. Most of these programs are specialized and highly sophisticated, offering functions and formulas beyond the needs of the average user. Accountants, for example, may use specific programs to track daily income and expenditures, to prepare quarterly and yearly tax returns, or to analyze the worth of a business. A marketing department can use spreadsheets to analyze current and potential sales; the personnel department can use spreadsheets to track the costs of personnel or health care; managers can use spreadsheets to develop budgets and track inventory.

Government uses spreadsheets at almost all levels, from planning to taxing. City planners can project growth—and its costs—by asking *What if*. What if the city grows by 5 percent over the next year? Over the next two years? Or five years? What would the projected costs be? How many new schools would

HOME SPREADSHEETS

Some people have the mistaken idea that a home computer is really just a calculator in a box. Although a computer does crunch numbers (and crunch them very well), home versions of spreadsheet programs can harness this power in much more creative ways, turning a home computer into a real labor-saving device. Easy-to-use programs can balance your checkbook, calculate mortgage payments and car payments, record travel expenses, and predict changes in property values or what stock would be the best investment over a period of years. Some spreadsheet programs can also produce graphs, flowcharts, and other visual aids to help interpret information. And—oh yes—the computer can help figure out your taxes, too!

be needed? How many service personnel would be needed? On the other hand, what if the city population decreased?

Such projections are important to taxing authorities also. How much would a 0.1 percent tax increase on industry bring in? Would this amount be enough to cover the projected expenditures? What would happen if industry left the area? Would an increase in real estate taxes curtail sales? The spreadsheet allows planners and taxing authorities to write best-case/worst-case scenarios and project the monetary results.

In these examples, use has been made not only of the routine mathematical functions but also of the spreadsheet's easy ability to recalculate results based on changes in the values entered—to ask *What if.*

• And, as mentioned earlier, spreadsheets can also be used to keep inventories: what's in the shop, the warehouse, the classroom, the office, the house, or the freezer.

SETTING UP THE WORKSHEET

Whether it is called a *spreadsheet* or a *worksheet,* the basic concept is the same: a grid of **columns** (usually identified by letters) and **rows** (usually identified by numbers). To distinguish between a spreadsheet program and the spreadsheet on which the work is performed, we'll use the word **worksheet** throughout this chapter to denote the latter. Just like the paper ledger sheet, the gridlines of an electronic worksheet are usually visible (although some programs let you hide them on the screen). Although programs differ in their specifics, the basic concepts, capabilities, commands, and terms are very similar.

• **The Cell.**   The intersection of a row and column, a cell, is identified by the column letter and row number; for example, A1 (Figure 7–3). This is called a **cell address.** Sequential cells—for example, cells A3 through A10 or cells A4 through Z4—are a **range,** usually indicated by a colon or two dots, as in A3:A10 or A3..A10 and A4:Z4 or A4..Z4.

• **The Cell Selector.**   The cell selector indicates the cell in use by (typically) highlighting the entire cell. It is moved by the arrow keys, the Tab key, or a mouse. Many programs have a line at the top or bottom of the screen that indicates the cell selector's location; this—or watching the cell selector's movement carefully—helps prevent you from entering data in the wrong cell.

• **The Grid.**   A worksheet can contain several hundred columns and several thousand rows—far more than can be shown on the screen, which can display only a small section of the work area at a time. The arrow keys, Tab, or mouse can move the cell selector to the desired location, with the worksheet scrolling through the screen.

A blank worksheet has default column widths, usually about 9 or 10 characters. This space is often too narrow to display all the desired data—or it may be wider than necessary. In either case, the width can be easily adjusted, either

Columns

	A	B	C	D	E	F
1						
2		Sept.	Oct.	Nov.	Dec.	TOTAL
3						
4	INCOME					
5	Work	450	450	450	450	1800
6	Student Loan	600	600	600	600	2400
7	TOTAL INCOME	1050	1050	1050	1050	4200
8						
9	EXPENSES					
10	Rent	350	350	350	350	1400
11	Tuition	1200	0	0	0	1200
12	Books	200	0	0	0	200
13	Food	150	141	130	170	591
14	Utilities	30	32	45	58	165
15	Transportation	45	51	49	51	196
16	Entertainment	80	80	80	80	320
17	TOTAL EXPENSES	2055	654	654	709	4072
18						
19	BALANCE	1005	396	396	341	128

Rows

Cursor   Cell

Figure 7-3
A typical worksheet. Note that columns are labeled with letters, rows with numbers. Any intersection of a column and row is called a cell; the highlighted cell is the location of the cell selector, where anything you type will be entered on the worksheet.

for a single column or multiple columns at once, to accommodate the display of data. Most spreadsheets allow alignment of data within the cell—right, left, center, or along the decimal point.

In addition to adjusting the width of a column, you can specify the way you want the worksheet to appear. You can choose the format for numbers (discussed later), and you can indicate boldface or italics for both labels and values. These enhancements are particularly effective on a color screen, where the column might appear in red. Too much of a good thing, however, will clutter both the screen and the eventual printout.

ENTERING DATA

Labels

Simply put, **labels** are the words used to name columns or rows or to explain or identify a formula or numeric entry (Table 7–1). A budget worksheet, for example, might categorize such expenses as food, medical, entertainment, auto, debts, and so on. The text is entered by typing it; the program automatically recognizes the letters as text.

The first column in the budget worksheet might include all the expense categories, with the months of the year entered across the page. Note that labels may contain numbers, such as dates, zip codes, or Social Security numbers, but these numbers cannot be manipulated mathematically. A journal or ledger

COMMUNITY SPREADSHEETS

Big projects are always easier when you have a little help from your friends, and spreadsheets are no exception. By using computer networks and telephone connections, people in different locations can now work on the same spreadsheet at the same time—an ideal way for a community charity, for instance, to finalize a fund-raising drive. Without leaving home, workers can give immediate feedback to each other, fill in gaps of knowledge, comment on each other's work, and approve changes made. Just the thing for a cold, rainy night!

Table 7-1

Examples of valid labels and values in Lotus 1-2-3.

Labels	Values
Johnson	3,234
NAME:	−34
October,	$1,352,345
Net Income	(3 * 150) + 50
R. Smith	.0075
Score 1	−89.6

spreadsheet might include transaction dates, which are treated as text by the program when a space or other character is entered first. Unless the program is told to treat the number as a label, entering 7/30 might produce .23 instead.

Values

Values are the numbers that are available for mathematical manipulation (Table 7–1). A $150 car payment in cell E12 (the transaction date might be in cell A12, the bank's name in B12) can be added, subtracted, multiplied, or otherwise manipulated with other numbers.

Although the values are often dollars and cents, it is not necessary to enter these symbols. Most spreadsheets offer a choice of formats: scientific, percentage, currency, and so on, as well as the number of decimal places to be shown.

Formulas and Functions

Formulas are the means for manipulating the numeric values in the cells (Table 7–2a). Rather than use the numbers themselves, you can instruct the program to add cell values. As noted earlier, most spreadsheets assume that letters are labels and numbers are values. To let the program know you are using a formula, it is necessary to begin with a special symbol such as +, @, or = (these indicate that the entry will be a formula). The formula might read

    =E4+E5+E6+E7+E8+E9+E10+E11+E12+E13+E14+E15

Once entered, the formula automatically performs its operation on the numeric contents of the cells specified, no matter how the values are changed. This capability allows you to ask *What if* and to see, for example, how an increase in the car payment would affect the total budget.

Functions are mathematical shortcuts that allow you to manipulate data—especially long strings of information—with very little effort (Table 7–2b). Even if you are willing to enter a long formula, most spreadsheets will not accept formulas longer than about 250 characters. The preceding formula can be rewritten using a range (E4:E15) and the SUM functions: =SUM(E4:E15). It will total the values and display the result at the cursor position.

Note the use of parentheses in formulas. Just as we use parentheses to show the order in which to calculate figures with paper and pencil, so do spreadsheet programs. For example, $(5 \times 3) + 4$ equals 19, while $5 \times (3 + 4)$ equals 35.

Formula	Explanation
=A1 + A2	The value of cell A1 added to the value of cell A2
=A1 − A2	The value of cell A2 subtracted from the value of cell A1
=A2 * B2	The value of cell A2 multiplied by the value of cell B2
=B1 / A1	The value of cell B1 divided by the value of cell A1
=(A1 + B1)/2	The sum of cells A1 and B1 divided by 2
=(A1 − B1) * =(A2 − B2)	The difference of cells B1 and A1 multiplied by the difference of cells B2 and A2

Table 7–2a
Examples of simple spreadsheet formulas.

Function	Explanation
=AVG (range)	Calculates the average of a range of values
=COUNT (range)	Counts the number of filled cells in a range of values
=MAX (range)	Determines the largest of a range of values
=SQRT (number)	Calculates the square root of a number
=SUM (range)	Calculates the sum of a range of values
=IF (condition, value, or formula)	Chooses between two possible values or formulas based on results of test

Table 7–2b
Common functions in Lotus 1-2-3.

Spreadsheets typically offer a number of other functions. =AVG (C12:C38) will average the values in cells C12 through C38; =SQRT(n) will find the positive square root of (n); =RAND generates a random number between 0 and 1. Standard deviations can be found with =STD and population variances with =VAR.

RANGES IN FORMULAS AND FUNCTIONS

Ranges are extremely useful in formulas and functions. A range can represent all or part of any column or row or several adjacent columns or rows. In fact, any rectangular section of cells in a spreadsheet can be described as a range or block. This gives you great convenience and flexibility when composing formulas and using functions. Most spreadsheet programs also let you name a range of cells. The row in which the budget spreadsheet calculates monthly totals can be specified (as B22:M22, for example) and named Totals. Then you can use the names instead of the cell designations when writing formulas. This makes the formulas far more readable. It is especially useful if you're modifying a spreadsheet you created long ago, and you're trying to remember what all those formulas you created back then mean.

*T*ALKING SPREADSHEETS

It's late and you are working on a spreadsheet, when suddenly you realize there is an easier way to analyze all the data. The only problem is that it will take a long time to write a memo explaining your idea to your boss. No problem. A recently introduced computer program allows users to record verbal remarks with their spreadsheets. By merely clicking on a cell, a second person can play back the verbal annotation. Obviously, this merging of voice and data technology could make working with spreadsheets a lot easier.

In many spreadsheet programs, giving a name to a range of cells also allows you to link that range to another worksheet, thereby automatically transferring the data. For example, if you're the statistician for your local softball or Little League team, you can keep individual worksheets for each player's statistics, and name the range of cells that represents that player's statistical totals. By linking all these named ranges to the master sheet that includes all the players, you can print totals for the team and all the players on one sheet. These named ranges can be dynamically linked; that is, every time the master sheet is opened, it retrieves updated information from the linked ranges in all the other worksheets, automatically keeping your master sheet information current. These techniques of naming and linking ranges apply to many other fields as well.

MANIPULATING DATA

Editing

Changing the contents of a cell before pressing the Enter key is as simple as editing with a word processor. Use the Delete or Backspace key to erase the numbers or letters, type in the correct data, and press the Enter key. Edit existing data by moving the cursor to the cell and retyping the information. Many spreadsheets let you edit part of a cell (there may be a function key that allows this) rather than making you retype the contents completely.

Copying and Moving

The value in cell B26 may also be needed in cell XX26; rather than retype it, you can copy the value and enter it where desired. Using the spreadsheet's ability to copy single or multiple cells lets you move all or part of the data to another worksheet (Figure 7–4). Once the headings for a budget worksheet have been entered, for example, you can copy the entire row of labels to the worksheet

Figure 7-4

By highlighting the cells you want and using the Copy command, you can copy an entire row of cells.

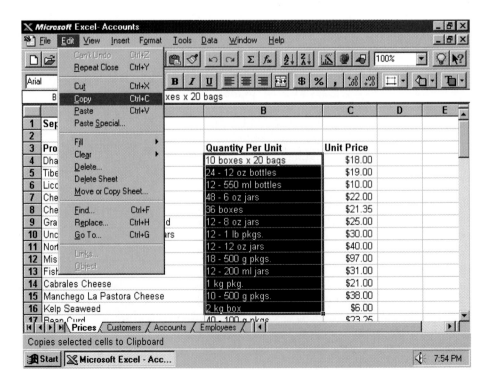

for the next month. You can copy formulas as well: when the expenditures for the month have been totaled (using =SUM, for example) in one column, you can copy the formula to each of the columns for the other months. Also, you can move the data and formulas, leaving the original cells blank.

An important consideration in copying formulas from one location to another is that of **absolute reference** or **relative reference.** For example, copying cell A44 containing the formula =SUM(A3:A43) to cell B44 as an absolute (unchanging) reference causes B44 to display the sum of cells A3 through A43. This can be a problem if the sum of cells B3 through B43 is desired; in this case, copy the formula as a relative (variable) reference, which will then change the formula to fit the data in the new column, =SUM(B3:B43). Note that relative references are assumed when copying formulas. To use an absolute formula, you generally have to specify that with a symbol; for example, =SUM($A$3:$A$43) instead of =SUM(A3:A43).

Inserting and Deleting Rows and Columns.   Most spreadsheets allow you to add columns and rows to an existing worksheet. Although some programs automatically adjust the formulas to reflect the change, others may require the insertion of values into specific cells. Columns and rows can also be deleted; again, formulas are often adjusted automatically. Beware when deleting columns or rows, however. Deleting a column or row in the middle of a range won't damage a formula, but if you delete data specifically used in a formula you will have to adjust the formula yourself—or the spreadsheet won't calculate properly.

Recalculating

Automatic **recalculation** is a time saver for the typical spreadsheet user: insert a new value in a cell and watch all the totals change. Large worksheets—those with hundreds of formulas that require multiple calculations—are another story. Adding new values may require that the program recalculate every one of those hundred formulas. This process can take several seconds—or several minutes—and will be repeated for each new value.

Manual recalculation, which means you control when the worksheet will be recalculated, can save time. Many spreadsheets offer this option, allowing you to make all the necessary value changes and then recalculate the entire worksheet at one time.

Determining the order of recalculation—that is, which formula is calculated first—is another choice offered by most spreadsheets. The typical choices are by column, by row, or what is called *natural calculation.*

The column-first method calculates the contents of columns before rows; the row-first method calculates rows first. Problems arise when a formula at the top of a column or the beginning of a row requires the results of a formula at the bottom of the column or the end of the row. Recalculating the top or beginning formula first will cause an error: the information on which it depends has not yet been calculated. Natural calculation (often the default setting) checks each formula in the worksheet to determine whether it requires information from another formula; if it does, the necessary formula is calculated first.

Sorting

A standard spreadsheet capability is the **sorting** of information numerically or alphabetically. Suppose you have a worksheet that lists your clients in one column, the items each client purchased in a second column, the amount billed in the third, and the purchase date in the fourth. You can sort this information by client name, by item name or number (this number would be entered as a label), by the dollar amount, or by the date(s).

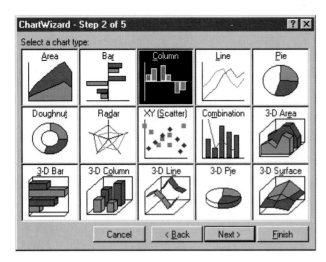

Figure 7-5

Creating a graph or chart in most spreadsheets is as simple as selecting the data you wish to use and clicking on the type of graph or chart you want.

SPECIAL FUNCTIONS

Graphs

Let us suppose the worksheet has been sorted, and the information, although complete, is very dull. Or perhaps there is so much that it is confusing. The graphics capability of many spreadsheets lets you display the data as a **graph:** a bar graph, a line graph, a pie chart, and so on. Creating a graph or chart is often as simple as choosing the data to display and the type of graph or chart, and entering the x- and y-axes (Figure 7-5). The process is repeated for each group of cells to be displayed, and the graph can usually be enhanced with x and y labels, headlines, captions, legends, and distinguishing patterns (for example, cross-hatched, striped, or solid).

Displaying the completed graph on the screen allows it to be previewed and changed as necessary. It can be printed (depending on the capabilities of the printer) and saved to file for later use—possibly as a slide or viewgraph.

Macros

Macros are predefined sequences of commands and keystrokes. Spreadsheet users—like word processor users—frequently use the same sequence of commands repetitively. Rather than type a long string of instructions every time you need to do something, you can write them once, define them as a macro, and use them over and over. Invoke the macro function, enter the desired sequence of commands, choose the key or keys that will recall the sequence, and save the macro. Once stored in the program library, the macro can be called up again as needed with a one- or two-keystroke command. This saves time and makes your spreadsheet use more efficient.

Templates

What a macro is to a sequence of commands, a **template** is to a frequently used worksheet. Using the template function, you can create a basic design with labels, functions, formulas, and other constant information. Once saved, the template can be used with different sets of values and by different users. A real estate firm may design a worksheet for customer analysis: the client's name, type of house wanted, desired price range, down payment available, and so on.

This template can be used by every agent in the firm—with one important warning. The original should be named appropriately—for example, Analysis—and each data-filled worksheet created from it should be saved and named separately. Calling the new worksheet Jones1 or Farber2 will prevent overwriting the template on the disk. You should always save a copy of the template on a backup disk.

SPREADSHEET GRAPHICS

Traditional spreadsheets can look intimidating with all those rows and columns of numbers. A new program called Walden can help the computer deal with this information in a more intuitive way—which also, incidentally, makes manipulating the data easier and faster. This is accomplished by building a spreadsheet that is completely graphical. Data are moved by pointing and clicking the mouse at various icons and tool bars. The main icon is an InfoBox. Objects such as graphs and forms are organized in Books or Documents with their related data so that materials can be grouped together. Users can even create scripts that will record a series of commands that are performed repeatedly.

SAVE, SAVE, SAVE

Just as a power failure can erase all your word processing or graphics data, so can it wipe out your worksheet and all the data on it. And, as in the example just given, saving a new worksheet under an old filename destroys the original data.

Save your work frequently; if you are updating a file, save it under the same name. If you need both the original and the new files, save the new one under a different name, changing Farber2 to Farber3, for example. At the end of the working session, back up the file and store the backup disk away from the original.

Many spreadsheet programs allow files to be written to disk (saved) in a word processing format. This lets you add the worksheet data to a word processing file where it can be edited and formatted as text. Saving the worksheet in this way does not affect the worksheet itself, which should then be saved in the regular manner.

It is also sometimes possible to import data from other spreadsheets, database programs, or word processors.

SPREADSHEET MOVIES

Working with a spreadsheet program can be intimidating, especially for a first-time user. But help is on the way, thanks to multimedia. A CD-ROM device now adds sound and images to illustrate basic spreadsheet functions. Need help figuring out how to go from one column to the next? Just click on "help," and an animated film example shows the way.

PRINTING THE WORKSHEET

Most spreadsheets offer a range of printing options; some, such as horizontal (or sideways) printing, depend on the capabilities of the printer. Generally, users can choose the default settings or change them to suit the content. The **default settings** are typically for standard 8½-by-11-inch paper and include top, bottom, and side margins; type size and style; headers; and page numbering.

With most programs, each of these settings can be changed to accommodate more or fewer columns, to compress more lines onto the page, to format the page so that it more closely fits in with those produced by the word processor, or to change the type style and size. Unless you have a color printer, the aqua italics and fuchsia boldface that distinguished the worksheet on the screen will translate to italic (or underlined) and simple boldface type.

And remember to save your work first. In some circumstances, a printer error can cause your computer to malfunction, and you will lose any unsaved work.

SUMMARY

- A spreadsheet program is an electronic ledger sheet that performs mathematical manipulations on numeric information.
- Its ability to perform complex operations quickly and accurately makes the spreadsheet an ideal tool for accountants, government agencies, schools, businesses, industry—in short, anyone who must work with numbers.
- Like a paper ledger sheet, a worksheet organizes data into rows and columns, forming cells into which labels, values, or formulas are placed.
- Functions and formulas manipulate the data and produce prompt answers to complex operations.

- The spreadsheet program's recalculating ability allows users to ask *What if?* questions about changes in income, expenditures, and growth.
- Macros, templates, built-in functions, and graphics add to the usefulness of most spreadsheets.
- Although spreadsheets vary in complexity, they all allow the user to enter, edit, and manipulate data—from basic arithmetic functions to the highly sophisticated offerings designed for the professional user.

KEY TERMS

absolute reference	functions	rows
cell	graph	sorting
cell address	labels	template
columns	range	values
default settings	recalculation	*What if?*
formulas	relative reference	worksheet

REVIEW QUESTIONS

1. Define a cell.
2. Name three types of data that can be placed in a cell.
3. Differentiate between absolute and relative reference.
4. Define a template.
5. How does the spreadsheet cursor move?
6. Name three typical spreadsheet users.
7. How should you enter a formula?
8. How should you enter text?
9. How should you enter numeric data?
10. How would you add together the values in cells A43 through A89?
11. Why is the order of recalculation important?
12. How often should you save your work?
13. What types of graphs are available through the spreadsheet program?
14. What is the first step to take when you enter data?
15. What is the purpose of a label?

SELF-QUIZ

1. In an electronic spreadsheet, a cell is
    a. the one place you cannot ask *What If?*
    b. the intersection of a row and a margin.
    c. the intersection of a row and a column.
    d. where addresses are located.
2. A cell address is indicated by
    a. the column letter and row number.
    b. the number of cells from the upper-left corner of the spreadsheet.
    c. the location of the worksheet in the CPU.
    d. the intersection of the entry bar.

3. The default column width of a spreadsheet is usually set at approximately
   - *a.* 5 characters.
   - *b.* 7 characters.
   - *c.* 9 characters.
   - *d.* 11 characters.
4. Labels are words used to name or identify
   - *a.* cell addresses.
   - *b.* a grid area.
   - *c.* a numeric entry.
   - *d.* the cell selector location.
5. Most electronic spreadsheets will not accept formulas longer than about _____ characters.
   - *a.* 100
   - *b.* 150
   - *c.* 200
   - *d.* 250
6. If you copy formulas from one location to another and the cell formulas adjust to the new locations, you are using
   - *a.* absolute reference.
   - *b.* relative reference.
   - *c.* positive reference.
   - *d.* temporary reference.
7. Which calculation procedure checks each formula in the worksheet to determine whether it requires information from another formula?
   - *a.* column calculation.
   - *b.* row calculation.
   - *c.* normal calculation.
   - *d.* natural calculation.
8. The sort command in most spreadsheets sorts data
   - *a.* alphabetically but not numerically.
   - *b.* numerically but not alphabetically.
   - *c.* only from low values to higher values.
   - *d.* either numerically or alphabetically.
9. Using a template is very similar to using a(n) _____; however, a template refers to the entire worksheet.
   - *a.* grid
   - *b.* macro
   - *c.* formula
   - *d.* function
10. One drawback to the use of spreadsheets is that a worksheet cannot be used in a word processing document.
    - *a.* true.
    - *b.* false.
11. _____ are the means for manipulating the numeric values in the cells of a worksheet.
12. _____ are mathematical shortcuts to formulas that allow you to manipulate data.
13. _____ are the words used to name columns or rows or to explain or identify a formula or numeric entry.
14. All or part of any column or row, several adjacent columns or rows, or even a rectangular section of cells can be described as a(n) _____ of cells.
15. An important consideration in copying formulas from one location to another is that of _____ reference or _____ reference.
16. _____ recalculation means the user controls when the worksheet will be recalculated.
17. _____ are predefined sequences of commands and keystrokes that can be implemented to minimize the input of individual keystrokes.
18. Data is always entered at the location of the _____.
19. _____ are the numbers that are available for mathematical manipulation.
20. A spreadsheet is an electronic _____ that lets you enter, edit, and manipulate numeric data.

SIMULATIONS

Scenario 1: Can I Graduate?

At most universities, the requirements for graduation are so complex that just figuring out if you have taken the required number of general education courses, major courses, minor courses, emphasis courses, related courses, required-related courses, and the like should be worth a degree. After all, you need a college degree to make this type of determination. One method of easing this difficult task is to create a spreadsheet that will help you track your progress through college. You can generate a list of courses, the number of credits for each course, grades earned, and credits earned. From this you can use the spreadsheet to calculate your grade point averages and quality point averages for each category, number of credits earned in a variety of subcategories, and totals for each.

Your assignment is to generate a spreadsheet to keep track of your progress toward a degree. Be imaginative. For example, you may want a section to total the number of courses and credits taken that do not count for your graduation. You may want to include the cost per credit hour so you can see how much you (or your parents) are actually spending on courses that do and courses that don't count. You might even want to include miscellaneous fees. Be sure to print a copy and save your work on disk.

Scenario 2: Teaching Teachers

Keeping track of student grades is often a time-consuming process. Teachers do not just calculate grades at the end of the semester. Often teachers are required to calculate grades several times a week. Parents call wanting to know how their child is doing, the administration wants periodic reports of progress on selected students, deficiency notices need to be processed, and coaches need eligibility lists. As a teacher you can spend considerable time each week calculating grades. To make this process easier you can develop your own grading system using a spreadsheet.

Your assignment is to generate a grade-reporting spreadsheet with at least ten entries for at least ten students. You will need to perform all necessary totaling and averaging as part of the spreadsheet. Be sure to print a copy and to save your work on disk.

HANDS-ON COMPUTING

1. Practice developing a spreadsheet. We have included some sample spreadsheet ideas. The exact format you use to develop your spreadsheet is up to you. Develop a spreadsheet that is both meaningful and useful to you. Here is a list of ideas. Maybe you can think of others.

   a. Baseball statistics.
   b. Semester budget.
   c. Tax information.
   d. Golf scores.
   e. Dating expenses.
   f. Music library (tapes, cds, records, etc.).
   g. Hobby data (stamps, coins, dolls, figurines, etc.).
   h. Check register (deposits, withdrawals, charges, etc.).
   i. Telephone directory.
   j. Aerobic exercise records.

2. The quality of a spreadsheet begins with content. However, the appearance, style, or format of a spreadsheet can help convey the information. Your task is to pick a spreadsheet you developed in the previous activity and create two different formats. Which format is more useful? Which has a more professional appearance? Which do you like best?

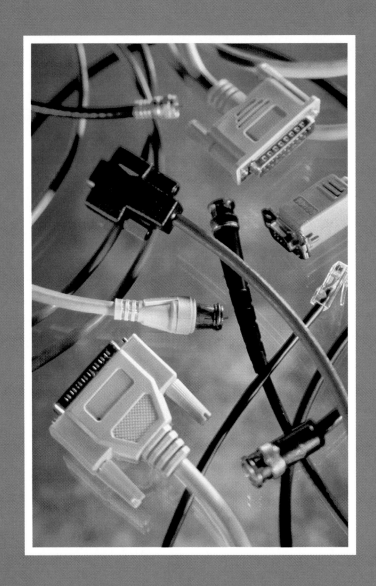

CHAPTER 8

Working with Databases

OBJECTIVES

After completing this chapter, you will be able to:

- Identify some major uses of database software.
- Differentiate database software from other types of application software.
- Identify the components of a database.
- Identify four common data types.
- Describe the role of planning in creating a database.
- Differentiate between indexing and sorting.
- Describe a data query.
- Describe the basic processes of the structured query language (SQL).
- Identify the six major types of database organization.

FOCUS

Before the advent of the computer, maintaining large collections of data was, at best, awkward. People stuffed documents into paper folders, stuffed the documents into file cabinets, stacked the file cabinets and stuffed them into a room—and then couldn't find the information they needed. The office of the registrar at any college was a good example: When a student enrolled, his or her name, address, and other pertinent data were typed or written on a form that was inserted into a file folder. Each semester, course information was added to the folder; at the end of the semester, the folder was manually pulled from the file drawer and grade information was entered. The grade-point average was calculated and entered, the information was manually entered on the transcript (possibly several days or weeks later), and the folder was put away—until the next semester (Figure 8–1). Mistakes were common. Folders were easy to misfile, and a graduate student applying for an assistantship might wait forever if her application went into the wrong folder or file drawer.

Computers—and computerized databases—have solved many of those problems. Mistakes can still be made, but the ease of both entry and access and the ability to scan many files (for that elusive assistantship, for example) can provide correct data almost instantly. The electronic database cannot really replace paper and pencil (and the hand-held calculator), but it can be used to compile and calculate and generate reports on a very wide range of topics with a few keystrokes. Database software allows the search committee to find and list the grade-point averages of all math majors or to locate all students who entered as sophomores or who have made the dean's list more than three times. And it can do these tasks in minutes rather than hours or days.

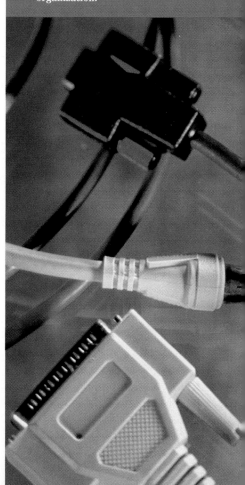

ELECTRONIC DATABASES

Word processors store primarily text; spreadsheets store primarily numbers. **Database software** can store virtually any form of data—documents from a word processor, mailing lists, accounting information, personnel records, salary schedules, Social Security numbers, places of birth, credit histories, military service records, high school and college grades, and political party affiliation. Anyone who needs to store and use large amounts of data will find database software useful.

Figure 8-1
Traditional methods of filing can be overwhelming when trying to maintain a large database. Just finding a file amid all the folders, drawers, and cabinets is a significant task, and maintaining many different individual files requires a tremendous amount of effort.

Law Enforcement Databases

Police departments keep track of outstanding local warrants, stolen cars, criminal records, and missing persons. A police officer who stops someone for a traffic violation enters that person's name directly into a database or calls it in to police headquarters, where a dispatcher checks the name against the police database. Within a few seconds, the information is reported back to the police officer. Many police departments also have access to national law enforcement databases to help identify and locate criminals and missing persons throughout the country.

General Business Databases

The number of business database applications is almost endless, from customer data, research and development, product ideas, and marketing results to order entry and corporate personnel directories.

One typical use of a customer database is the creation of mailing lists. If you purchase a set of golf clubs at a sporting goods store, the merchant enters data about you and your purchase into a customer database. The sporting goods store can then notify you when golf shoes or shirts go on sale.

Businesses also develop market research data with database software. A list of items purchased can help identify which products are selling faster, which need to be removed from inventory, and which need to go on sale. Databases can be used to identify market trends and help businesses make better decisions.

Government Databases

Government agencies collect and store data on individual citizens. The IRS keeps data on salaries paid by employers. Individual tax returns can be checked against these records to show whether people are claiming all their earnings. The FBI database maintains information about crimes and criminals. In investigating a crime, the FBI can compare aspects of the crime with details about other crimes stored in the database, and can generate a profile of the perpetrator as well as a list of suspects.

Bank Databases

Banks store data about customers' checking accounts, savings accounts, indebtedness, and credit history. If a customer requests a loan, the bank uses this information to help determine the likelihood of repayment. Bank examiners use databases to uncover illegal loans, fraud, embezzlement, and unethical banking practices.

Home Databases

Students can use database software on their home computers to store and access research notes for assignments, from term papers to dissertations. A home database can contain phone numbers and addresses of friends and relatives. Because additions and changes are simple to make, the directory can easily be kept current. Using one field to identify people who should receive Christmas cards, it is easy to produce an accurate and current Christmas card list.

Database software is useful for even the simple organization of tape and CD collections, books, travel logs, and lists of household goods for insurance.

Communications with Databases

Through communications links, users at one location can access a computer and database at another location. For example, it is possible to connect a home computer to a database containing current airline flight schedules and prices. A bank loan officer can use the bank's computer to access a credit bureau's database to determine whether the bank should lend an applicant money. And the credit bureau's computer can receive data on the bank's credit customers. Although data transferred in the credit bureau's database is often shared with other banks or credit-giving organizations, federal regulations offer some protection against unauthorized access to these records (see the discussion on privacy later in this book).

DATABASE DESIGN

Databases have three levels of organization: files, records, and fields (Figure 8–2).

Files

A **file** is similar to a physical file cabinet; it consists of a group of records. For example, the university's student history file contains each student's academic record. A student file contains each student's personal record, including name, address, and date of birth; date of enrollment; courses taken; and so on. A

Last Name	First Name	City	State	ZIP
Rogers	Mark	San Francisco	CA	94914
Seaver	Laura	Baton Rouge	LA	34169
James	Frances	Tumwater	WA	74761
Rhodes	Joe	New York	NY	65165
Stone	Kerry	Miami	FL	77137
Towers	Alan	Tempe	AZ	87842

File   Field   Data item   Record

Figure 8-2
When viewed in list format, a typical database file looks like a table. Each record occupies a row, and field names are listed across the top; each column represents a field, and the cells (like those in a spreadsheet) contain data items. This format works best with relational and flat-file databases.

THE RÉSUMÉ BANK/ DATABASE

All job seekers wonder if anyone really reads their résumés, but frustrations run high on both sides of the interviewing process. One of the nation's largest companies, Johnson & Johnson, is using computer software to help cope with the problem. "We know we have a gold mine of people out there," says Catherine King, Johnson & Johnson's manager of employment, "but finding the right person has been darn near impossible." Now a computer program that reads and files résumés has created an in-house database of prospective employees. Candidates are called up by words used on their résumés that match the description of the job being filled. Another side of the process is résumé job banks, such as Banc One Corporation in Columbus, Ohio, which has an employment kiosk where people can fill out applications on screen. Employment manager Greg Burk points out, "Every time a search is done, everyone in the database is considered equally and consistently based on their qualifications. Even though you apply for a specific job, you might be considered for vice president strictly based on what you say your skills are."

course file contains a record of each course that the university offers.

Records

A **record** is similar to a paper file folder containing one student's data. A record stores a group of data relating to a single specification such as a person, place, or thing; each item is stored in a separate field.

Fields

Each **field** in a record stores specific data. For example, each student's record in the university's student file contains a name field, an address field, and an identifier field (a unique name or number). Each field is further assigned a field type, field name, and field size.

A **field name** describes the field; for example, LASTNAME. The name typically can consist of a limited number of characters, including digits and underlines, and must start with a character.

The **field type** tells the computer whether the field data are to be manipulated mathematically, stored alphabetically, compared to other dates, or used for making IF-THEN comparisons. Field types are numeric, alphanumeric, logical, or date.

- **Alphanumeric data** include any alphabetical character, number, or symbol entered from a keyboard. The numbers in this case are treated as descriptive characters rather than those with a mathematical quality. That is, they cannot be added, subtracted, or subjected to any other mathematical operation. For example, we would classify zip codes, driver's license numbers, Social Security numbers, and credit card numbers as alphanumeric because we do not add or subtract them. They can, however, be sorted alphabetically or numerically.

- **Numeric data** are numbers used in mathematical operations. Numbers in an alphanumeric field cannot be subjected to mathematical operations; numbers in the numeric field can. For example, a student's grade is entered as a number in a numeric field so that the grade-point average can be calculated.

- **Logical data** entries identify one of two alternatives—true or false (yes or no). Logical data are used to make IF-THEN comparisons for decision making. For example, a logical field named CHRISTMAS may contain a Y(yes) or an N(no). The user can generate a Christmas card list based on CHRISTMAS fields containing a Y. If a Y is in the CHRISTMAS field, then send a Christmas card.

- A **date field** indicates to the software that the numbers used are a date. This lets the software make comparisons and calculations based on the occurrence of an event. It can compare a target date with the date field in every record, producing a list of customers based on when each purchased a given product. Six months after purchasing a product, the customer can be sent a letter inquiring about product satisfaction.

Field size specifies the maximum number of characters allowed in the field. To decrease processing time, assign the smallest possible size to each field; the computer requires less time to read a 15-character field than a 30-character field.

Planning a Database

Planning is the single most important step in creating a database that works. A poor plan and design can make manipulating and controlling data difficult or impossible.

Let's look at a plan for a university registrar's database. Figure 8–3 shows a layout that describes the fields for each record in the registrar's student file. For each field, the table displays the field type and field size.

An essential step in the planning process is determining precise search factors. If a field called NAME contains both the first and last names, for example, it will be difficult to search for records based on just the last name. In this case, designating two fields— F_NAME (first name) and L_NAME (last name)—in the initial design makes it possible to search for records based on either a first or last name.

It is also important in planning a database to determine all the fields needed. For example, including a TITLE field allows you to indicate whether a person is to be addressed as Mr., Mrs., or Ms. This is useful for such greetings on letters as Dear Mr. Smith or Dear Ms. Smith. Without the TITLE field, the greeting might say Dear Joe Smith or Dear Jane Smith.

If, after the database is established, you realize you've forgotten an essential field, you can add it quite easily with some types of software, but other programs present major difficulties. In any case, an added field generally means adding new data to every record in the file.

When all the fields are defined, the next step is to assign each record to a file. With most databases, it is more efficient to group a small number of related

TRACKING CLIENTS

Every salesman knows how vital it is to keep in contact with clients. Thanks to computer database programs, nothing could be easier. No more frantic racking of the brain to remember the names of the client's children or favorite baseball team. It's all in the computer. If Donald Trump sells a casino to a new customer, one Madaas Mussuh, he could enter the following information into his client database. Interests: casinos, racehorses, almond M&Ms. Also fond of toy poodles and late-17th-century artwork. May be looking for a condo in Miami for next Spring. Financial: Casino negotiated at 450. Final deal on 9/26. Last contact: 8/3/92. Trump could set up any categories he pleased and add new information to the existing file on Madaas. To call up the information, he could enter the date they last spoke, the casino name, or the name Mussuh. By pressing autodial, the computer could even dial the phone for him. In addition, to mail out his Christmas letter, Trump could have the database fill in the blanks with each client's name and address.

Description	Field Name	Field Type	Field Size
Student Number	ID	Numeric	5
Last Name	L_NAME	Alphanumeric	20
First Name	F_NAME	Alphanumeric	10
Street Address	STREET	Alphanumeric	20
City	CITY	Alphanumeric	20
Zipcode	ZIP	Numeric	5
Date of Birth	DOB	Data	8
Minority Status	MIN	Logical	1

Figure 8-3

This plan for a school registrar's database shows the thinking that must go into database design. The table shows what information is to be stored, how it will be labeled as fields, what type of data each field is to contain, and what size the fields should be.

CHANGING JUNK MAIL?

Computers have certainly contributed to the growth of junk mail, thanks to swelling databases of mailing lists that companies swap or sell to each other. But Phil Herring, a direct-mail marketer, suggests that computers can also help solve the problem of annoying junk mail by properly using database technology. These databases would only contain the names of people who want to be on it, who bought specific products in the past, or who contacted the company for information. To help companies further target their mailings (and thereby get more return for their money), Herring says the databases should also include consumers' buying patterns and changes in income. Since more than 600 legislative bills were pending in 1992 that addressed direct-mail marketing, Herring thinks it's a good idea for the industry to regulate itself before the government steps in. For starters, companies can use recycled paper and mention that fact prominently on the mailing. Who knows? Maybe junk mail could become something people would like to see in their mailboxes!

fields in each record and to assign a manageable number of records to a file. For example, the registrar's database needs all students' course grades as well as their names, addresses, dates of birth, and so on. Rather than placing all this information in one huge file, it is better to break up the course history information and the personal data into two separate files such as a student file and student history file. Using a common field name—for example STUDENT_ID—in each file allows the software to look up data for that student in both files.

After the hard work of creating a detailed plan for the database structure, the actual process of creating a database is easy. Depending on the software, once the structure has been defined, building the database is as simple as entering the record name, each of its field names, and each field name's field type and field size. The rest is data entry.

DATA ENTRY

Data entry is generally the simplest part of using a database. Once you've planned your database and defined all the fields, the software will provide you with an on-screen data entry form to directly type in data. You can move from one data field to the next, generally with the Tab key or the arrow keys. Some database software packages provide a list view that shows several records at once. This view generally places each record in a row, with fields in columns (Figure 8–4). This way you can compare data in several records and modify the information as needed.

Data are also entered in a database by reading a data file. To do this, the file must be organized according to the fields you've defined in your database. The data file is usually plain text (although some databases understand other file formats), with information for each record in one paragraph and the fields separated by tabs or commas. If the data file is properly formatted, it can be imported to the database quickly, giving you immediate access to a large amount of information.

SORTING AND INDEXING

One important and useful feature of a database is its ability to transform randomly entered records into a more organized and useful form. For example, in a physician's office, patients' names are entered into a database in the order they come into the office. Rather than keeping the patient list in this random order, it makes more sense to alphabetize it. Database software uses two methods for alphabetizing or otherwise changing the order of records: sorting and indexing.

Sorting is a permanent reordering of the organization of a database, changing the actual arrangement and order of each record in the database. For example, a file sorted on the field LAST_NAME is permanently reorganized into alphabetized LAST_NAME order.

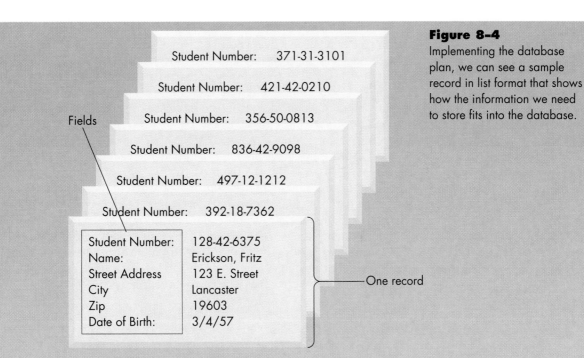

Fields

Student Number: 371-31-3101

Student Number: 421-42-0210

Student Number: 356-50-0813

Student Number: 836-42-9098

Student Number: 497-12-1212

Student Number: 392-18-7362

Student Number:	128-42-6375
Name:	Erickson, Fritz
Street Address	123 E. Street
City	Lancaster
Zip	19603
Date of Birth:	3/4/57

One record

Figure 8-4
Implementing the database plan, we can see a sample record in list format that shows how the information we need to store fits into the database.

Another way to visualize a database is as a list or table. Each row of the table is a record. Each column of the table is a field.

One record   One field

	Student Number	Last Name	First Name	Street Address	City	Zip	DOB
1	128-42-6375	Erickson	Fritz	123 E. Street	Lancaster	19603	3/4/57
2	392-18-7362	Vonk	John	908 Elm Street	LeSalle	40361	3/4/61
3	497-12-1212	Smith	Sarah	810 OakAve.	Minor	93716	4/19/64
4	836-42-9098	Jones	Alice	916 3rd Ave.	Eastville	48313	5/16/65
5	356-50-0813	Doud	Jan	410 St. Joe	Minor	93716	8/13/65
6	371-31-3101	Ruth	Jenna	973 Main St.	Millville	47147	9/3/71
7	421-42-0210	Andres	John	911 Lotus Ave.	Orange	48131	7/14/70

Table or list

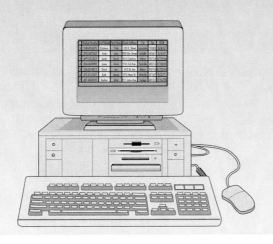

Sorting is useful when the organization of a database must remain constant. For example, a car dealer may enter the names and addresses of all customers visiting the dealership each day and then sort the data according to the specific criterion, by type of trade-in, by date, or by type of car desired.

The major disadvantage of a sort is time. Depending on the type of equipment and the number of records in the database, a sort can take from several minutes to hours.

Indexing organizes data temporarily. The results of indexing appear the same as sorting; however, the first record displayed may actually be (and remain) the 150th record in the database.

Because indexing is a temporary sort, it is possible to create multiple indexes for the same database file. For example, a file can be indexed alphabetically by last name, alphanumerically by zip code, and in date order by purchase date, allowing customer listings to be produced in each specific order.

Multiple indexes also let you produce lists alphabetized in more than one field at a time. For example, a customer file indexed on CITY and LAST_NAME can produce an alphabetical list of customers within a city:

Chicago,	Bepper
Chicago,	Lowell
Chicago,	Meridith
New York,	Jones
New York,	Kale
New York,	May
New York,	Provall
San Francisco,	Allen
San Francisco,	Berger
San Francisco,	Valdez

Indexing is normally much faster than sorting, and it provides greater flexibility. Indexing allows more than one kind or organization within one database file; permanent sorting tends to limit a file's organization.

KEEPING TRACK OF THE VOTERS

Elected officials can use databases to maintain better contact with their constituents. Since computers can store almost unlimited information, legislators can have lists of voters in their district segmented demographically or according to a voter's interests. For example, Senator Seymour knows that Henry Wallach hasn't voted for the past three elections, that Lilia Wallach opposed the logging of the Mendocino coast, and that Jerry Wallach contributed money to his last campaign. Accordingly, Jerry Wallach gets a letter every three months and Lilia gets a letter extolling the senator's support of the environment and informing her about current legislation he has introduced to save the spotted lizard. If Henry sent Senator Seymour a letter about crime in the streets, he might get back a letter describing the senator's ideas on gun control.

DATA QUERIES

A request for data in a database is a **query.** Queries can be as simple as searching for a specific name in a field or as complex as searching for all customers who meet a precisely detailed set of specifications.

In a simple query, the first step is to identify the field to be used. For example, searching for a record of a specific customer is usually as simple as entering the customer's name or identification number.

The more precise the query entry, the more accurate the information located. Querying a large database using the last name Smith, for example, will return all Smiths in the database. Querying the same database for Smith as the LAST_NAME, Colorado as the STATE, and snowshoes in PURCHASE will produce all Smiths in Colorado who purchased snowshoes.

Queries work with database indexes to produce appropriately organized lists of data. Suppose you wish to find all customers who purchased a new car in 1992. If the file is not indexed, the query will produce a list based on entry order rather than alphabetical or date order. If the file has been indexed by customer name, however, the query will produce a customer list in alphabetical order. If the file has been indexed by purchase date, the query will produce the list ordered by purchase date.

Structured Query Language (SQL)

Various databases approach the process of querying differently. Just as different word processors use different commands to accomplish the same task, different database programs use unique command sets for locating data. A standardized approach to data querying, the **structured query language (SQL)** crosses these barriers. Software that supports SQL can locate data within a variety of microcomputer and mainframe databases. Because SQL was designed for querying remote databases, not local ones, database software programs that implement SQL on microcomputers generally use it for accessing databases on mainframe computers and computer networks. Since these areas of microcomputing are growing fast, SQL has become more and more popular.

Structured Query Language is based on a series of standardized query expressions to specify the criteria for a data search. These expressions look very much like the commands in a programming language. It is beyond the scope of this book to teach you all the expressions in SQL and how they interrelate to produce queries; however, the following few expressions will give you some understanding of the basic SQL process.

Most SQL expressions have at least two **clauses.** For example, the SELECT clause determines the fields to use from the database and the FROM clause specifies which file will provide the fields.

```
SELECT TITLE, FIRST_NAME, LAST_NAME, STATE, AMOUNT
FROM CUSTLIST
```

This produces a list of all customers from the CUSTLIST file. It displays their titles, first names, last names, states, and purchase amounts.

Adding the WHERE clause puts a search restriction on an SQL expression.

```
SELECT TITLE, FIRST_NAME, LAST_NAME, STATE, AMOUNT
FROM CUSTLIST
WHERE STATE = 'MI'
```

This limits the query to customers in the state of Michigan. The name in single quotation marks in the expression identifies the data in fields that must match for the record to be included. The single quotation marks show that the data are alphanumeric (data without quotation marks are numeric).

Another useful clause is AND. AND follows the WHERE clause to show that two conditions must be met for a record to be included in the results of the query. For example,

ART DATABASE

A new art history database in Rome provides scholars comparing sculpture, painting, and architecture in the ancient world and the Renaissance with a phenomenal amount of information in both text and visual form. Data can be viewed on two screens simultaneously, so that an ancient Greek work of art can be juxtaposed against a Roman copy from the 1450s. Any combination of images and text can be called up and compared. This is especially helpful to scholars of the periods, since it is unclear how much Renaissance artists knew of ancient art. The database—stored on a video disk—was developed over ten years with the help of museums and libraries in three countries.

```
SELECT TITLE, FIRST_NAME, LAST_NAME, STATE, AMOUNT
FROM CUSTLIST
WHERE STATE = 'MI'
AND AMOUNT > 15000.00
```

produces a list of all customers in Michigan who purchased a car valued at more than $15,000.

Several clauses are used to change data in the database. The clause INSERT places a new record into a database. DELETE removes a record, and UPDATE changes the contents of a record. For example,

```
INSERT
INTO CUSTFILE
VALUES ('DR.', 'Bill', 'Smith', 5634.23)
DELETE
FROM CUSTFILE
STATE = 'CO'
UPDATE CUSTLIST
SET COMMISH = .20
WHERE AMOUNT > 15000.00
```

will insert a new record for Dr. Bill Smith into the CUSTFILE, delete all records from the state of Colorado, and set the commission rate at 20 percent when the purchase amount exceeds $15,000.

*T*HE GLOBAL JUKEBOX, A SINGING DATABASE

Want to find out how many people bought Madonna's latest hit, play Gregorian chants, or find the notation of Middle Eastern music? The world's greatest jukebox (more than 4,000 songs from 400 countries) allows the user to access statistical data, charts, graphs, dance videos—and most of the world's music. Intended as a research tool for museums and libraries, the Global Jukebox uses Cantometrics, a system of code words that define and analyze music. This computerized file cabinet for music and dance across time and cultures is part of New York City's Hunter College. Says Alan Lomax, director of Hunter's Association for Cultural Equity, "What we did was similar to the classification of plants and animals. We developed methods to describe and classify performances. And we can show the various cross-cultural evolutions of song and dance styles." Do lights flash while the Global Jukebox plays your request?

GENERATING REPORTS

A **report generator** controls the display of information both on the screen and on paper. The simplest type of report is a list of the data in the database. More complex reports include titles, page numbers, subtotal and total calculations, column and row headings, and a variety of other information to make a database report both functional and attractive.

A database program's report generator contributes significantly to its overall usefulness. After all, it's not enough just to be able to store all this information; the information is useless unless you can get precisely the information you need and print it in a useful form. Together with queries, report generators are the primary method of extracting specific data from a database; their capabilities are crucial.

DATABASE ORGANIZATION

There are six major types of databases: relational, flat file, HyperCard, hierarchical, network, and free form.

Relational Databases

The database file in Figure 8–4 is a table showing a relation where the rows correspond to records and the columns correspond to fields. **Relational data-**

bases organize information in this manner, which allows maximum flexibility of querying based on relationships between different fields.

By using this table structure, you can access and control more than one file at a time. Changes made to one record in one file automatically update linked records in another file.

Flat-File Databases (File Managers)

Many microcomputer users need only a simple method for storing limited amounts of data. To meet this need, **file managers,** sometimes called **flat-file databases,** are available.

Flat-file databases are **single-relation databases.** That is, these databases work with only one file at a time; there are no linkages with other files. One major advantage of flat-file databases is their ease of use: It is easy to set up a database, store records, and generate queries and reports. Another advantage is that flat-file databases are almost always much less expensive than any other type of database. As long as there is no need to cross-reference files, flat-file databases can be very efficient.

HyperCard

One fairly recent development in database management is a program called **HyperCard** (a limited version comes with the Macintosh). HyperCard combines many aspects of traditional database design with advanced graphics and the Macintosh environment.

HyperCard allows users to create individual screens filled with text from a word processor, other data, and graphics. Each screen displays a particular set of information with access to other screen displays. The term **card** describes an individual screen display, and a group of cards linked together form a Hyper-Card **stack.**

A card is equivalent, in database terms, to a record. Unlike traditional database records made up solely of fields, however, a card can be made up of fields, text from a word processor, or graphic images. For example, a user might design one card to welcome users to a database of the animal kingdom and another card with text about elephants, a picture of an elephant, and specific statistical elephant data. An individual card could be developed for each animal in the animal kingdom.

Linking cards in any order based on any criterion gives HyperCard its strength. A **button** links cards into a stack. A button can appear as a simple statement such as Continue, Next Card, Search, or even Change Kingdoms. It can also appear as a small picture or icon; moving the mouse pointer onto the icon and clicking causes a new card to appear. Buttons can cause cards to display sequentially or randomly.

One of HyperCard's features is its Englishlike language for setting up links between cards. Users do not have to be database or programming experts to use HyperCard, which—like its competitors, such as Linkway for the IBM—is very easy to learn and use.

Hierarchical Databases

Hierarchical databases are used mostly with mainframes. Data are organized with the broadest grouping at the highest level, followed by more specific subgroups (Figure 8–5). The structure is very similar to a family tree or DOS directory structure, where a parent, or root, directory houses several children, or subdirectories. In turn, each subdirectory can house additional subdirectories. The top-down organization eliminates searching through all records; the pro-

Figure 8-5
Hierarchical databases organize information in a treelike structure, with each category of information containing subcategories. Here, brands A, B, and C are subcategories of Tomatoes, itself a subcategory of Canned Goods under the San Diego Store. This structure provides good organization of large volumes of information, but limits the ways in which you can access it.

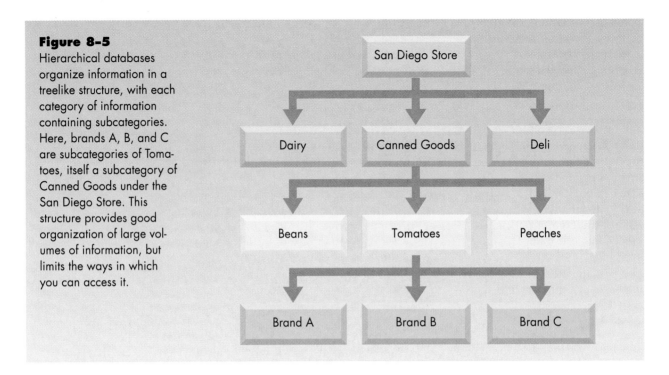

gram searches only the specified groups of data. The disadvantage is that, unlike relational databases, every relationship and link must be predefined. Adding any new field requires a complete redefinition of the database.

Network Databases

Network databases are similar to hierarchical databases with the additional feature of each subgroup having more than one root. That is, each child in a family tree can have more than one parent group. Network databases can branch from one group to several others or from one owner to several other members, making the search process easier.

Free-Form and Encyclopedic Databases

Except for HyperCard, all the databases discussed so far involve the storage of individual data in predefined fields. These are known as **record-oriented data-bases.** For many data applications the individual size of a record or a field within a record can cause problems; storing the Gettysburg Address in a table, for example, would be very difficult. **Free-form databases** are used for data that consist of large volumes of text.

Data entry in free-form databases is normally accomplished by moving word processing files into the database. Rather than using specific fields, the search process uses **keywords,** words entered by user to determine the scope of the search. **Encyclopedic databases** are large databases, or data banks, containing information on a vast array of subjects. These databases are generally subscription services, allowing users access to the data (through communications links) for specific charges. Users begin their search with keywords. Any record that contains a specified keyword is included in the results of the search. For example, using the keyword *insects* causes the database to return a list of all records about insects. In a comprehensive biology database of research articles, this one word could produce a listing of several thousand records or articles.

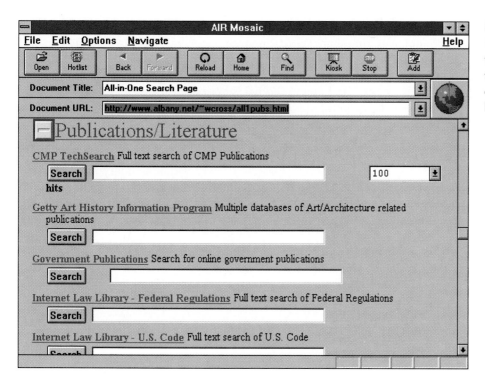

The amount of time the host computer spends on this initial search varies according to the specificity of the keyword. For example, the keyword *baseball* will produce a much longer list of articles and citations than the keyword *Babe Ruth*.

Adding a third criterion such as *homeruns* to *baseball* and *Babe Ruth* will cut the number of citations even further. Each service provides guidelines to make searching the database more precise—and less costly.

Users with CD-ROM (compact disk–read only memory) drives can buy CD-ROMs with encyclopedic databases. The disks include tremendous amounts of instantly accessible information, including photographs, about an almost unlimited number of topics.

SUMMARY

- Database software makes it possible for computers to store and retrieve large amounts of data.
- A database is organized into three levels: files, records, and fields.
- A file, the electronic equivalent of a file cabinet, contains a group of records.
- A record, (like a paper file folder) stores a group of data items, or fields, relating to a single specification, such as a person, place, or thing.
- Each field has a field name, size, and type.
- The field name is a unique identifier. Field size determines the maximum number of characters or numbers that can be stored in a field.
- Data type determines the kind of operation the computer can perform on the data; data can be alphanumeric, numeric, logical, or date.
- Alphanumeric data, such as addresses or Social Security numbers, can be alphabetized and sorted numerically.
- Numeric data are numbers used in mathematical operations.
- Logical data identifies one of two alternatives—true or false, yes or no.

- Numbers stored in a date field represent a calendar date.
- Planning is the single most important step in creating a database that works.
- One of the most important steps in database planning is determining search factors and making the fields specific.
- Data is entered in the database through an on-screen entry form or a data file formatted to match the already-defined fields.
- The order of records can be permanently changed by sorting or temporarily changed by indexing.
- A request for data in a database is a query. A simple query involves identifying a field and searching for all records that match the field name.
- Structured query language (SQL), a standardized language for querying, is based on a series of expressions that specify the criteria for a data search.
- Six major types of databases are relational, flat file, HyperCard, hierarchical, network, and free form.
- Relational databases organize information in relational tables and let users manipulate or control more than one file at a time.
- Flat-file databases work with single-file applications.
- HyperCard combines text and graphics to produce individual screens called cards.
- A hierarchical database organizes data into a family-tree formation, with the broadest grouping at the parent (root) level; specific subgroups appear as children (subdirectories).
- Network databases are similar to hierarchical databases; each group has more than one parent.
- Free-form databases accept large amounts of text without specifying data type or size.

KEY TERMS

alphanumeric data	hierarchical databases
button	HyperCard
card	indexing
clauses	keywords
database	logical data
database software	network databases
date field	numeric data
encyclopedic databases	query
field	record
field name	record-oriented databases
field size	relational databases
field type	report generator
file	single-relation databases
file managers	stack
flat-file databases	structured query language (SQL)
free-form databases	

REVIEW QUESTIONS

1. What is a database field?
2. What is a database record?
3. List five ways a physician could use a database.
4. What is a file?

5. List four types of data stored in a database and briefly explain each one.
6. Describe an encyclopedic database.
7. How does a keyword access a database?
8. Describe the similarities between a file cabinet and a computer database.
9. What is a report generator?
10. Explain the difference between indexing and sorting.
11. What is a relational database?

SELF-QUIZ

1. In a university database, a student's address is a
    a. record.   c. field.
    b. file.   d. field type.
2. In a university database, all the information about a single student is called
    a
    a. record.   c. field.
    b. file.   d. field type.
3. In a university database a student's academic records are kept in a
    a. record.   c. field.
    b. file.   d. field type.
4. Which of the following are considered numeric data?
    a. Social Security numbers   c. Zip codes
    b. street addresses   d. grade point averages
5. Data that identify one of two alternatives, such as true or false are called
    a. alternative data.   c. bilateral data.
    b. alphanumeric data.   d. logical data.
6. A permanent reordering of the organization of a database, changing the actual arrangement and order of each record in the database, is called
    a. sorting.   c. querying.
    b. indexing.   d. report generating.
7. A temporary reordering of the organization of a database is called
    a. sorting.   c. querying.
    b. indexing.   d. report generating.
8. Which of the following is faster and provides greater flexibility?
    a. sorting   b. indexing
9. A standardized approach to data querying is called
    a. standardized query forms.   c. structured query language.
    b. structured query forms.   d. standardized query language.
10. With the form of database referred to as HyperCard, a group of cards linked together form HyperCard
    a. button.   c. hierarchy.
    b. stack.   d. file.
11. _____ is the single most important step in creating a successful database.
12. _____ specifies the maximum number of characters allowed in a field.
13. _____ data includes any alphabetical character, number, or symbol entered from a keyboard.
14. _____ is a permanent reordering of the organization of a database.
15. A request for data in a database is a(n) _____.
16. A(n) _____ controls the display of information both on the screen and on paper.

17. The _____ tells the computer whether the field data is to be manipulated mathematically, sorted alphabetically, compared to other dates, or used for making if-then comparisons.

18. A(n) _____ field indicates to the software that the numbers used are a date.

19. The need for storing limited amounts of data can be met with _____ managers, sometimes called flat-file databases.

20. With HyperCard, a(n) _____ is used to link cards into a stack.

SIMULATIONS

Scenario 1: Tracking Customers

Keeping track of customers has always been a difficult and time-consuming task, but one that is critical for success in sales and business in general. As the newest sales member of Honest Abe's Discount Fine Automobiles, you want to make a positive impression. You also want those big commissions, and you want to win the free January weekend trip to Nome. Fortunately, you know that the way to be successful is to keep track of every prospect you meet, the type of automobile he or she is interested in, when he or she last bought a car, etc. You also know that you have only two days to close a sale before the potential customer is lost to another dealer. You decide the solution to sales success is a database (a smart decision).

Your task is to create a customer-tracking database using any of the popular database programs available. In your database you need to include the following customer information fields:

First name	Car type
Last name	Type of trade
Address	Amount down/trade-in
City	Previous purchase date
State	Contact date
Zip code	Prospect rating
Initial contact date	Buy (Y/N)

Print a simple report that lists all customers in your database.

Scenario 2: Customer Sorts

Now that you have the foundation for a customer-tracking database, you can generate some meaningful reports. After all, your customer database is of little value unless you can retrieve data in a useful and meaningful fashion. One of the key elements of your customer-tracking database is the prospect-rating field. When you come into work each day, you want to be sure to contact customers with the highest prospect ratings. Therefore, you need to produce a report that lists all your prospects sorted in ascending order based on the prospect-rating field. In fact, that is your task. Produce a simple report that is sorted in an ascending order according to prospect rating.

Scenario 3: Customer Limits

At some point a customer contact fails. In the automobile business, two days is the limit. After that, the contact has either purchased a car from another dealer or was not really very interested in buying a car. Therefore, you need a report sorted in ascending order based on the prospect rating that includes only those customers with a contact date that is less than two days old. Generating this report is your next task.

No matter how hard you try or how experienced you are, you never get the number of fields correct. It is only after you begin to use a database that it becomes evident that you either need to add or remove fields. What other fields could you add to the customer-tracking database to make customer tracking easier, more efficient, or produce better reports? Use your imagination and creativity to think of different fields to add to your database that will enhance the value of your reports.

Scenario 4: Modify

Now that you have been salesperson-of-the-month for the past five months, everybody, including your boss, wants to know your secret. You are a bit reluctant to share your customer-tracking database since it did help you win the trip to Nome. However, in the interest of cooperation and because you are a decent person and getting a $2,000 bonus for your secret, you decide to share your database. The problem is, you never really cared how the database looked, but sharing the database means you want it to look as good as possible. Your task is to clean up and improve the overall appearance of your database. You want the style of the database to reflect the quality of the design. Again, it is up to you to make your database look as good as it works. Once you complete this task, share your database design and format with others in the class. It always helps to share database design ideas.

Scenario 5: They Want Your Database

HANDS-ON COMPUTING

1. Database management can be especially useful for keeping track of your music CDs or tapes, model train collection, stamp collection, or any other home hobby. Create a database for any hobby you desire. It is important to remember that each piece of data must be stored in its own field. For example, it is better to have individual fields for CD title and CD artist than to combine the two pieces of data into one field. Once you create this database, print a simple report.

2. You can combine your knowledge of computers with database management by creating a database for selecting a computer to purchase. Create fields for computer type, model number, microprocessor, clock speed, RAM, monitor type, price, guarantee, service rating, and any other fields you think may be useful. From this database produce a report that is sorted on a variety of criteria, such as price and microprocessor.

3. Databases can be useful for keeping track of friends and families. Create a personal database that contains the names, addresses, birthdays, telephone numbers, and other information about your friends and family members.

4. Develop a financial database to track your checking account. (Use fields such as purchase, account number, and amount.) From this database produce a report by account number to see where all your money is being spent. You may wish to use the graphing capability of your database software to generate meaningful charts and graphs.

5. A database can be an excellent tool for tracking all the movies that you have seen. Develop a movie database that contains the movie name, type, rating, and review. Once you create the design, enter a variety of movies. Use the query function to search for movies based on the type and rating. Be sure to print a report of your findings.

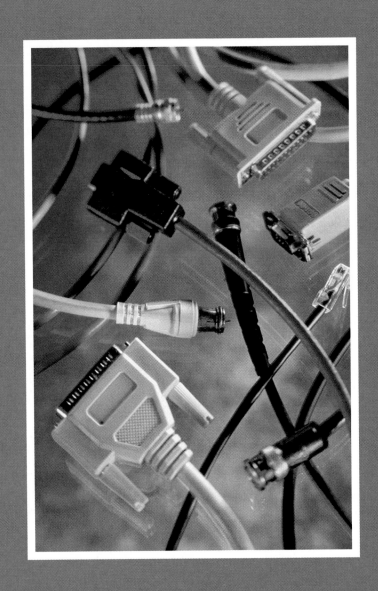

CHAPTER 9

Working with Communications

FOCUS

When a microcomputer stands alone, not connected to another computer, the only information it can provide is on the hard disk or on a manually inserted floppy disk. But if you connect that computer to other computers, you multiply its capabilities and gain access to a world of information.

The transfer of data from one computer to another is known as computer communications. This chapter describes the two most common microcomputer communications systems: telecommunications and networking.

Telecommunications, which uses the telephone to connect computers to each other, takes on many forms for many uses. Chief among these are electronic mail, which sends messages from one computer to another; internet access, which allows you access to tens of thousands of computers and millions of computer users; access to various services, including on-line databases for supplying information; bulletin board services for posting public messages, sharing data files and software, and electronic conversation; and general on-line services, such as America OnLine, CompuServe, and Prodigy, among others, which provide a whole range of services, from financial information to on-line shopping.

Networking, which uses special wiring to connect computers locally and a mixture of private and public connections to connect computers over a wide area, is primarily used for sharing data, programs, and most importantly, processing power in a working environment. A local area network connects computers over short distances, say, within an office or between adjacent buildings; a wide area network connects computers and local area networks over many miles. Networks can be configured in a number of structures, called topologies: bus, in which all computers are on a single line of cable; star, in which computers are connected on branching lines from a central hub; and ring, in which computers are connected in a loop. Networks can also be administrated in one of

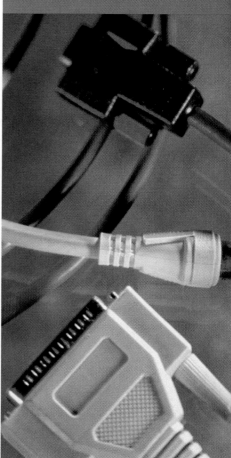

two ways: client-server networks use a central computer to run the network and provide shared resources, and peer-to-peer networks give all computers on the network equal status and direct sharing of resources.

TELECOMMUNICATIONS

Telecommunications is the process of sending and receiving electronic data using a telephone. This makes it possible for a computer to share and exchange data with another computer connected to a telephone almost anywhere in the world. Users can communicate with each other directly, send and receive electronic mail and facsimiles (faxes), participate in electronic bulletin boards, and access large national databases.

Internet

A network is a collection of computers tied or linked together, usually to achieve some common goal. In most cases, networks allow users to share information. In business, networks enable a computer user to send messages to any other computer user on the network. For example, a business may have a network that allows users to access inventory files, new product announcements, and demonstrations of services. In schools, networks allow users to access student record files, library catalog listings, and class registrations. Internet is no different from any other network—except it's bigger. It exists to provide access to information (see page 174 for more on networks).

Internet is a network of networks. Internet is a group of networks linked together using rules that allow any one user to connect to and use any available network or computer connected to it. This means that accessing any computer connected to Internet provides access to all computers connected to Internet. In other words, connecting to Internet means connecting to tens of thousands of other networks, millions of individual computers, and tens of millions of other computer users.

The Internet Connection. Internet is a communication system. It involves the physical connections (usually through telephone lines, direct wires, fiber optics, satellite transmissions, etc.) that link one computer network to another. It is also a standard of communication (called a protocol) that enables one computer network to "speak" to another. In the early days of networking, there were many different types of networks and many different ways that computers communicated to one another. The problem of linking networks together was not so much one of running cable from one network to another as one of establishing a common communication language (protocol). In the 1980s a new protocol emerged called **Transmission Control Protocol/Internet Protocol** (**TCP/IP**) that established a communication standard. Any computer network could communicate with any other network as long as it followed TCP/IP standard protocol.

AHEAD OF THE NEWS

During the 1991 attempted military coup in the former Soviet Union, information in faxes and e-mail often reached other countries ahead of the news media. Westerners who had been communicating via computer with Soviet citizens suddenly found themselves in an electronics cross-fire of anxious messages. "The shooting has begun," read one e-mail message. "There have been many explosions outside the parliament building. The siege is underway." Since communications inside Russia were fragile, people in Europe and the United States could, in turn, relay what they had learned from TV, radio, and newspapers, offering encouragement and support for the freedom fighters. This vital electronic pipeline of information was greatly valued by those receiving it. "The new junta will try to impose censorship and cut the flow of information from our country," read one fax. "I suggest you take some measures in order to continue operating, even under highly adverse conditions."

Once TCP/IP was established, it became relatively easy for networks to communicate. The National Science Foundation (NSF) set up an initial link of networks primarily for governmental agencies and universities to communicate and share research information. This initial link of university networks to five supercomputers (called an NSFnet) became the foundation of Internet.

The real strength of NSFnet and TCP/IP was that their designs made it very easy for other networks to join. Originally, NSFnet did not allow other (especially commercial and for-profit) networks to join. However, new rules were adapted and soon it became very easy for commercial entities to join and participate on Internet. This move opened up the world to Internet.

The rules that govern Internet rest with the Internet Society, a voluntary organization run by a board that meets to set standards and determine resources. For example, it is the Internet Society through the Internet Architecture Board (IAB) that determines addresses and rules for accessing and using addresses.

Addresses. What makes Internet possible is a standard of addressing set by the IAB. Internet addresses are in some ways similar to home addresses. Every network and every computer user must have a unique address; otherwise, information would become lost and confused. The structure of an Internet address is, therefore, very important.

The address system for Internet is actually quite easy. It uses a process called **domain name system** (**DNS**). A domain is a location. Every domain is separated by a dot (.). For example, marauder.millersv.edu has three domains. The first, marauder, is the domain (or name) of the computer system. The second is the domain (name) of the network. Finally, edu identifies the network type. In this case edu stands for educational institution. In short, this name is read backwards as the educational institution, Millersville University, using the Marauder computer. There can be more than three domains and very often there are. The key point is that the address is specific to a computer.

Domains

.com	commercial
.edu	educational
.gov	governmental
.mil	military
.org	organization
.net	network resources

Since Internet is worldwide, a domain may designate a country. For example, a domain ending with .ca is Canada, a domain ending with .uk is the United Kingdom, and so forth.

In addition to identifying and locating a specific computer system on Internet, it is also important to be able to identify specific individuals who have accounts or use specific computers. This is the reason for the @ (at) symbol. For example, ferickso@Marauder.millersv.edu indicates a specific individual (Fritz Erickson) at (@) the Marauder computer at Millersville University, which is an educational institution. Of the millions of people using Internet no one has exactly the same address. Therefore, if you want to write to either Fritz Erickson or John Vonk (javonk@bentley.univnorthco.edu), all you need know is our Internet address.

Points of Access. Of course, the basic premise of Internet is that connecting to any one computer allows you access (if you have permission and access codes) to any other computer on Internet. Most university computers are connected to Internet. You can also gain Internet access if your company computer is connected, if you work for the military, or if you join a provider.

The growing popularity of Internet has created a demand for service providers who, for a fee, provide the general public with access to their computer, which is connected to Internet.

The World Wide Web.   Accessing Internet is accomplished through several processes. One of the most popular is called the **World Wide Web.** Web (as it is commonly called) users use a graphical interface and a series of addresses to locate particular information. The Web uses a standard for transferring information called the HyperText transfer protocol (http). This protocol allows users to post and retrieve documents, images, and sounds. Http allows users to access information graphically over Internet.

To use the graphical features of the Web, you must have browser software, such as Mosaic. Mosaic offers a full-color graphical interface that allows you to use a mouse to point and click to obtain information through the World Wide Web. The popularity of the Web is growing because it is very easy to use and operate. However, the protocol differs from TCP/IP and is not available from all providers. In the case where Mosaic is not available, a text-based system for searching the Web, called Lynx, may be available. This provides full Web access but does not provide the ability to display graphics or use a mouse to point and click.

Gophers.   Another method for searching for information on Internet is called **Gopher.** A gopher is simply a tool for navigating Internet through a series of menus. This is often a very easy system to use that does not require a graphical interface.

Veronica.   Locating gophers is accomplished with **veronica.** Since there are thousands upon thousands of gophers available, finding a gopher for a particular topic can be difficult. Veronica is a process for searching for gophers related to specific or selected topics.

Telnet.   One of the major advantages of having access to Internet is that you can connect directly to any other computer connected to it. For example, if you want to use a computer located at another university, you can telnet to that computer; then your computer acts as a terminal of the connected computer. Of course, when you telnet to another computer, you must have a password and permission to access that computer.

File Transfer Protocol (ftp).   Accessing information on Internet is enhanced by a feature that allows you to send and receive files. This is the purpose of File Transfer Protocol, or ftp. With ftp you can retrieve files and print them on your own computer. You can download files that are located on Internet and save them on your own disk. You can even use ftp to send files to other computers connected to Internet.

Electronic Mail

Electronic mail, or e-mail, is the sending and receiving of messages from one computer to another over a telephone or across networks to other computers, computer bulletin board systems, and on-line services (Figure 9–1). Using e-mail software, such as ccMail or InBox, you can write a short message with

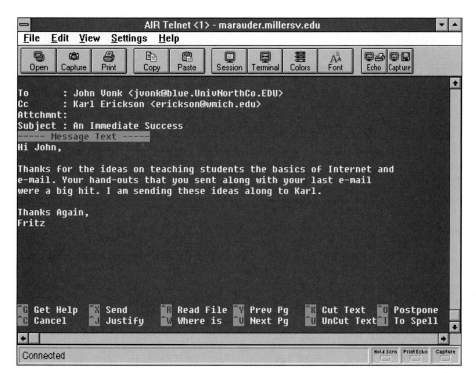

Figure 9-1
E-mail packages such as Pine let you send messages to anyone with an e-mail account as long as they are connected to Internet.

a text editor (similar to a word processor) and address it to a particular person or group of people. You can also attach items such as word processing files, graphics, or other computer files to your message and send them electronically, much like—but considerably faster than—mailing paper documents through the U.S. Postal Service.

Suppose an author in New York City is working on a manuscript and wishes to have input from a colleague in San Francisco. It is 9:00 AM in New York, but it is only 6:00 AM on the West Coast—too early to send the chapter directly. In addition to their computers, both the author and the colleague have e-mail software that can access a common **network** or on-line service (such as MCI Mail, an electronic mail network; Internet; or on-line services such as CompuServe). The writer can create a message and attach the manuscript file, then send it electronically, in a matter of seconds, to the service they use. After dialing into the service and receiving and editing the manuscript, the colleague can send the file from San Francisco back to the service, from which it will be picked up by the author in New York City.

Figure 9-2
The fax card allows you to send and receive faxes on your computer just as you would on a fax machine.

Facsimile Transmission

Popularly known as a fax machine, a **facsimile** machine is essentially a copier that sends and receives copies over the telephone. An inexpensive alternative to a stand-alone fax machine is a fax card installed in a microcomputer. This arrangement generally allows you to use the card as either a fax or a modem (Figure 9–2).

With a computer fax, however, only computer files, rather than paper hard copies, can be transmitted. The faxed files differ from e-mail files in that, unlike

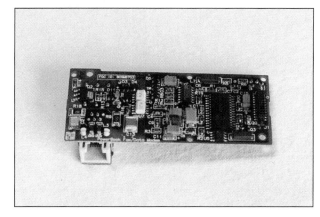

a word processing file, faxes are received as graphic images and cannot be changed. Optical character reader utility programs convert the fax to a text file; they also print the faxes. Sending an already printed page requires a scanner and software to convert the scanned image to fax file format, enabling the fax card to transmit the scanned page.

Databases

Telecommunications provides access to news wire, financial, consumer product, and encyclopedic databases. Instead of calling a stockbroker for a stock quote, investors can get their own current information and can even schedule a stock trade. Users can reach others interested in trading products and services, shop by catalog, get information about topics from aerospace to specific laws, and make hotel and airline reservations.

Bulletin Boards

An electronic **bulletin board** serves the same purpose as any other bulletin board: it is a location for public messages (Figure 9–3). It provides a vehicle for users to share ideas ranging from computer use and software applications to stamp collecting and genealogy.

Subscribers access a bulletin board and scan the database for information. Job applicants, for example, can search for positions according to occupational groups, geographic locations, or salary requirements. For each job vacancy, an electronic mailbox indicates where applicants can send their résumés.

Computer user groups—groups of people who use the same type of computer equipment or software—are frequent users of bulletin boards. These groups use bulletin boards to announce meetings, ask each other questions, and offer solutions to computer problems. Some bulletin boards give users access to public domain software (which can be freely copied and used) and share-

Figure 9-3
Software companies often provide bulletin boards so you can access and download the latest files and software fixes.

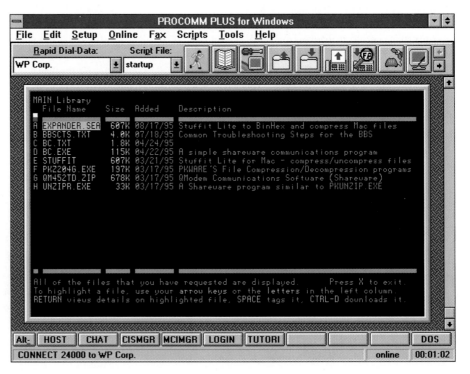

1.
To: All
From: Fritz Erickson, ferickso
Subject: Graphics Help!

I have been trying for two weeks to convert a graphics file from the Microsoft Windows 95 clipboard to an encapsulated postscript format. All the programs I have tried produce the graphics in Microsoft Windows 95 native clipboard (.clp) format or bit mapped (.bmp). Does anyone know of a program that can help?

2.
To: Fritz Erickson, ferickso
From: John Vonk, jvonk
Subject: Graphics Help!

One of the interesting features of Windows 95 is that graphic file formats (as well as any file format) are hidden. If you have a graphic in the clipboard, do not use the clipboard viewer. Instead, use Pbrush, then select the Paste command from the Edit menu. This will allow you to import the file into Pbrush. At that point you can save the file on disk.

Figure 9–4
Bulletin boards and List-servs on Internet can be used to discuss a variety of topics, from current social issues or information on home repairs to questions about Mozart.

3.
To: Fritz Erickson, ferickso
     John Vonk, jvonk
From: Jack LaBonde, jlabon
Subject: Graphics Help!

John got the answer partially correct. However, when you save a graphics file in Pbrush from Windows 95, it automatically saves it as bit-mapped file. The easiest solution is to save the file as a bit-mapped (.bmp) file, then go in and use any of the popular file conversion programs written for Windows 3.1, and import the .bmp file and convert to encapsulated postscript.

4.
To: Jack LaBonde, jlabon
From: John Vonk, jvonk
Subject: Graphics Help!

You are correct, Jack. I forgot about some of the limitations. However, it seems that there should be a way of converting graphics file formats directly in Windows 95. If anyone out there has any ideas, please let me know.

5.
To: Jack LaBonde, jlabon
     John Vonk, jvonk
From: Fritz Erickson, ferickso
Subject: Graphics Help!

I gave the Pbrush solution a try and it seems to work OK. I guess .bmp bit-mapped format will work just fine for my needs. I really like being able to modify the graphics with Pbrush.

Thanks for your help.

ware (these also can be freely copied, but if they are used, compensation for the programmer is requested). Much of this is available at little or no cost.

Unfortunately, bulletin boards are also the primary method of transferring computer viruses. Viruses are computer programs, developed by unethical programmers, that destroy data stored on disk or otherwise interfere with the operation of your computer. They are discussed in the chapter on social issues. An infected bulletin board file copied to your computer can destroy all data on your disk. Before using a bulletin board, be sure to install software that can detect and destroy computer viruses.

CAFE LINK

Not all communities have geographic boundaries; some only have networks. Thanks to electronic mail, there are communities of people around the world bound together only by shared interests and their computers. People discuss Kierkegaard or sell kittens via e-mail. People have even met through e-mail and married.

Cafe-goers in Paris, Budapest, and San Francisco now have their own network, Cafe Link. For $1 users buy 20 minutes of interfacing time. The brainchild of a computer and cafe lover, the network can be accessed from home, as well as from cafes. One of the users who accesses Cafe Link from his home is Don Caca, who is blind. He uses a computer equipped with a voice synthesizer and a Braille keyboard. Not all cafe lovers are enamored with the service. They say cafes are supposed to be havens from modern life. But users of Cafe Link say it's just another sort of haven.

NATIONAL BEDROOM COMMUNITIES

Once upon a time people lived in bedroom communities to escape from their jobs. Once on the 5:23 train home, work was no more. That was the idea anyway. But now, thanks to networked PCs, modems, and faxes, an opposite trend is developing: people who take their work home with them in a new way. At its most extreme are the urban professionals who commute several time zones to work a few days a week, and take care of business the other days by computer, such as Sherri Abend-Fels, a psychologist who lives four days in Los Angeles and three in Santa Fe. Some small towns are designing communities with state-of-the-art fiber-optic networks, regional microwave systems, and satellite links—all built into new homes. Opponents decry this creation of "yuppie ghettos," but supporters argue that such places will attract more tax dollars for the community.

Some bulletin boards, such as the WELL, offer users the opportunity to communicate with each other, either by leaving messages in public forums (generally organized according to topics) or by directly typing messages back and forth (what's called *chat mode* or *CB mode* on some systems). Using these capabilities, users can discuss anything from the news of the day to social issues, intimate affairs, and trivia. Computer bulletin boards have been the medium for social groups, political movements, clubs and organizations, and even dating and marriage. Thus, **virtual** or **on-line communities** develop among people who have never actually met but know each other better than their own neighbors.

On-Line Services

On-line service companies provide access to Internet, electronic mail systems, bulletin boards, and databases. Individuals who subscribe pay a flat fee or use fees. Popular on-line services include the following.

CompuServe. **CompuServe** provides a broad spectrum of business and non-business information, including

- *The Official Airline Guide.* Subscribers can examine airline schedules, request information about specific flights, reserve seats, and even arrange for automatic credit-card billing.
- *Restaurant guides.* Users can select a restaurant according to price, name, type of food, features, and geographic location.
- *Hotel guides.* Users can select a hotel according to price and features; they can make their own reservations.
- *On-line shopping.* Users can access the catalogs of hundreds of merchants selling a broad spectrum of products and can purchase items directly.
- *Financial information.* CompuServe also provides stock quotes and other financial reports.
- *Internet access.*
- *Computer-oriented services.* CompuServe is the leading forum for on-line technical support provided by producers of microcomputer hardware and software. CompuServe also offers large libraries of public domain software and shareware, and many of its on-line shopping vendors are computer suppliers.
- *On-line encyclopedias and databases.* Users can access a tremendous range of information and articles on subjects of general and technical interest.
- *Electronic mail and on-line conversation.*
- *Computer games.*

America OnLine. **America OnLine** (AOL) (Figure 9–6) is an information service that provides access to a wealth of information. Some of the features of AOL include access to local news stations, national sports networks, and financial information. America OnLine also provides free graphical software that makes accessing and using Internet very easy. America OnLine contains many of the features found in other on-line services and is designed for easy use.

Prodigy. **Prodigy** is a telecommunications partnership between IBM and Sears. It is more family oriented than other services; children as young as eight or nine can easily use the service because of its graphical interface. Unlike other services, Prodigy sells on-screen advertising to a variety of companies, many of which are also on-line as Prodigy merchants. Subscribers to Prodigy can

Thanks to computer communications, pregnant women can use their home telephones in new ways to get hospital help when they most need it. Pilot projects at Purdue University in Indiana and at Pennsylvania Hospital in Philadelphia have created a computerized phone system to monitor mothers at risk for early labor while they stay at home. The patients can answer questions by punching the numbers on their phone; the answers get sorted, recorded, and analyzed by a computer, which also alerts a nurse if necessary.

- Book their own seats on airlines, purchase tickets when there are discount opportunities, and make hotel reservations.
- Shop electronically from major stores and catalogs.
- Track stocks.
- Access electronic games.
- Access an encyclopedia, the *Weekly Reader,* and *Consumer Reports* abstracts.
- Access news and weather information.
- Access *USA Today.*
- Participate in home banking services, including paying bills without writing checks, transferring funds, and checking their account balances.

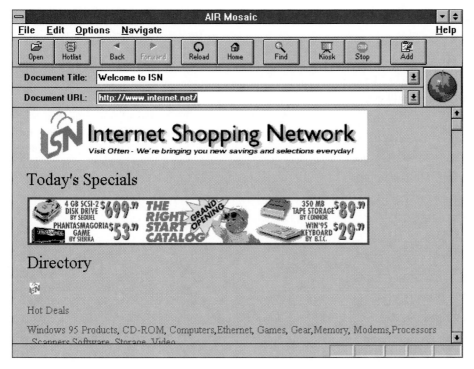

Figure 9-5

Internet can provide you with access to thousands of products.

Figure 9-6
America OnLine's many consumer-oriented features include access to the EAASY SABRE airline booking service.

TELECOMMUNICATIONS HARDWARE AND SOFTWARE

To communicate using telephone equipment, a microcomputer needs both a modem and telecommunications software.

A **modem** is an absolutely essential piece of equipment for telecommunications (Figure 9–7). A modem translates binary (digital) information to audible (analog) tones for transmissions over telephone equipment; it also receives these tones from the telephone and translates them back into binary information the computer can use (Figure 9–8).

Controlling the flow of information to and from the modem requires **telecommunications software.** A variety of telecommunications software packages are available for microcomputers, each with specific capabilities, such as linking to several different types of modems, providing automatic controls for accessing different computers with modems, and a host of technical features. As with all software, the more demanding the requirements, the greater the need for a package with sophisticated capabilities.

Synchronous and Asynchronous Communications

Synchronous communication is a method of transmitting data in serial fashion (one bit at a time) in which the bits are sent in digital form at a constant rate. To make this work, both ends of the transmission, the sender and receiver, must know the data transmission rate and what kind of data to expect (binary numbers, ASCII characters, etc.). Synchronous communication thus can operate at very high speeds

COMPUTER BIDDING

Now companies can advertise their garbage by computer. An Ohio firm, Team-W, provides an on-line service that lists companies' recyclable waste material and lets other companies bid for it. If Acme Yogurt has some leftover corrugated cardboard that Flowers First can use, the florist can use the computer to arrange to pick up the cardboard and give the yogurt company $25. Not only does the service save landfills from unnecessary objects, it's good for business. A similar service allows art lovers to bid on works via computers. Using an ID number to log on, they can browse through available works by title or by artist. Bids are made by punching in the code for the work, and sales are finalized by fax—all without ever leaving home.

(up to several megabits per second); however, it requires special communications lines and equipment, which are generally too expensive for use with microcomputers. Synchronous communication is therefore used mainly for communicating in large computer networks and, within a computer, between its various components.

Asynchronous communication is the most common pattern for telecommunications with microcomputers. In asynchronous communication, the hardware assumes that the data coming over the line has no particular interval. Therefore, as the data come over the line one bit at a time, the modem must have some way to know when a character starts and stops. A **start bit** indicates that the next set of bits forms a single byte, or character, and a **stop bit** indicates the end of a byte. For each byte of data that is sent, asynchronous communication confirms that the byte received was actually the byte sent. This ensures accuracy over telephone lines that have static, called **noise.**

Asynchronous communication can be implemented with inexpensive hardware and software, and in most cases can meet the needs of the individual user. That is why it's so widely used on microcomputers. However, the disadvantage of asynchronous communication is speed. Its maximum transmission speed is slower than can be achieved with synchronous communication over dedicated (used only for this purpose) lines. Recent developments in asynchronous communication include data compression and error-checking standards that allow modems to pack more information into the bits they transfer, allowing for effective transmission speeds in excess of 100,000 bps.

Figure 9-7

An external modem is a self-contained unit and requires connection to the microcomputer through a serial port; the internal modem occupies an expansion slot on the microcomputer's motherboard.

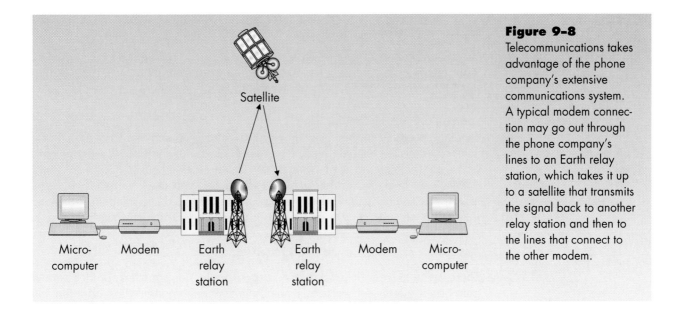

Satellite

Micro-computer   Modem   Earth relay station   Earth relay station   Modem   Micro-computer

Figure 9-8

Telecommunications takes advantage of the phone company's extensive communications system. A typical modem connection may go out through the phone company's lines to an Earth relay station, which takes it up to a satellite that transmits the signal back to another relay station and then to the lines that connect to the other modem.

GETTING OUT OF A JAM

Drivers may soon be able to use a computer in their cars to avoid those seemingly endless traffic jams. Some people already use the Global Positioning System, a computer mounted in cars, boats, and bicycles, to tell them exactly where they are. But a pilot project in Los Angeles, home of the country's first freeway, takes this idea the next logical step. The Department of Transportation has begun testing a program that picks up data from the California Highway Patrol, sensors and television cameras on the road, air surveillance, and information from radio stations. A screen mounted on the dashboard of the car allows the driver to access a map that highlights alternative routes that avoid reported trouble spots. Right now it is only being tested on a 14-mile stretch of road in Los Angeles and in Japan, but it seems like an idea whose time has come.

With asynchronous communications, users of the sending and the receiving computers must agree on three pieces of information:

- **Byte length,** the number of bits that make up a byte. Most modems and telecommunications software support bytes of seven and eight data bits.
- **Parity,** the method used by the computer to check that the byte sent was the byte received. Parity can be set to even, odd, or none.
- The number of stop bits, which indicate a byte has been sent. This can be set to one or two.

The term 8N1, meaning an eight-bit byte, no parity, and one stop bit, is the most common telecommunications software setting for microcomputer users.

Selecting Transmission Speed

Modems can operate at several transmission speeds. The unit of measure for data transmission speed is the **baud** (named after the telegraphy communications pioneer, J. M. E. Baudot), which approximately equals the number of bits that are transmitted each second (bits per second—**bps**). With the 8 bits that form a character byte, plus the bits used to signal the start and stop of each character, it usually takes 10 bits to send a single character. Thus, modems operating at 14,400 bps can send data at 1,440 characters per second (cps). 28,800 bps is about 2,800 characters per second. The actual data transfer rate may be higher depending on data compression techniques.

The data-transmission rates for both the sending and receiving computers must match. If one modem normally operates at a higher rate, the telecommunications software must be adjusted so that it transmits at the slower speed. Most telecommunications software packages can detect the transmission speed of the other modem and adjust the speed to match it.

Setting Duplex and Echo

Microcomputers can use one of two **duplex** settings: full duplex or half duplex. With a half-duplex setting, data are sent in only one direction at a time. With a full-duplex setting, the most common, data can be sent and received at the same time.

Echo settings determine whether or not the characters you type on-line are not only transmitted, but also show up on your own screen. They also determine whether the characters sent by the other end of the transmission link are sent back (echoed) to verify that they've been received.

Problems in these settings are indicated when you can't see what you type or get double characters when you type. If either of these happens, changing the duplex or echo setting on your computer will usually solve the problem.

Setting File Transfer Protocols

There are a variety of procedures, or **protocols,** for transferring files to and from other computers. Protocols specify how one computer will send a file and how the other computer will receive it. Protocols inform the computers on each end of the transmission that they're dealing with a file to be read and stored, for example, rather than simply text to show on the screen. File transfer protocols (ftp) also let each end of the transmission verify that the file received exactly matches the file sent. The protocols organize the bits of the file into groups, called **blocks,** or **packets,** and give each block a key code that allows the receiving computer to check that the block received is what was sent. If the block doesn't check out, the receiving computer requests that it be resent until it is correct; this allows the file to be transmitted without errors.

As with other asynchronous settings, it is important that both the sending and the receiving computers have their telecommunications software set to the same file transfer protocol. Some of the more popular file transfer protocols are **XMODEM, YMODEM,** and **ZMODEM,** each offering advantages and disadvantages. XMODEM, for example, one of the first protocols designed for microcomputers, is reliable but very slow. YMODEM, based on XMODEM, is faster, but less stable and more susceptible to line noise. ZMODEM is designed to make XMODEM more efficient and flexible by using larger data blocks, allowing the sending computer to command the receiving computer; it also allows several files to be sent in one transmission. It sends the file names and sizes to the receiving computer, allowing the receiver to monitor transmission speed and estimate the time remaining for completion; this is very useful for transmitting large files. Another increasingly popular protocol is **Kermit,** which was developed on mainframe computers and is widely used on microcomputers to transfer information to and from mainframe databases. It is also becoming popular for micro-to-micro file transfers. Its sophisticated control language permits a variety of custom file transfer operations to be controlled by the user.

You can also capture incoming data using a **capture buffer,** a special allocation of computer memory controlled by the telecommunications software. Turning on a capture buffer lets the receiving computer store text or data there; this special memory can also be turned off at any point. For example, if you were receiving bibliographic citations from an encyclopedic database, the citations could be stored rather than sent directly to a printer. You could turn the capture buffer on when the desired information was being received and turn it off for information that you didn't want. After completing the telecommunications with the database, you could print the contents of the capture buffer or save it on a disk for future use and reference.

Setting Terminal Emulation

When a microcomputer accesses a large mainframe, it often needs to act like a specific type of terminal directly wired to the computer. Many telecommunication software packages support **terminal emulation** for a variety of different types of terminals. Thus your IBM PC can "think" it is a DEC VT100 or VT102 terminal, a VIDTEX, and ANSI, or another terminal required by the mainframe you are accessing. This lets you run applications on remote mainframes and control the screen, rather than just watching text scroll down the screen in one stream. A plain terminal, with no screen control, is usually called a TTY terminal and is controlled entirely with standard ASCII characters.

Dial Control and Packet-Switching Services

An important consideration when using telecommunications software is the method of calling another computer. For example, some software lets users create automatic dialing and access menus. Users record the phone number and all other appropriate settings for a particular computer. Then, all the user need

#&%)}????

Computer people *do* speak another language—it's called emoticons and it's very serious indeed : −). If you tilt your head to the side and examine that last punctuation sequence, you'll see it resembles the ubiquitous smiley face of the seventies. On an electronic bulletin board it has a more nineties meaning, such as "NOT!" or "just kidding." Also called smileys, emoticons first started showing up ten years ago, but with the popularity of e-mail, the range of emotions conveyed by emoticons has also grown. Writers on the subject say emoticns convey nuances, individuality, or charisma that is otherwise lacking in computer conversation (: # = my lips are sealed). Movie critic Roger Ebert believes that "smileys might be a real help for today's students, raised on MTV and unskilled at spotting irony without a laugh track." (5: −)= I'm Elvis). David Sanderson has been collecting smileys for years and currently has 664 of them from around the world. His favorite? C=>:* *)). Guessed yet? It's "I'm a drunk demonic chef with a cold and a double chin."

do to contact another computer is select the desired item from the menu; the software does the rest.

Using a computer, a modem, and telecommunications software to access other computers has one major drawback: telephone toll charges. To decrease expenses, several communications services provide direct connections to distant computers through local telephone numbers.

One of the most common methods for providing such access is through a **packet-switching service,** which allows several computer users to share the same line. Charges are usually much lower than standard long-distance charges. Two of the most common packet-switching services, **Tymnet** and **Telenet,** charge as little as $2 per hour to access national information services. Standard long-distance toll charges might cost $10 to $15 per hour.

NETWORKING

Instead of telephone company equipment, networks use specially designed cables that physically connect two or more computers. This makes it possible for one computer to house all the application software for all the computers in an office. Each connected, or **networked,** computer can share information from one central computer, access the same printers, and send electronic mail messages from one user to another.

The dedicated cables connecting a network carry information in a digital format, unlike the analog transmission over a telephone. This provides high-speed synchronous transmission of data.

Two types of computers make up the most common type of network, the **client-server network:** a host computer and a workstation (Figure 9–9). The **host** computer, or **file server,** is the central computer with all the network's files and programs. All computers on a network are connected to the host, which is usually the network's most powerful computer, requiring a great deal of disk storage capability. The host computer controls who can have entry to the network, which programs are available for operation, and file sharing. With its large hard disk, it also provides a common data storage space for users. In the past, a mainframe or minicomputer was used as a host computer. Today, high-speed microcomputers with large-capacity disk storage capability can serve as hosts.

Workstations are all the microcomputers that are linked to the host computer. Typically, the host computer requires workstation users to enter an identification code and password for security protection. This is known as logging on to the network. Once a workstation user logs on, the user can access programs and files stored in the host computer.

Because passwords are assigned to users rather than workstations, an authorized user can use any workstation on the network. Users can have differing levels of authorization; for example, some users can access any word processing files and others can access financial records. By limiting who has access to which programs and data, the network provides additional data security.

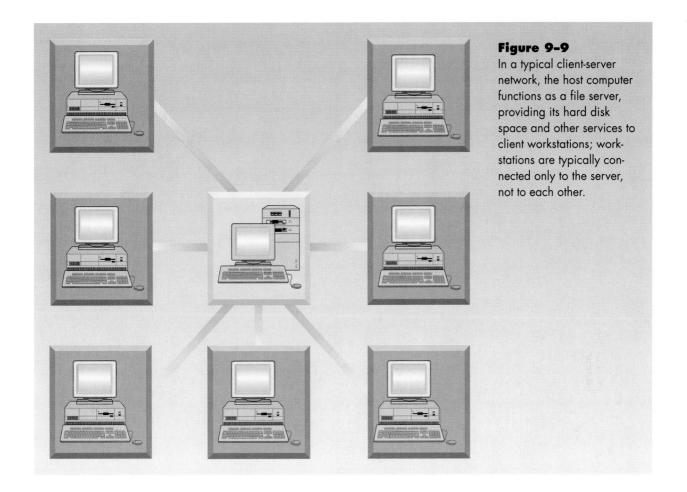

The primary disadvantage of this type of network occurs when the host computer becomes damaged or disabled. All access to information and programs on the network stops when the host stops. Another type of network, often used by businesses and organizations, is the **peer-to-peer network.** Here all stations on the network have equal status, and individual stations can choose whether to make their disk storage available to other users. As no station is host, the network doesn't stop when the host computer is off or damaged. Peer-to-peer networks, however, generally have less sophisticated services for the station. They also provide less security, as files are transmitted directly instead of through a host computer. Anyone whose disk is accessible is thus susceptible to having data lost or damaged.

LANs and WANs

Another way to describe networks is in terms of the area covered. A **local area network (LAN)** connects computers in the same building or within about a one-half-mile radius around the host computer. A **wide area network (WAN)** can serve computers several—or hundreds—of miles apart (Figure 9–10).

Local area networks are more common than wide area networks. Because WANs often connect over long distances via dedicated communications lines and satellites, they tend to be expensive. The LAN is less expensive, but it is an option only when an organization's networking needs can be met by connecting the computers in one location or adjacent locations.

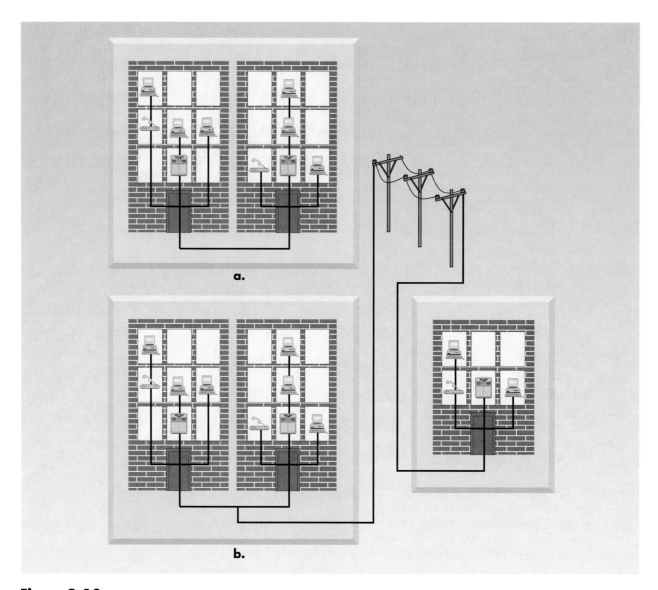

Figure 9-10

LANs and WANs: (a) A LAN connects computers within a building or between buildings near each other. (b) A WAN connects computers (including LANs) across long distances, even thousands of miles.

Network Design

A network's **topology** is the way the various elements of the networks are wired together. The most common network topologies are bus, star, and ring.

Bus Network. In the **bus network**—the simplest network topology available for microcomputers (and common in peer-to-peer networks)—all computers are connected with a single line cable (Figure 9–11). For example, a 50-foot cable might connect a series of five computers, with the first computer at one end of the cable and the fifth computer at the other end. Data on a bus network travels from one computer directly to another.

Star Network. The **star network** is most commonly used to connect a central host computer to workstations in a client-server network. Each workstation

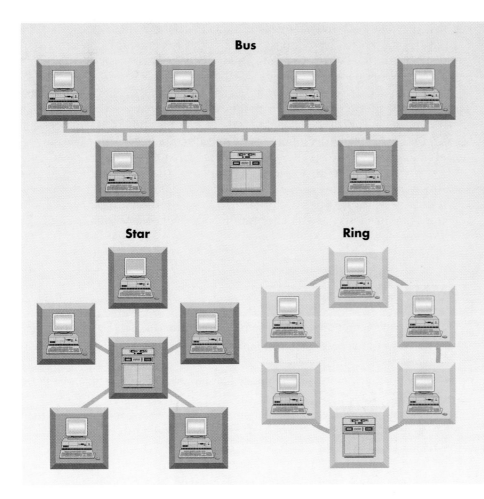

Bus

Star

Ring

Figure 9-11
The three basic network topologies: bus, in which all computers on the network are connected to a single communications cable; star, in which client computers are individually connected to the central file server; and ring, in which the computers pass information around a central ring cable.

is connected to the host computer by a separate table (Figure 9–11). Each workstation communicates directly with the host; workstations cannot communicate directly with each other.

Ring Network. In a **ring network,** all computers are connected on a central cable ring (Figure 9–11). This configuration is similar to the bus network, except there is no beginning point or ending point. The ring configuration is becoming more common for local area networks, because adding computers is a simple process and the ring provides an efficient flow of data. Much as traffic flows on a highway around a major city, data enters the ring cable and travels around until it finds its desired computer, or exit. Both client-server networks and peer-to-peer networks use this topology.

Distributed Processing

In traditional network designs, all common processing is handled by one host or file server. **Distributed processing** is a decentralized approach in which processing requirements are shared among several smaller computer systems. Distributed processing uses more than one host; each computer has a different data processing role. The distributed processing network allows data sharing, but most computer operations remain independent of one another. Thus, while separate computers may perform accounting, research and development, inventory control, and marketing functions, they can still share other activities and resources through networking.

A distributed processing system has several strengths. Failure of one computer does not interfere with the operation of other computers. In addition, each department can work independently without worrying about the processing needs of other groups. This differs from centralized networks in which several departments in a business can compete for processing time on the host computer and activities must be prioritized. Distributed processing also incorporates the strengths of a stand-alone system. Each independent computer in the system can have software specifically tailored to fit its user's exact needs and requirements. Because the computers are independent, there is no need to use standardized software.

SUMMARY

- Connecting computers allows computer communications.
- Two ways to connect microcomputers are through networks and telecommunications.
- Telecommunications uses telephone lines and modems to send and receive data.
- Telecommunications allows people to send and receive electronic mail (e-mail) and facsimiles (faxes), participate in bulletin boards, and access databases.
- On-line services provide one or more of these services to their subscribers and also include access to stock and bond data, encyclopedia information, news, sports, and airline schedules.
- Data communications is either synchronous or asynchronous.
- Synchronous communications is faster, but it requires more expensive and specialized equipment and, therefore, is most commonly used in mainframe communications and networks.
- Asynchronous communications is slower but less expensive and easier to implement; it is the most common choice for microcomputer telecommunications.
- Telecommunications software controls the speed at which data are transferred.
- Software controls whether the data flow in one direction (half duplex) or both (full duplex).
- Software controls whether you see what you type or only what the other computer sends you (echo).
- Software controls the file transfer protocols (XMODEM, YMODEM, etc.) that help ensure error-free transmissions.
- Software controls emulation choices that make your computer act like a specific terminal attached to a mainframe computer.
- Networking involves physically connecting two or more computers with special cables.
- Networking makes it possible for one computer to house all the application software for all computers in an office.

- A client-server network includes the host, or file server, and the workstation.
- The host computer is the central computer that maintains and controls access to the files and programs used by all other computers—the workstations—on the network.
- Two types of networks are commonly used with microcomputers: a local area network within a limited physical space and a wide area network in which the components may be hundreds of miles apart.
- Local area networks commonly use three types of topology: bus, star, and ring.
- Distributed processing is a decentralized approach to networking in which processing requirements are shared among several smaller computer systems, each with a different processing role.

KEY TERMS

America OnLine	packet-switching service
asynchronous	parity
baud	peer-to-peer network
blocks	Prodigy
bps	protocols
bulletin board	ring network
bus network	star network
byte length	start bit
capture buffer	stop bit
client-server network	synchronous
CompuServe	Transmission Control Protocol/Internet
distributed processing	Protocol (TCP/IP)
domain name system (DNS)	telecommunications
duplex	telecommunications software
echo	Telenet
facsimile	telnet
file server	terminal emulation
File Transfer Protocol (ftp)	topology
gopher	Tymnet
host	veronica
Internet	virtual (on-line) communities
Kermit	wide area network (WAN)
local area network (LAN)	workstations
modem	World Wide Web
network	XMODEM
networked	YMODEM
noise	ZMODEM
packets	

REVIEW QUESTIONS

1. What is the difference between half duplex and full duplex?
2. What is the difference between asynchronous and synchronous communications?
3. What is the purpose of a local area network?

4. What is the difference in characters-per-second (cps) speed between a 2,400 baud modem and a 9,600 baud modem?
5. Name the three common network configurations.
6. What is electronic mail and what are the advantages of using it?
7. To use telecommunications, a computer must have two important elements. What are these elements and how do they work?
8. What is the advantage of using a packet-switching service such as Tymnet or Telenet?
9. Name three popular information services.
10. List five activities common to information services.
11. What are the differences between client-server and peer-to-peer networks? What advantages do client-server networks have over peer-to-peer networks?
12. What is distributed processing?
13. What does baud mean?

SELF-QUIZ

1. Transmitting data in serial fashion, one bit at a time, at a constant rate is called
   a. synchronous communication.   c. full duplex communication.
   b. asynchronous communication.   d. half duplex communication.
2. The most common pattern for telecommunications with microcomputers is
   a. synchronous communication.   c. full duplex communication.
   b. asynchronous communication.   d. half duplex communication.
3. With asynchronous communications, users of the sending and receiving computers must agree on which of the following pieces of information?
   a. byte length, parity, and stop bits
   b. byte length, parity, and noise
   c. parity, stop bits, and switching service
   d. byte length, parity, and switching service
4. The static that occurs on telephone communications is called
   a. asynchrony.   c. noise.
   b. synchrony.   d. parity.
5. Which of the following forms of telecommunications is faster?
   a. synchronous communication
   b. asynchronous communication
   c. multisynchronous communications
   d. monosynchronous communications
6. The method used by the computer to check that the byte sent was the byte received is called
   a. asynchrony.   c. parity.
   b. synchrony.   d. sender-receiver agreement.
7. Stop bits are usually set to
   a. odd.   c. none.
   b. even.   d. any of the above.
8. What type of procedures organize the bits of the file into groups called blocks or packets?
   a. duplex settings   c. emulations
   b. bauds   d. protocols
9. In a client-server network, a host computer is also known as a
   a. file server.   c. LAN.
   b. workstation.   d. distributor.

10. Which of the following file transfer protocols (ftp) was developed on mainframe computers and is widely used to transfer information to and from mainframe databases?
    a. XMODEM   *c.* ZMODEM
    b. YMODEM   *d.* Kermit
11. A(n) _____ translates binary data to analog data for transmission over telephone equipment.
12. Controlling the flow of information to and from the modem requires _____.
13. A(n) _____ indicates that the next set of bits forms a single byte, or character.
14. A(n) _____ indicates the end of a byte.
15. If you cannot see what you type or get double characters when you type, you probably have to change the _____ setting on your computer.
16. _____ specify how one computer will send a file and how the other computer will receive it.
17. A(n) _____ is a special allocation of computer memory controlled by the telecommunications software.
18. The way the various elements of the networks are wired together is referred to as a network's _____.
19. A(n) _____ network occurs when all stations on the network have equal status and individual stations can choose whether to make their disk storage available to other users.
20. In _____, the network has more than one host; each computer has a different data processing role.

SIMULATIONS

Scenario 1: The World of Internet

There is no doubt that you are the company computer genius. After all, you can surf the net and locate vital business information and loads of recreational data. You know how to explore the world using the World Wide Web. You can use gophers to find specific resources. With all of this knowledge, you have an obligation to help others use Internet as a valuable information resource. Bringing the world into your office is now easier than ever before. With Internet and other on-line tools, you can provide your colleagues with the opportunity to explore the world.

Your assignment is to identify, using the appropriate address (e.g., http:), seven resources for a specific topic. For example, if you want to research horses, identify seven locations for information on horses on Internet. Pick any topic you like but make sure you use some of the navigational tools to help you locate information. In the space provided below list the topic and each of the addresses.

Topic _____

Address 1 _____

Address 2 _____

Address 3 _____

Address 4 _____

Address 5 _____

Address 6 _____

Address 7 _____

Scenario 2: Accessing Extremists

Being an extremist is becoming easier every day. In the old days extremists had a difficult time communicating. They had a hard time figuring out who else was an extremist, identifying other extremists with similar views, finding extremists with opposite views, or engaging in general communication with anyone. The postal system was expensive and not very conducive to contacting others with similar interests. Today, extremists have a very easy time locating and communicating with other extremists. All that is needed is access to Internet.

Even if you are not an extremist, it is always interesting to find out what information others are disseminating. Surf Internet to determine what type of extremist information is being posted and is readily available to anyone with Internet access. Be prepared to report on your findings.

HANDS-ON COMPUTING

1. Locating information on Internet is fast becoming a standard practice in business, in school, and in everyday life. The best way to learn about Internet is to simply explore. It is a good idea to note the addresses of interesting topics in case you ever want to return to that site.

2. There is a lot of information out there on the information superhighway. However, not all of that information is appropriate. There has been much in the popular press about the sexually explicit graphics, bomb-making recipes, and hate-group activities flourishing on line. As you surf Internet, take note of the information you can obtain. Is it appropriate for children to have free access to this information? Is the information physically dangerous? Can people claim that there is a danger when perhaps there is no evidence of a danger? Be prepared to share your findings and ideas with the rest of the class.

3. One of the great advantages of surfing Internet is learning what you do not know. List five interesting pieces of information that you found while surfing that you did not previously know.

4. Internet, while very popular, is not the only source of valuable on-line information. There are a variety of information services, such as Prodigy and CompuServe, that offer either free or inexpensive ways to explore their services. It is worth the effort to explore some of these services.

5. Networking is a very popular method of communicating within an office or company environment. Besides the advantage of shared resources (printers and hard drives), networking offers users the opportunity to quickly and efficiently perform daily communications. Some suggest that handwritten office memos will become a relic of the past. Take some time to explore a networked environment. At many school computer labs, computers are networked for efficiency and cost effectiveness. What are the capabilities for internetwork communications?

6. Electronic mail (e-mail) is fast becoming a standard communication device. In fact, many view electronic mail as important as a telephone. Because

you can send mail almost instantly to anyone or any group of people who have e-mail accounts, it is often easier to use than the telephone (no more telephone tag). If you have access to an e-mail account, send some mail. If you don't know anyone with an e-mail account, use Internet to locate the address of your congressional representatives. They would like to hear from you.

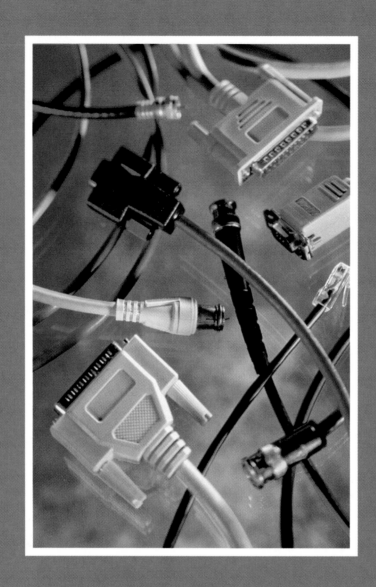

CHAPTER 10
Programming

FOCUS

The most effective use of many popular software applications requires some knowledge of programming. In particular, spreadsheet, database, telecommunications, and some word processing programs encourage you to apply programming procedures when using them. Spreadsheet and word processing "power users" in business, finance, and scientific industries pride themselves on their extensive macro creations. Accountants and librarians create unique and customer-specific data input forms with elaborate report-generating capabilities from their database applications. And some telecommunications enthusiasts have set up extensive electronic bulletin boards.

This chapter provides an overview of the program development process. It focuses on the definition of a program and programming, describing the programming process and the different types of programming languages. It is not meant to teach programming, but to provide an understanding of programming concepts that can be applied in many areas of microcomputer use.

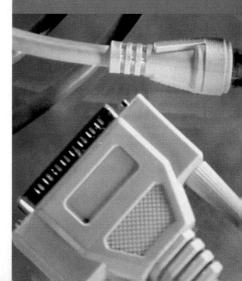

PROGRAMS AND PROGRAMMING

A **program** is a set of instructions written in a language designed to make a microcomputer perform a series of specified tasks. These instructions tell computers exactly what to do and exactly when to do it. A **programming language** is a set of grammar rules, characters, symbols, and words—the vocabulary—in which those instructions are written.

Programming is the designing and writing of programs. It is a process that involves much more than writing down instructions in a given language. The process begins with identifying *how* a program can solve a particular problem. It ends when the written documentation has been completed.

THE PROGRAMMING PROCESS

The program development cycle involves five processes: problem definition, algorithm development, coding, program testing and debugging, and documentation (Figure 10–1).

LIVING COMPUTER PROGRAMS?

Tomorrow's state-of-the-art computer software won't be written; it will be grown. At least that's the current thinking of a number of computer scientists who are involved with open-ended programming. First developed to model weather patterns and global economics, open-ended programming was next turned toward the field of artificial life. Scientists treat the computer as an environment and the programs as organisms that must evolve over time or die. Programmers give the software certain traits and then design constraints within which the software will evolve. "All we do is define the puzzle," says one programmer. "We don't have to be smart enough to figure out the way the program solves the puzzle." At UCLA Rob Collins and David Jefferson used artificial life programming to build a computerized colony of ants who must go out, find food, and bring it back. Some ants never left the nest; others found food but did not bring it back. Only those colonies whose ants found food and brought it back thrived. Artificial life is not only changing computer programs, it is changing computer programmers. As one observer put it, "Programmers will be more like gardeners than engineers."

Defining the Problem

The first step in developing a computer program is determining exactly what it is that you want the computer program to do. What tasks will it perform? What kind of data will it use, and where will it get its data from? What will be the output of the program? How will the program interact with the computer user? Answering these questions, and thereby defining exactly what you want the computer to do, is what we call *defining the problem.*

To define the problem, programmers meet with the intended users to develop the program's objectives. The resulting outline includes information about what the output should look like, what kind of data the program will use as input, and the processing requirements (how the data will be manipulated and what kind of hardware will be used to run the application). The more information programmers can learn at the beginning of the programming process, and the more specific that information is, the more likely the resulting application will meet users' needs.

To help in defining the problem, users are also asked to draw a picture of how they wish the final output to appear. The programmer can then begin to plan what input, data, and processing are necessary to get the desired results from the application.

Constructing the Algorithm

An **algorithm** is a prescribed set of well-defined instructions for solving a problem in a finite number of steps. The programmer, knowing how a microcomputer works, decides how data must be entered, how

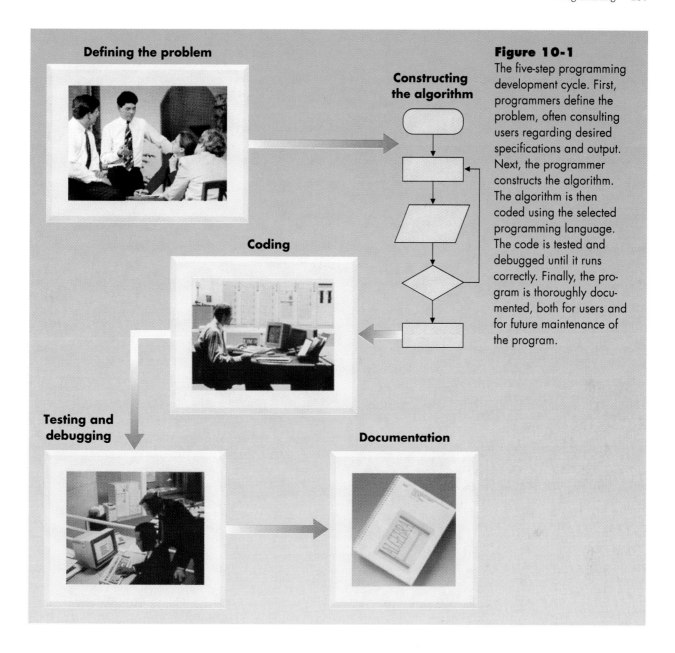

Defining the problem

Constructing the algorithm

Coding

Testing and debugging

Documentation

Figure 10-1
The five-step programming development cycle. First, programmers define the problem, often consulting users regarding desired specifications and output. Next, the programmer constructs the algorithm. The algorithm is then coded using the selected programming language. The code is tested and debugged until it runs correctly. Finally, the program is thoroughly documented, both for users and for future maintenance of the program.

they must be processed, and how the data must be presented to produce the required output. The algorithm spells out when the computer is to start and stop the program, where input is needed, where output is needed, when to perform arithmetic operations, and when to perform comparison operations. It also indicates what the microcomputer is to do if certain answers are derived from these operations.

To control the sequence of steps the algorithm performs, the programmer uses **logic structures,** the rational constructs that control the steps from beginning to end (Figure 10–2). Logic structures control the sequence of events, when a decision must be made, and what to do after the decision is made. The **sequence** structure is the simplest logic structure: One program statement follows another, instructing the microcomputer to perform tasks in a linear (sequential) manner. When a choice of actions is possible, a selection structure is written into the algorithm; this calls for the computer to make a

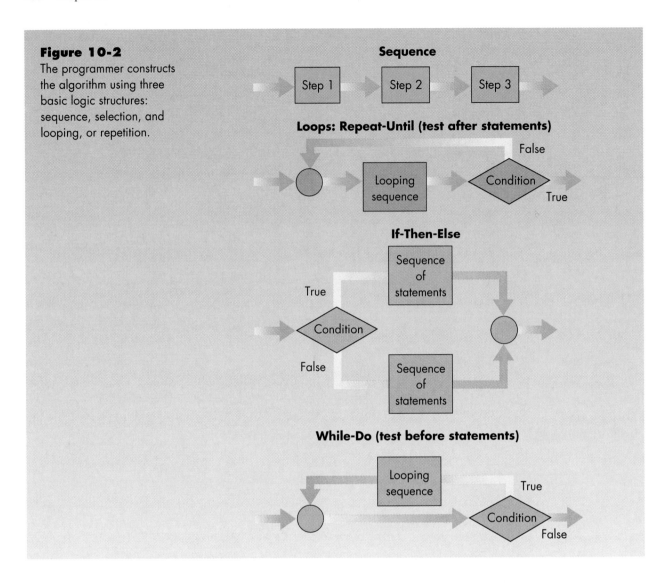

Figure 10-2
The programmer constructs the algorithm using three basic logic structures: sequence, selection, and looping, or repetition.

decision and act accordingly. For instance, IF the data is within a given range of values, THEN use the data, ELSE (otherwise) do not use it. The algorithm may also require that a particular sequence of steps be repeated, either for a given number of repetitions or until a particular condition is met. This repetition requires a **looping** structure.

When working out the precise description of the algorithm, the programmer can write it in pseudocode and/or draw it in a flowchart. **Pseudocode** is a narrative description of the flow and logic of the intended program, written in plain language that expresses each step of the algorithm (Figure 10–3). A flowchart is a diagram, using symbols, lines, and arrows to show the movement of logic through the algorithm (Figure 10–4). Both methods of working out program logic are useful; which one is used is generally the programmer's choice. In a commercial programming environment the choice is often a matter of policy.

In constructing the algorithm, programmers use the techniques of top-down design and structured programming. **Top-down design** is the process of starting with the most general outline of how the algorithm will work, refining it by sketching in the details on smaller and smaller scales. Once a general outline is constructed, the programmer treats each of the steps as another algorithm to be developed and thus creates an algorithm for executing all the steps in the

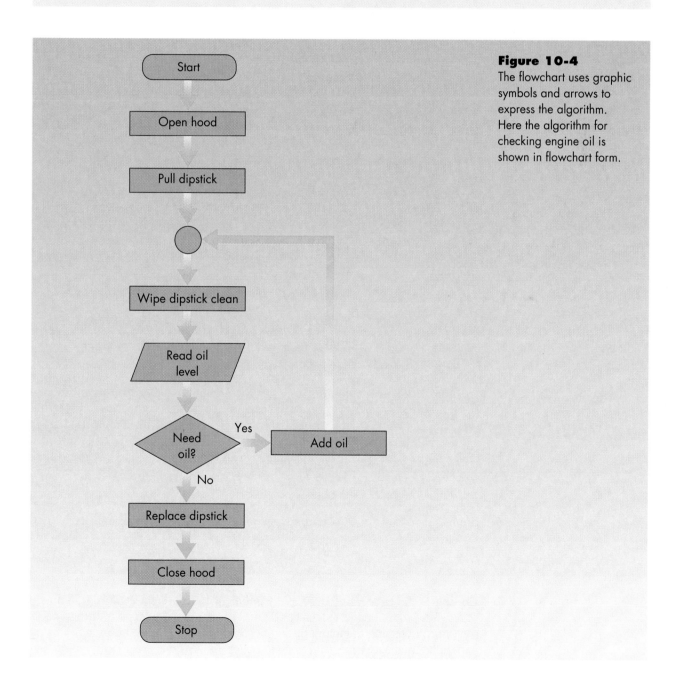

Checking Engine Oil

Open hood.
Pull dipstick.
Repeat:
    Wipe dipstick clear;
    Dip dipstick;
    Read oil level;
    If oil level is low, add
    appropriate amount;
Until oil level is correct.
Replace dipstick.
Close hood.

Figure 10-3
An algorithm can be developed for performing any task. Here is a simple algorithm for checking engine oil and adding oil if needed.

Figure 10-4
The flowchart uses graphic symbols and arrows to express the algorithm. Here the algorithm for checking engine oil is shown in flowchart form.

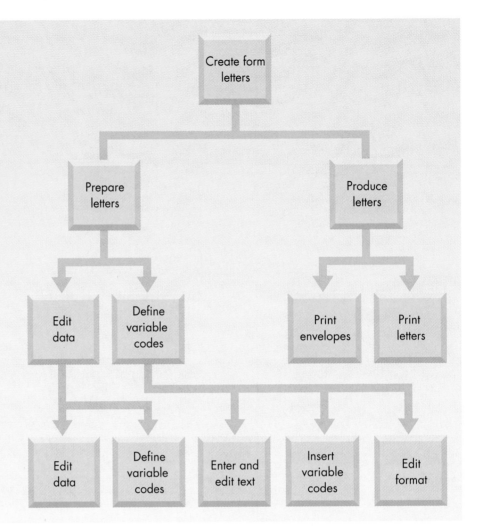

Figure 10-5
Structure charts are a different way of looking at the algorithm, showing not the sequence of steps to be performed but the way the steps are organized. Each successive level of the structure chart shows a greater level of detail in the algorithm, and the program is structured according to the form of the chart.

general outline. By continuing to refine each step at lower and lower levels of the program, the programmer creates a plan for how the program should be organized. This is often drawn up on a **structure chart** (Figure 10–5).

Structured programming uses a programming language to organize code according to the top-down design. Most programming languages today let the programmer define each part of the program as a separate, self-contained block of code called a **procedure.** Procedures are written for each task the program must execute. These small procedures are grouped under larger procedures, and all the procedures are called in sequence by the main body of the program, which is written to implement the top level of the program design. By providing a means of organizing code according to the logic and structure of the algorithm, structured programming makes programs easier to develop, debug, and document.

Coding

Coding is the process of translating the algorithm into the syntax (grammar) of a given programming language (Figure 10–6). In developing its programs, a software publishing company often specifies that its programmers must use a particular language, especially as most major applications are a group effort that involves many programmers. Independent software developers often choose a

```
Program in Pascal:                              begin (Power)
                                                    if base = 0.0 then
Program Exponential (input, output);                    Power: = 0.0
                                                        else if base > 0.0 then
var     number, exponent: real;                             Power: = Exp(pow *Ln(base))
                                                            else Power: = 1.0/Exp(pow *Ln(base))
function Power (var base, pow: real): real:     end; (Power)


                                                begin (main)
                                                    writein ("This program computes the result of raising a");
                                                    writein ("number to a power. Please enter two numbers");
                                                    writein ("separated by a space, e.g. 3 6");
                                                    readin (number, exponent);
                                                    writein ("The result is", Power(number, exponent))

                                                end.
```

Figure 10-6

Once the algorithm is constructed, it must be translated into a programming language: this is called coding. This algorithm performs the mathematical function of raising a number to a power; e.g., $2^2 = 4$.

favorite language to work with for most of their projects. In some cases (such as a program developed for a specific client), which programming language to use is decided according to the needs of the user, who may refine or modify the program later. When possible, the decision should be made objectively; different programming languages have their strong and weak points that make them better for some programming tasks, worse for others. In any case, selecting a programming language is a crucial decision in the program development cycle. Programming languages are discussed later in this chapter.

Testing and Debugging

Program **testing** means running the program, executing all its functions, and testing its logic by entering sample data to check the output. **Debugging** is the process of finding and correcting program code mistakes. The term comes from an episode in the early days of modern computing when programmers for the Mark I computer in 1945 were trying to discover why their program didn't work. Examining the computer, they found a moth stuck between the contacts of an electrical relay. Nowadays any error in code is called a *bug*. Two general types of errors are syntax errors and logic errors.

A **syntax error** is a transgression (breaking) of the grammar rules of the programming language. As with all languages, programming languages have rules of grammar. A programming language's grammar is stricter than most languages, however, and any deviation from the rules causes a program to not work.

A **logic error** is a transgression of the basic logic structure. It can involve missing a step in the algorithm, having an error in the algorithm's logic structure, using an erroneous formula, or any number of other subtle problems with the design or execution or the program steps. If the microcomputer cannot follow the logic, at some point the program will not operate properly. Logic errors can be so serious that entire programs must be redone.

The testing and debugging process follows a least-risk procedure (Figure 10–7). First the programmer reads the code in an attempt to edit (correct) any errors. Next the programmer tries to follow the program's procedures by hand, possibly using a calculator and sample data, to see whether the algorithm produces the outcome desired *without* the microcomputer. Next, because the program must be translated into machine code in order to use it, the programmer tries to have the code translated by the translating program. If it cannot be translated, it has syntax errors; even if it is translated, however, it doesn't mean the code is free of logic errors. Finally, the program is tested by running the program using sample data. If the program operates correctly and produces the desired output, logic errors are ruled out. If there are logic errors, here is where structured programming gives the programmer an advantage: Because the program is organized into short modules, it's easy to trace problems in logic to the specific procedure involved, rather than having to search the whole program for a single erroneous statement.

Another round of testing involves actual software users. **Field testing** involves letting users operate the software with the purpose of locating problems, which can range from minor details to the broad approach of the software. Logic errors show up better under actual real-life use of the program— and the testers may find the program too difficult for its intended users to use.

Documenting the Program

Program documentation is a written record of the program's development; it is also a set of directions for using the program.

Internal documentation consists of instructions and comments within the program itself, for use by the programmer and other programmers when they are looking at the program code (Figure 10–8). It includes comments that explain the program's logic, identify the significance of variable names, and highlight specific codes responsible for key features. If other programmers wish to make changes in the program, they need to know the meaning of acronyms and other abbreviations used by the original programmer. When testing the code or modifying it later, the original programmer may also need reminders of what various things mean and how the program works.

External documentation is the printed set of instructions (the manual) describing how to operate the program. Early drafts of external documentation may occasionally be written while the program is being developed. Many programmers, however, wait to write precise instructions until after debugging the program with test data. Many good programs fail, not because of poor design or coding, but because the documentation is inadequate. Documentation explaining how to use the program is as important for most users as the program itself.

Many sophisticated applications add a third type of documentation that is directly accessible to users while operating the program. **On-line documentation** often provides—or amplifies—much of the information found with external documentation, in the form of help keys, topic indexes, and other features to guide users to successful operation of the software.

TYPES OF PROGRAMMING LANGUAGES

Programming languages are classified as first-, second-, third-, fourth-, or fifth-generation languages, according to when they were developed and how sophisticated they are. The first- and second-generation languages are very difficult

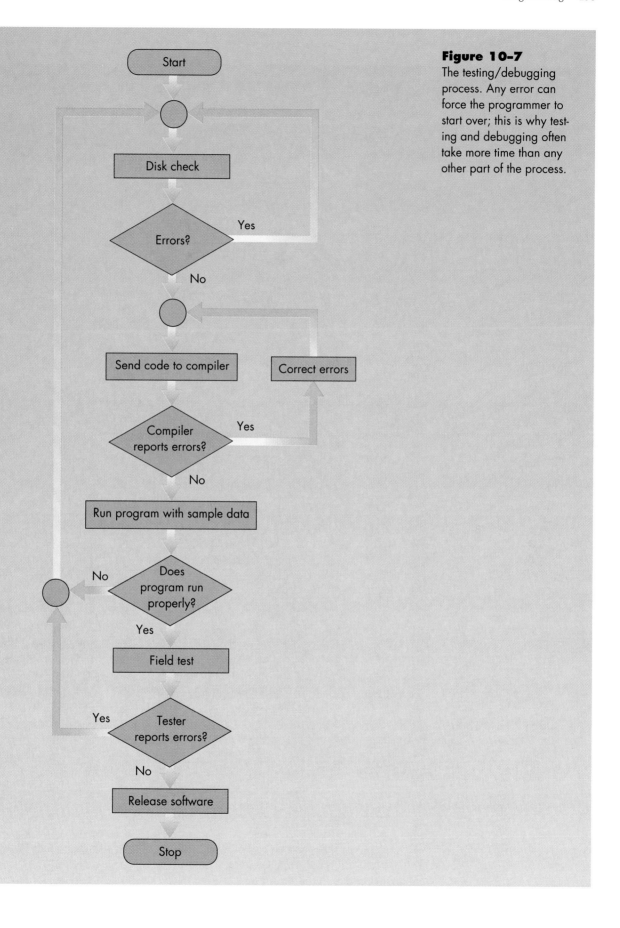

Figure 10-7
The testing/debugging process. Any error can force the programmer to start over; this is why testing and debugging often take more time than any other part of the process.

Figure 10-8
This Pascal program shows use of internal documentation. All text enclosed in braces is commentary, explaining what the program is for and what various parts of the program do.

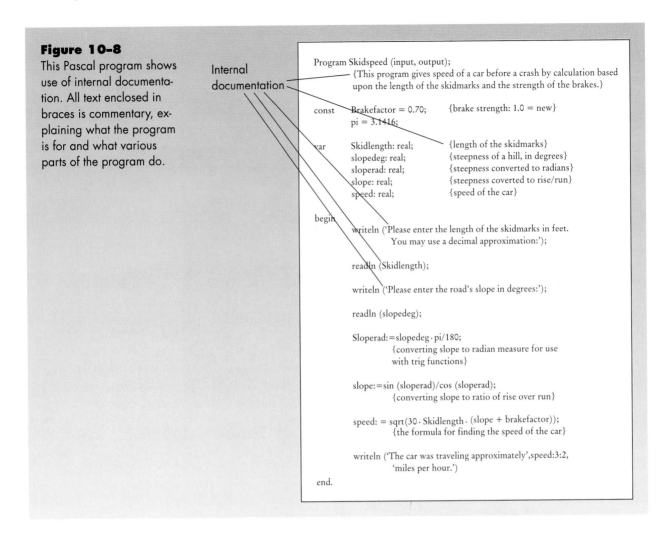

to use and are considered low-level languages. The others are sometimes called high-level languages.

Machine Languages

Machine languages are the first generation of programming languages; these languages consist of instructions the computer is actually built to execute. At the hardware level, computers understand only binary notation (1s and 0s), so programming with a machine language requires writing out the binary values of the program instructions. A simple machine-language command might be "10101001 10101010 1011101011010100." Machine languages vary from one model of computer to another, as each model of processor is built differently. Machine languages are difficult to understand and use, so they are rarely used directly by programmers today. Since the computer understands only machine language, however, any program written in any other language must be translated into machine language in order to run.

Assembly Languages

Assembly languages are second-generation programming languages and are the first to use alphanumeric symbols to write code. The creation of assembly languages depended on the development of an assembler. An assembler is a program that translates the assembly code into machine language. It is necessary to have one assembler for each kind of assembly language and for each kind of computer used.

Assembly languages are the simplest improvement over machine language; their commands are simple mnemonic codes that stand for the binary instructions of machine code. When programmers need to deal with the computer directly, they use assembly language; because it is so close to the hardware level, it is possible to write very efficient programs in assembly language. That same closeness to the hardware level, however, is what makes assembly language difficult to use for large programming projects. Therefore, most assembly programming today is used for writing small modules that can be included in larger programs written in more convenient languages.

Procedural Languages

Procedural languages are third-generation languages. They are also called **high-level languages** because they represent a higher level of abstraction from machine code than assembly languages. Procedural languages employ more humanlike words, and each has its own set of syntax rules. They are also more efficient, allowing the programmer to express with one statement what would take several commands in machine language. They are called *procedural languages* because they allow the programmer to create procedures that implement structured programming. Procedural languages are, by far, the most widely used programming languages.

The development of procedural languages was started by the invention of translation programs that could convert the syntax of the high-level language to machine code that the computer could execute. These translators are compilers and interpreters. A **compiler** converts an entire program written in a high-level language to machine language, storing it in what is called an *executable file,* to be run later at the user's discretion. The original code is then called the *source code,* and the machine-language code is called the *object code.*

An **interpreter** reads each high-level program statement, then translates it to machine language and instructs the computer to execute the statement immediately. It creates no object code and no executable file. From the programmer's or user's standpoint, the computer executes the original code. This method of execution gives the programmer more immediate control of the machine and lends itself to an interactive method of programming and refining code and testing it immediately. The interpreter program does not permanently change the code, allowing users or programmers to make additions and other modifications to the program more easily. However, interpreting the code takes more processing than running a compiled program, so interpreted programs generally run slower than compiled programs.

Some of the most frequently used procedural languages include the following:

BASIC. The Beginner's All-purpose Symbolic Instructional Code (**BASIC**) is a high-level programming language developed in 1964 at Dartmouth College. An interpreted (rather than compiled) language, it is the first language designed to

TOOLS FOR PROGRAMMERS

The cost of developing an information system for a large company is staggering, but the cost of doing a bad job is even worse. Computer-assisted software engineering (CASE) tools have been touted as the savior of corporate programmers since they incorporate all kinds of software tools into a single package. But there are still problems. For example, CASE tools are designed to foster structured programming, but in doing so they can force programmers into predefined structures that do not necessarily suit the needs of the system being developed. Another problem with CASE tools is that they are notoriously difficult to learn. Finally, programmers are generally used to working alone, and CASE tools encourage team effort, forcing users to change their style. But CASE tools are still in their infancy, which gives programmers hope that more sophisticated CASE tools will be even more useful.

A FLOWERING COMPUTER

Computers are aiding a new branch of mathematics, biomathematics, which seeks to use numbers to describe nothing less than the growth of plant life itself. Sets of mathematical formulas describe not only the plant's outer shape, but also duplicate the way the plant grows. The result is a series of biologically correct computer pictures that trace the life of the plant from a tiny seed to maturity. One advantage of these computer programs is that processes that cannot be observed in nature can be visualized through computer modeling. Another advantage is that as the programs become more sophisticated, scientists can watch a 500-year growth cycle within a few minutes on a computer screen.

make programming easy for the novice programmer. It is a general-purpose language used for microcomputer programming and developing business data processing and education applications. BASIC's simple syntax is easy to learn, but its lack of sophisticated structural features makes it less useful for commercial programming applications. In the microcomputer era, BASIC has been popularized as the programming language packaged with the computer, but it has also suffered from the fact that many different versions of it exist, making it difficult for programs to be used on different computers. New versions of BASIC, such as VisualBASIC for Windows, promise a new generation of novice programmers an easy tool for developing applications.

Pascal. **Pascal** (named after the French mathematician Blaise Pascal) is a programming language developed in the late 1960s specifically as a teaching tool. It has subsequently developed into a very popular language for use with a variety of programming applications, because of the clarity of its syntax and its strong features for structured programming development. Standard Pascal is used on mainframes and minicomputers; the microcomputer programming field is dominated by Turbo Pascal for both DOS and Windows and ThinkPascal for the Macintosh. The latest versions of these Pascal packages include object-oriented programming features (see discussion later).

C. One of the fastest-growing high-level programming languages is **C,** developed in the early 1970s. Its developers were especially conscious of the flow of data to and from storage devices. Because C can control this flow especially well, it is a popular language for developing database software, operating systems, and general applications, providing both strong structured programming features and tools for close control of the hardware. C has spawned new versions, C+ and C++, for use in object-oriented programming, and it has become the most popular language for developing Windows and Macintosh software.

COBOL. The COmmon Business-Oriented Language (**COBOL**) is a language used for business applications such as accounting, inventory control, payroll, and banking systems. Initially developed in 1959 by a panel of government and business experts, COBOL was designed around the needs of common business reporting. Programs are based on four major divisions: identification, environment, data, and procedure. The identification division states the name of the program, who wrote it, and other distinguishing data. The environment division states the computer or computers to be used. The data division lists the data used in the program. The procedure division is the actual algorithm. While COBOL has never achieved great popularity in microcomputer use, it is still one of the most important programming languages for mainframe computers in business.

FORTRAN. The FORmula TRANslator (**FORTRAN**) language was the first high-level programming language, developed in 1954 for applications in mathematics, engineering, and science. As its name implies, FORTRAN works very well with sophisticated mathematical formulas. FORTRAN has gone through several revisions, keeping it up-to-date with advances in programming techniques and hardware development. FORTRAN is still the most popular language for scientific and engineering applications in business, institutional, and government settings and is used frequently by microcomputer programmers in these fields.

Ada. **Ada** (named after Ada Lovelace, the first programmer) was developed from the foundation of Pascal, and is primarily used in the defense industry for developing weapons systems and in industrial environments for controlling real-time systems and automation. Ada is very highly structured, which forces programmers to use a standard procedural approach for program design. This programming language is still primarily used in the defense industry, with its larger computer systems. Because of its highly structured approach, however, it is gaining popularity in other areas.

RPG. The Report Program Generator (**RPG**) is a business-oriented programming language designed to automate many input and output features. Users are encouraged to use it to retrieve data and generate reports. Many of the processes used to input and output data are integrated into small sets of commands. Using these small sets of commands allows programmers to avoid writing protracted instructions for each programming task. RPG is popular among programmers who need to design sophisticated reports from well-defined input. RPG's automation of input and output functions and use of standardized procedures served as a precursor to later techniques of object-oriented programming and authoring systems.

*H*ARD TIMES FOR
RUSSIAN PROGRAMMERS

Since the collapse of the Soviet Union, the plight of the Russian computer user has been unpleasant at best. Personal computers are far from a household item, and the falling ruble has made it almost impossible to buy foreign-made hardware. The big-name software titles are especially tough to find because companies selling them are wary of the widespread software piracy in the commonwealth of independent states. The country did not pass its first law protecting software copyrights until June 1992. Under communism, the best programming jobs were with the government or the universities (which were, of course, controlled by the government). Now that public money is drying up, those jobs are suffering. Nonetheless, talent seems to abound among Russian programmers, who are, of necessity, quickly learning the Western skill of marketing their talents.

LISP. The list processing (**LISP**) language was the first interpreted language. Although a structured language, LISP is nonprocedural in the sense that the programmer doesn't implement a sequence of algorithmic steps, but instead develops a group of functions that work together to solve the programming problem. LISP syntax consists primarily of lists, where the first item in the list is the name of a function, and the other items in the list are data items on which the function operates. LISP is also unique in that the programmer can not only define new functions, but also rewrite the language's built-in functions. Together with the fact that the program is interpreted, this allows programs to modify both themselves and the language—a crucial component of intelligence. Since its inception, LISP has been used primarily for artificial intelligence research and the development of expert systems (where a computer is programmed to function as an expert resource in a given subject area or occupation). It has also been used for some commercial applications, such as databases. LISP has not become very popular on microcomputers yet, but that may change as hardware becomes increasingly sophisticated and thus better able to handle the processing demands of the language.

Problem-Oriented Languages

Fourth-generation languages, the **problem-oriented languages,** are a mixed bag of strategies to make programming easier and place them within the grasp of nonprogrammers. They were created to solve specific user and programming

A BRAINLESS ROBOT

For years scientists have used computers to try to create artificial intelligence by mimicking the human brain electronically. But at MIT researchers are trying a vastly different approach, called "bottom-up" AI, and the result is Genghis, a six-legged, foot-long robot without a brain. What Genghis does have is a network of small, simple control programs, each dedicated to a single function: say, lifting one limb. Though the programs operate independently, they communicate with each other rather like bees in a hive. Genghis is programmed to learn through avoiding negative feedback, a vastly simplified version of an infant learning to walk by not falling down. Information is provided by sensors in the robot's belly that provide feedback to the small programs that lift and lower its legs and change its direction. Scientists hope that someday collections of such robots could be used to do such things as clean up oil spills or explore other planets.

problems rather than to achieve the broad general usability of procedural languages. This group of languages includes object-oriented languages, application generators, authoring systems, HyperTalk, and query languages.

Object-Oriented Programming. **Object-oriented programming** (**OOP**) takes a different approach to creating applications. Traditional programming treats data and instructions as separate items with the instructions controlling the data. The instructions are active controls on passive data. In object-oriented programming, an object is created by joining data and instructions in a process known as *encapsulation.* Once an object is made and debugged, it will work. Objects can then be linked together with messages (*calls* to the object to implement its instructions on its data) to form full-fledged applications.

Common OOP languages include C++, SmallTalk, Loops, and Objective-C. OOP is contributing greatly to the development of the newest GUIs, including programs using the Macintosh, OS/2, and Windows operating systems as well as the operating systems themselves.

Application Generators. **Application generators,** also called *programming environments,* can be used to create programs without writing any code. An application generator provides an example of the interface for the intended environment. A Macintosh application generator first shows a standard Macintosh window with menu bar and slide bars; a Windows application generator shows a Windows interface. A DOS or UNIX character-based application generator may have a menu bar, but it could be much more limited. With Windows and Macintosh, for example, you can name menu items, pull down the menus, click on an add-command message, and be given a dialog box to name a new command and designate what the command will do. When you finish, the application generator writes the code necessary to add that feature to the application. You can also design the window and dialog boxes as you go along. Then, at any time in the process, the code can be tested for syntax and logic errors, and these can be brought to your attention. You can even type the code directly, in a text editor provided by the tool. This editor, using the search and replace feature, is a great help when you are making broad, sweeping changes.

Authoring Languages. **Authoring languages,** also called *authoring systems,* are popular application generators for creating educational and instructional software. They are designed to create question-and-answer screens and develop instructional material according to principles of instructional design. For example, an authoring system may be used to create an instructional module on forecasting economic trends. This type of module may display a screen that asks a question and provides four different answer options. As the user selects an option, a message such as *correct,* followed by a brief reinforcing statement, may be displayed.

HyperTalk. The **HyperTalk** programming language, a control language for the HyperCard system (see Chapter 8) combines the GUI with object-oriented programming. Behind HyperTalk is the concept of **hypertext,** which uses the microcomputer's ability to present information in a nonlinear way. Books and other written material can generally give information only in a linear, straight-line method. Computers can present text, images, sounds, and actions in any order and can be controlled by the user from moment to moment. In hypertext development software, users and programmers are given objects represented by index cards on screen. These cards may have lists of people or animals or other data; they may also have graphics; and they have one or more buttons with pictures or text that tell what pushing each button will do. You link these cards together to make new applications.

HyperCard is a programming application that implements hypertext on the Macintosh. Several Windows and OS/2 programming environments, such as Smalltalk, Toolbook, and IBM's Linkway, make use of the hypertext concept as well.

Query Languages.   **Query languages** are used specifically within the realm of databases. These languages are designed to instruct the computer to retrieve and manipulate database information and can be used to develop specific applications based on databases, such as database publishing and project management. The most important query language is structured query language (SQL; see Chapter 8), but most major database packages for the microcomputer have their own sophisticated query languages.

Macros.   Although not, strictly speaking, a language, macros use the ability of existing applications such as Lotus 1-2-3, Excel, WordPerfect, and dBASE to automate tasks. Many programs now come with *scripting languages* for users to write macros. Others have macro recorders. Extensive macros can be used to query database information and to generate many of the outcomes that in the past required programmers to write new programs. Macros can even be compiled with macro compilers.

Natural Languages

The fifth and final generation of programming languages does not involve the generation of any code. These **natural languages** use the normal grammar of the spoken language to create programs. Some natural programming languages include Intellect, Broker, and Explorer. Although they don't yet meet their inventors' ideal, they are showing promise, and continued advances in this area may someday radically change the way we use computers and how we create programs.

SUMMARY

- A program is a set of instructions written in a programming language. It is designed to make a computer perform a series of specified tasks to solve a problem or achieve a specific goal.
- Programming is the act of designing and writing programs in a development process that has five stages: problem definition, algorithm development, coding, program testing and debugging, and documentation development.
- In defining the problem, programmers meet with users to identify the desired output and discuss other requirements for the software.
- An algorithm—a prescribed set of rules for the solution of the problem—can be written in pseudocode or drawn as a flowchart.

- The algorithm is coded, or translated, into statements in a programming language. The choice of programming language may be critical to the success of the program.
- Once written, the program is tested to find bugs, or errors, in the syntax, or logic, of the program.
- Internal documentation describes the meaning of lines of code and the flow of logic. Internal documentation is embedded in the code.
- External documentation is prepared for user manuals to explain the processes used by the program.
- Programming languages are classified as first-, second-, third-, fourth-, or fifth-generation languages.
- The first generation of languages, machine language, is written in binary zero and one values the microcomputer can process directly.
- The second-generation assembly languages use alphanumeric mnemonic codes to replace machine commands and need an assembler to translate their codes to machine language.
- The third-generation procedural languages dominate the programming field and require compilers or interpreters to translate their codes to machine language. Popular third-generation languages in use today include BASIC, Pascal, C, COBOL, FORTRAN, Ada, RPG, and LISP.
- The fourth-generation problem-oriented languages bring programming more within the reach of nonprogrammers. These languages include object-oriented programming, the use of application generators and authoring systems, and the use of HyperTalk and query and scripting languages.
- The fifth-generation natural languages do not produce code; they follow human language grammar rules.

KEY TERMS

Ada
algorithm
application generators
assembly languages
authoring language
BASIC
C
COBOL
coding
compiler
debugging
external documentation
field testing
FORTRAN
high-level languages
HyperTalk
hypertext
internal documentation
interpreter
LISP
logic error
logic structures
looping

machine languages
natural languages
object
object-oriented programming (OOP)
on-line documentation
Pascal
problem-oriented language
procedural languages
procedure
program
programming
programming language
pseudocode
query languages
RPG
selection
sequence
structure chart
structured programming
syntax error
testing
top-down design

REVIEW QUESTIONS

1. What is a program? What is programming? What processes are involved in programming?
2. How does a programmer define the problem? What information does a programmer need to begin the programming process?
3. What is a program's algorithm? In constructing an algorithm, what logic structures does a programmer use? How do these logic structures appear in pseudocode and on a flowchart?
4. What is structured programming? What is a top-down approach?
5. What is coding? How does a programmer choose a programming language for any given program?
6. What is program testing? What is debugging? What kinds of errors are found in program code? Describe the errors.
7. What kind of documentation is necessary for programs? How is each used?
8. What are the low-level languages? What does an assembler do?
9. What are the procedural languages? How do they differ from first- and second-generation languages?
10. What do compilers do?
11. List and describe five popular procedural languages.
12. What are the fourth- and fifth-generation languages? Describe object-oriented programming and two other fourth-generation programming strategies.

SELF-QUIZ

1. A set of grammar rules, characters, symbols, and words make up a
   a. programming language.   c. program.
   b. programming vocabulary.   d. pseudocode.
2. Determining what task a program will perform, what kind of data will it use, and where it will get data are called
   a. defining the problem.   c. developing program code.
   b. constructing the algorithm. d. writing pseudocode.
3. A logic structure refers to the rational constructs that control the steps of a program from beginning to end. The simplest logic structure is called the
   a. pseudocode.   c. beginning structure.
   b. structure chart.   d. sequence structure.
4. A sequence of steps that are repeated until a given condition is met requires a(n) _____ structure.
   a. sequence   c. logic
   b. looping   d. top-down
5. When each part of a program consists of self-contained blocks of code, these blocks of code are called
   a. code.   c. structures.
   b. algorithms.   d. procedures.
6. An example of a logic error in a program is
   a. an error in syntax.   c. an error in grammar.
   b. missing a step in the algorithm. d. looping.
7. The first generation of programming languages consists of instructions written in
   a. binary code.   c. assembly code.
   b. mnemonic code.   d. procedural code.

8. A(n) _____ reads each high-level program statement, translates it to machine language, and instructs the computer to execute the statement immediately.

9. _____ languages are third-generation languages.

10. _____ consist of instructions and comments within the program itself for use by programmers when looking at program code.

11. A(n) _____ is a set of instructions written in a language designed to make a microcomputer perform a series of specified tasks.

12. A(n) _____ is a set of grammar rules, characters, symbols, and words in which instructions are written.

13. A(n) _____ is a prescribed set of well-defined instructions for solving a problem in a finite number of steps.

14. _____ is a narrative description of the flow and logic of the intended program.

15. A(n) _____ is a diagram that uses symbols, lines, and arrows to show the movement of logic through the algorithm.

16. _____ is the process of translating the algorithm into the syntax (grammar) of a given programming language.

17. Program _____ means running the program, executing all its functions, and testing its logic by entering sample data to check the output.

18. Program _____ is the process of finding and correcting program code mistakes.

19. A(n) _____ error means breaking the grammar rules of the programming language.

20. A(n) _____ error means breaking the basic logic structure in the program.

SIMULATIONS

Scenario 1: High School

A lot of students today take computer courses in high school. In fact, you may be one of them. There is a great deal of variation in high school computer courses. Some courses focus on the fundamentals of application software, some focus on business uses and typing, and others center on using computers as learning tools. However, the most dominant curriculum in high school computer courses teaches the fundamentals of computer programming.

Teaching programming in high schools has long been controversial. Some critics suggest that most students who leave high school with a programming background never use those skills again. If you ask a room full of college students who have taken computer courses in high school if they have written any programs, the vast majority will indicate that they never use their high school programming experience.

The other side of the argument suggests that if you really want to learn to be a fluent computer user, understanding the fundamentals of how a computer "thinks" is critical. Programming teaches users how to use a computer and software applications more effectively and efficiently.

You have been hired recently by a major school district as a computer consultant. The argument over whether or not to teach programming rages throughout the district. Your job is to make a recommendation concerning the teaching of programming in the district. Should programming be taught? If so, to whom? If not, why? You must develop a position paper to explain and support your position. Just saying teach it or drop it is not enough. You need to submit a complete report in order to receive a several-thousand-dollar honorarium.

You must have access to LOGO to be able to complete this assignment. You have achieved your lifelong dream—to become an elementary teacher. While you were prepared for the long hours, frustrations dealing with parents and administrators, and low pay, you were not prepared for the general computer illiteracy among your teaching colleagues. The district hired you because you understood some of the fundamentals of programming. But you have never had the opportunity to develop programming skills that you can use with elementary students. To cope with your lack of knowledge you decide to learn a bit about elementary programming by using a graphical programming language designed for young children—LOGO. After all, if LOGO is designed for use in the primary grades how hard can it be?

Scenario 2: LOGO

It's embarrassing. LOGO was designed for young children, yet you are having some difficulty mastering the language. To demonstrate that you have competence in using LOGO you must demonstrate that you can use primitive and routines (procedures) to create a variety of objects.

Your assignment is to create the following design. You must print a copy of both the graphic and the procedures you used to create the graphic.

Create five procedures:

Sun
Birds
Waves
Boat
Sail

Combine all of these procedures into one procedure called picture so that when you execute picture it creates a single graphic.

HANDS-ON COMPUTING

1. Flowcharting is an important aspect of programming. A flowchart provides a graphical representation of the logic behind a particular program. But flowcharts can also be made for nonprogramming or noncomputer activities. Your task is to develop a flowchart of the steps for riding a bike. Think of as many variables as possible and responses to a variety of situations. What happens if you are riding and you come to a cliff? What are the possible decisions? Where do they branch?

2. Many application-software packages come with their own built-in programming languages, usually called macros. Macros allow you to automate repetitive procedures. For example, a macro can be used to enter a particular phrase in a word processor, to search for a series of text in more than one file, and even to automate the process of entering and editing large sets of texts. If you are going to be literate about using software you need to understand the process of building and using macros. Using a word processor, develop a macro that will produce your name every time you execute the macro.

3. Documentation is an important part of programming because it provides users with a written guide (external documentation) to the operation of the software and it provides other programmers with explanations about critical elements within the program (internal documentation). Your task is to generate external documentation for the process of riding a bike. In other words write a series of instructions for riding a bike. Be sure to include every detail. Did you forget any steps? Were the steps in the correct order?

Maybe after this activity you will have a greater appreciation for what it takes to develop instructions that are both easy to follow and useful. You may want to vary this activity by developing instructions for using a piece of software, eating lunch, or assembling a swing set.

4. The Recorder program in Microsoft Windows will record a series of selections and keystrokes in the order in which they are used. This is a specialized form of a macro and can be a very useful tool. One problem with the Recorder program is that you must be precise. Use the Recorder program in Microsoft Windows to create a macro for starting the File Manager and obtaining a directory of a disk in the A: drive.

5. If you completed activity 4, see if you can edit what you recorded. To accomplish this task you may want to use the help feature of the Recorder to guide you through the editing process. If you become adept at creating and editing Microsoft Windows macros with the Recorder, you will find that you can automate many redundant Windows tasks.

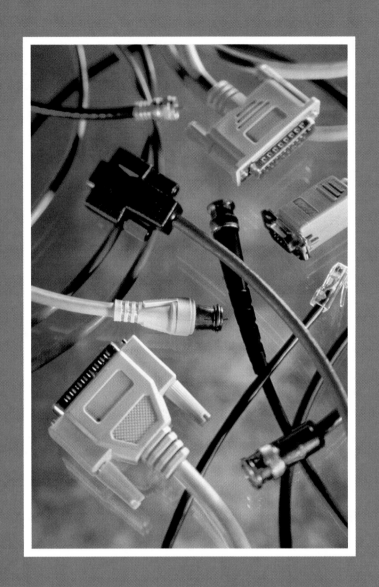

CHAPTER 11
Microcomputers and Social Issues

OBJECTIVES

After completing this chapter, you will be able to:

- Describe the various types of computer crime.
- Discuss how the use of computers relates to problems of privacy.
- Identify some organizations that acquire and store personal information.
- Discuss the reasons for and against sharing such information.
- Identify the dangers inherent in electronic trespass.

FOCUS

As you've read this book, you've seen the many uses to which computer technology has been and can be applied. We've looked at hardware, software, and operating systems; explored word processing, graphics, desktop publishing, communications, and databases; and discussed many aspects of programming.

Like most other technological advances, the computer is a tool, one that can be used for good or ill. You can save time with computers, write better—or at least better spelled and better typed—papers. You can balance budgets, from the personal to the professional; input, store, process, and output all kinds of information; and send it around the world as fast as telephone lines and satellites can carry it. You can also use computers frivolously. You can use your computers to spy. To lie and cheat. To steal. To do harm.

These last uses are the uses that concern us in this chapter. As the power of even the smallest laptop microcomputer increases, the danger of misuse also increases. We have an obligation to use computers responsibly—in ways that are not harmful to the society in which we live and work.

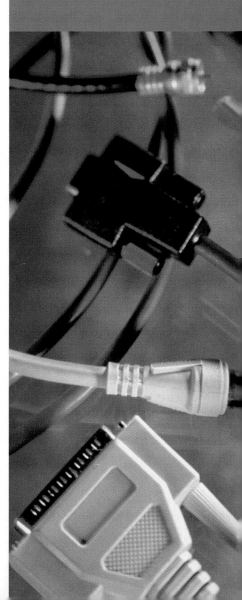

COMPUTER CRIME

As technology has outpaced the law, it is sometimes almost impossible to prosecute computer crimes, which often fall into rather gray legal areas. Some fraud is straightforward; for instance, forging checks with magnetic ink character recognition (MICR) numbers at the bottom, or the false inputting of data. Such crimes can easily be prosecuted as forgery, theft, or extortion. However, consider the case of a studio employee who sold story ideas and gossip to the tabloids. The information came from the studio's database, but there were no company guidelines on how the database should be used, so no rule had been broken. Criminal cases against hackers are often lost because, although it is easy to prove intentional access, it is almost impossible to prove intentional damage. Hackers contend their motivations are intellectual rather than criminal and that they are an annoyance rather than a serious threat to business. Britain has recently passed the Computer Misuse Bill and the Data Protection Act in an effort to cope with computer crime. But it remains to be seen how successfully these laws will deter computer criminals.

COMPUTER CRIME AND SECURITY

The headlines tell us about **computer crimes** after they have been discovered. Hackers are arrested for using telephone and credit card numbers other than their own to acquire goods and money; someone with a distinctly different sense of humor infects software with a virus that causes fish to swim across a spreadsheet. Another someone changes all the scholarship information in the financial aid office, and yet another uses the company computer—on company time—to do a little freelance writing or software development for an outside client. These are not jokes. They are crimes.

Electronic Trespass

Although peeking at someone's private records may not seem a heinous crime, **electronic trespass** is a crime. Peekers who gain access to a co-worker's personnel file or to a neighbor's checking account records are trespassing, just as if they were physically in the file or the bank. They have entered another's computer system or file without permission—hence, illegally. Among its other provisions, the Computer Fraud and Abuse Act of 1986 makes it a felony to willfully access a computer without, or in excess of, authorization.

The problem of trespassing is compounded when data is altered or destroyed. Although there may sometimes be no intent to alter data and the changes are only the result of striking the wrong key, this is a very rare occurrence. In most cases, the trespasser has something to gain from the alterations. The gain may be real, as in changing bank records to reflect a higher balance (discussed

Figure 11-1
You and your computer are vulnerable. Obviously someone can steal your hardware, but they can also take your software and data files, often without you even knowing.

later), stealing company secrets, erasing long-distance charges, or changing that grade from an F to an A. The gain may be strictly personal and vengeful: changing hospital records or credit ratings, destroying social security records, or inserting false and defamatory information in a personnel file. These crimes are serious, and they are costly.

Electronic Funds Transfer (EFT) takes money from one account and moves it to another. Banks do this when authorized to do so by legitimate customers. But bank employees have also been known to do it without authorization, directing the funds into their own accounts or those of an accomplice. The transfer of a million dollars will be quickly noted, but the transfer of one-tenth of a cent from every customer's monthly interest will not—and those fractional cents can quickly add up to many dollars.

Business and industry also have much to lose through electronic trespass. Information about new products, stock transfers, plans to acquire another company—or to head off such an acquisition—and other proprietary information can be worth millions of dollars to the company or its competitors.

Data encryption—using a code—when transmitting information is one way to help stop would-be electronic thieves. The data encryption standard, a code that was considered unbreakable a dozen years ago, has been broken. It is still in use, however, because the high cost of intercepting the coded data pushes would-be intruders into using less costly and more detectable methods. More recent advances offer codes based on the product of two large prime numbers and on the use of quantum theory. The latter uses some aspects of the uncertainty principle to encode messages; both new methods are currently considered extremely difficult to break.

Internal Security

Protecting data from electronic invaders is one thing—but how do you protect your data from people inside the organization? One obvious control is to limit access. Personnel who use computers must be carefully screened—just as they would be for any sensitive position within the company. Just as auditors inspect a company's financial records, so too can they inspect a computer log to determine who has had access to what, and when. Have there been too many data corrections? Are the same people who wrote the programs running them? An old data security rule was never to let the programmer operate the computer—and beware of any computer operator who refused to take vacation or sick days.

Passwords are one of the oldest means that still work for limiting access to data on programs. If you share a computer or are in the habit of leaving it on while you go to lunch, you can foil trespass by making entry into the program or file contingent on a password. True, passwords can be guessed or worked out by determined spies, but changing them frequently makes such exercises more difficult. Other cautions include not posting your password on the computer or jotting it on the edge of your desk calendar and not using such easily guessed combinations as your birthdate or your mother's maiden name.

Waste—from used printer ribbons to printouts— should be routinely shredded or otherwise disposed of safely. If it isn't done routinely, the day you forget

*H*ACKERS THREATEN INTERNET SECURITY

One or more hackers waited until Christmas afternoon before using a weakness in Internet system to penetrate the computer of one of the world's preeminent experts on computer security. The intruders copied more than 20,000 files that could help them break the complex security systems of computers around the world. This breach of security has slowed down Internet's eagerness for full commercial activity and has spurred interest in the development of encryption. Encryption allows data on Internet to be encoded (secure) even if Internet is not secure.

LAPTOP THEFT

As computers become more popular, so does computer crime. And now that laptop computers have shrunk in size, swiping a computer has become even easier. Laptops have been stolen from people like the chairman of Compaq Computer Corporation, Ben Rosen, and even from General Norman Schwarzkopf! The real danger for many corporations is not so much the loss of the equipment, as annoying as that is, but the loss of valuable—perhaps irreplaceable—information. Thieves can earn $10,000 per laptop, provided it belongs to the correct corporate or government official. Companies do, of course, have ways of protecting themselves from such crime. Methods range from the computer equivalent of locking a bicycle up with a chain, to elaborate procedures to ensure a stolen laptop cannot be connected to the corporate database.

COMPUTER AMENDMENTS

Harvard law professor Laurence H. Tribe has called for a 27th amendment to the U.S. Constitution to protect privacy and other individual rights being threatened by the spread of computer technology. Because the law has not kept pace with technology, Tribe says it needs to be made clear that the Constitution as a whole "protects people, not places." Speaking before high-tech cops, computer hackers, civil libertarians, and corporate security experts at a California conference on Computers, Freedom, and Privacy, Tribe pointed out that it took the government over 40 years to recognize that conversations on telephones were as protected by the Constitution as any other form of speech. Cyberspace, the nonphysical area where communication and business take place via computers, is equally in need of protection, Tribe said. Though normally wary of Constitutional amendments, the professor feels the computer revolution has created "substantial gray areas" that need to be carefully explored.

to do it will be the day proprietary secrets land in the wrong basket.

Any microcomputer—not just a laptop—can be picked up and moved out of the door and into a waiting car or truck. Too often, a uniform or a smudged signature on an official-looking form is enough to gain a thief entrance. To prevent such thefts, microcomputers can be locked to desks; laptops can be placed in secure closets. And proprietary data can be kept on floppy disks that can also be locked away, rather than allowed to remain on the hard disk.

Many microcomputers have locks that will keep unauthorized personnel from even turning them on. Identification badges with photographs or magnetic stripes, combination or card locks, sign-in and log-on sheets, and physical means of identification such as fingerprints, voice recognition, or retinal scanning—all these can limit unauthorized access to computers.

Although many of these deterrents seem more suited to a computer center than to one small computer sitting on your desk, neglecting computer security at any level is a costly error.

Safety

Although today's microcomputer is sturdy, it is not indestructible. Dropping ashes or liquids into it is frowned upon; so is using magnets to hold messages to it, clipping disks together with magnetized paper clips, or placing the disk you just spilled coffee on in front of an electric heater. Surge protectors—usually multiple-outlet extension cords with built-in circuit breakers—are wise investments. They prevent electrical spikes from harming either the computer or your data; some also protect your telephone-modem line. Uninterruptible power sources provide backup power that will keep the computer running at least long enough to save your data; some let you keep working even longer.

Fire is another danger. Large computer centers are generally protected by smoke detectors and fire extinguishers; they often use commercial off-site storage for their backup records—especially copies of sensitive data and customized software. Smoke detectors and fire extinguishers are a good idea in general; placing them conveniently close to your own computer may make it possible for you to extinguish a small fire quickly with no danger to yourself. Off-site storage of your backup records—even if it's in a barn or a friend's closet—can also save you grief and hours of trying to reconstruct lost files.

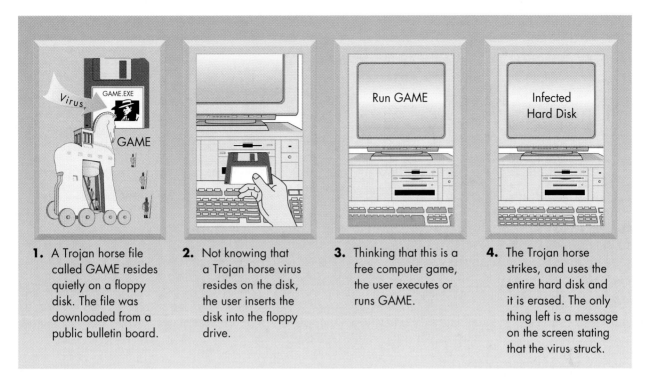

1. A Trojan horse file called GAME resides quietly on a floppy disk. The file was downloaded from a public bulletin board.

2. Not knowing that a Trojan horse virus resides on the disk, the user inserts the disk into the floppy drive.

3. Thinking that this is a free computer game, the user executes or runs GAME.

4. The Trojan horse strikes, and uses the entire hard disk and it is erased. The only thing left is a message on the screen stating that the virus struck.

Viruses

Computer viruses, like physical viruses, are insidious and often deadly. They're programs on a computer disk that generally remain undetected until their damage is done; they move from an infected source (usually a floppy disk) to the system disk or another disk in the system, and they replicate themselves, turning data into unusable nonsense when they become active. The damage is typically permanent, and anyone who has lost important files to a virus understands how serious the problem is. Other viruses have been created that aren't quite so deadly to your data, but do such things as slowing your computer to a crawl, putting prank messages on the screen, and the like. Some viruses wait until a particular date or other condition before becoming active; others act immediately to inflict harm on your computer.

Viruses are often spread through shared disks, however some telecommunication services, such as bulletin boards, can become infected and unknowingly pass viruses on to subscribers who download files—or even simply log on to the system. Some viruses, known as **Trojan horses,** are designed to act like a legitimate piece of software when first used; once on your system, though, they usually destroy all your data (Figure 11–2).

The effect of a **worm** is much like that of a virus: you lose disk space and computer capability. The difference—which doesn't much matter if you've lost the use of the computer—is that a worm does not attach itself to other programs while it spreads. It does, however, write itself to each computer it encounters in a network, establishing itself on the hard disk, and using up memory until the affected computer becomes disabled.

Recovering data that has been lost can be expensive and time-consuming; it can also be impossible. In addition to more recent versions of operating system software, a number of software vendors have developed specific programs that detect viruses on a new or suspect disk and can then clean the disk. The cost of

Figure 11-2

A Trojan horse is a hidden computer program designed to alter or destroy computer data at a specified time or when a specific computer operation occurs.

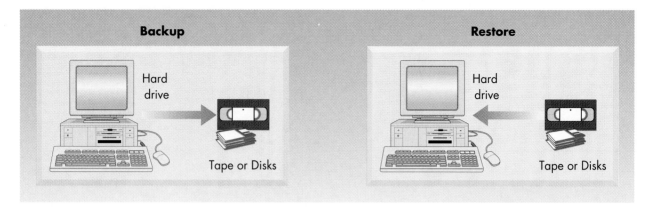

Backup

Hard
drive

Tape or Disks

Restore

Hard
drive

Tape or Disks

Figure 11-3

Backup procedures allow you
to store data on floppy disks
or on magnetic tape.

this specific software ranges from virtually free (public domain) to $100 or more (from some established vendors). The major limitation, aside from cost, is that the programs may be virus-specific; that is, they can detect and destroy only already-known viruses. New viruses, worms, and time bombs will undoubtedly be written and new detection software will follow; although the cost of acquiring the latest virus-killer may be high, the cost of not using it may be even higher.

Piracy and Counterfeiting

Not too many people would buy a book, photocopy it, and then return the book to the store. Yet many otherwise honest citizens buy a software program, copy it, and return the original to the computer store. Or they buy a program that is so useful they wish to share it with all their friends and classmates, passing out multiple free copies.

Sometimes illegal copies of software are sold as original work; this is **electronic counterfeiting**—a more sophisticated crime than sharing your new spreadsheet—and often involves a major criminal effort. It is a surprisingly big business. The package is hard to distinguish from the original, the disks may perform well, and the manual may be a direct copy of the book in the original box. The initial outlay by the dealer and consumer is lower, of course, but the users who couldn't resist the bargain of the century may find themselves with no backup—or recourse—when the program fails.

Given that software prices are often high, we must still remember that those prices include development costs, testing at several levels, and, usually, technical support. Like other authors and publishers, those who develop and publish software have a right to be compensated for their work; whether we call copying software without paying for it **piracy** or theft, it is still a crime. And it is, in part, responsible for the high prices charged.

There are, of course, legitimate copies that can be made of software: shareware and public domain software. Shareware, which can be purchased inexpen-

COMPUTERS, A HAZARD TO THE ENVIRONMENT?

Computers were supposed to create "the paperless office," but things don't seem to have worked out that way. The spread of the PC, plus high-speed copiers, laser printers, and FAX machines, have all dramatically *increased* the consumption of paper in the office. Many companies are recycling their paper, and some paper products are made using recycled materials, but paper is only one of the problems. In an effort to recycle hardware components, some companies are now accepting empty toner cartridges and selling refurbished ones. Batteries are another problem. Though they only constitute two-tenths of one percent of the total volume in landfills, their toxic heavy metals make them account for 20 percent of the hazardous waste from households and offices. Some companies are collecting worn-out batteries and others are developing batteries that do not use heavy metals.

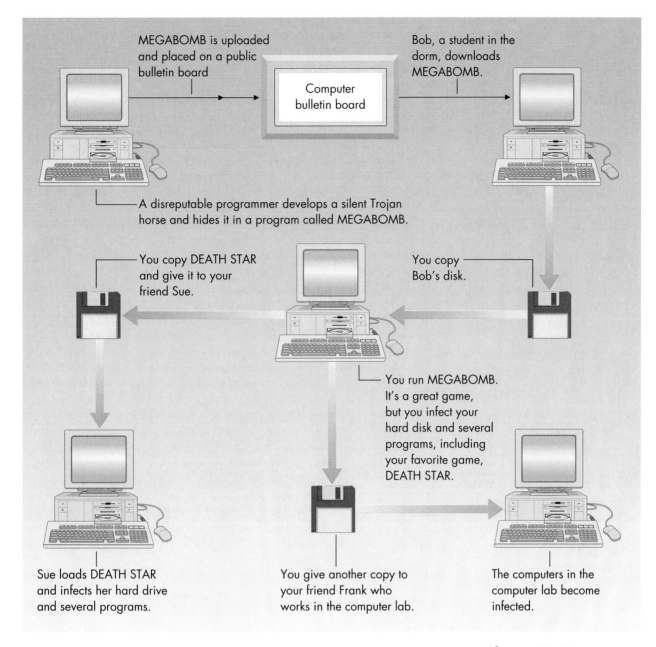

MEGABOMB is uploaded and placed on a public bulletin board

Computer bulletin board

Bob, a student in the dorm, downloads MEGABOMB.

A disreputable programmer develops a silent Trojan horse and hides it in a program called MEGABOMB.

You copy DEATH STAR and give it to your friend Sue.

You copy Bob's disk.

You run MEGABOMB. It's a great game, but you infect your hard disk and several programs, including your favorite game, DEATH STAR.

Sue loads DEATH STAR and infects her hard drive and several programs.

You give another copy to your friend Frank who works in the computer lab.

The computers in the computer lab become infected.

Figure 11-4
An infectious process.

sively both in stores and through mail-order catalogs, ranges from games to databases. Some of these programs cost no more than the small purchase price, but the software usually includes a request for an additional small payment to the software writer. Public domain software is generally spread from friend to friend—no one quite remembers who originally wrote the neat little program that blanks the screen or lets you type with one hand, but there's rarely a charge (maybe the cost of a disk), and it's all quite aboveboard and legal. A word of caution: check the disk immediately to make sure it carries no viruses or worms.

It is also legal in certain situations to copy commercial software: to make backup disks, for example, or to make licensed copies for many users in an organization. In the latter case, the company gets a multiuser license or site license; the particular arrangement varies with the vendor, who receives a given percentage of the cost of a single package for each additional user.

*B*ORDER CROSSINGS

In Europe, plans to create a continentwide database that would contain information on terrorists, criminals, illegal immigrants, and asylum seekers have triggered objections from civil rights groups and others. Opponents contend the system may criminalize legitimate refugees. By tracking people who seek asylum, governments are keeping records on innocent people that might be used against them unfairly. Opponents also say the database may violate human rights and run counter to principles of national public accountability. Three different systems have been proposed. One is based in Strasbourg, France, with satellites in six other countries. Police and immigration officials would have access to information such as fact of sighting, place, time, route and destination of journey, passengers, vehicle used, luggage, and context of the sighting. Another system would concentrate on criminal records and details of visas. The third proposed database would code people who have sought asylum many times so that, after a certain amount of time, they would be denied access to a country.

Stealing Time

At first glance, it doesn't seem like much of a crime: a little solitaire or a quick battle to save the home planet before you start work. If it's your own computer on your own desk—and if you are not charging anyone else for the time you spend—it's not a crime. But if you use your employer's computer on your employer's time to play games or do a little outside consulting work, it is a crime. It's theft, and it's wrong—even if you're only doing a flyer for the church rummage sale. Although this is more of a problem in organizations with mainframe computers, where access is limited and time is rationed, the company computers—of any size—should be used only for the company's business. At the very least, ask permission.

PERSONAL INFORMATION: STORAGE, USE, AND ABUSE

If you have bought a battery at a widely known chain store and given the clerk your name and address, you are listed in a computer database. If you've applied for insurance or subscribed to a magazine or filled out a warranty card, you are listed in a computer database. It is almost impossible for anyone to avoid having personal information stored in a computer. Businesses collect personal data about current and potential customers to increase sales and reduce credit losses. Government agencies collect and store a vast amount of information, from tax records to driving records to criminal records. Most of the time the information and its uses are benign and sharing it can be beneficial. Sometimes, however, sharing or releasing such information can be harmful.

A number of laws have been enacted to guarantee privacy. Some federal acts forbid the exchange of personal data (**data sharing**) between government agencies. Others restrict access to such information to authorized users only; loopholes and exclusions, however, often make these laws virtually ineffective. Some states have also passed laws dealing with computer crime and privacy.

Credit Bureaus

Credit bureaus collect data about people from banks and other financial institutions, department stores, small businesses, and credit card companies; they also supply data to them. The data include indebtedness and loan-repayment history, marital status, whether the person's residence is rented or owned and how long he or she has lived there, next of kin, military service, employment history, and other personal information. The Fair Credit Reporting Act of 1970 allows you access to your record and grants you the right to challenge it, to explain marks against you, and to have incorrect information changed.

Although the individual's authorization is supposedly required before any personal information is released, such permission may be part of a charge card application or presumed by the bureau itself. Problems arise when the record contains false or incorrect information or when there is illegal access—electronic trespass—or when the information is simply no one else's business.

Banks

The repayment record of your student loan not only is reported to one or more credit bureaus but becomes part of the bank's own database. This allows access to your credit history when you apply for a credit card, a mortgage, or another loan. Your credit record at Bank A thus becomes part of your record at Bank B—and accessible to an additional group of people. There are some limitations, however. The Right to Financial Privacy Act of 1978 limits the government's access to your bank records; the Comprehensive Crime Control Act (1984) goes even further in keeping other unauthorized users from accessing those protected records. It also forbids the unauthorized use, disclosure, manipulation, and so on of information stored in the government's computers.

Internal Revenue Service

It seems that everyone tells the IRS everything; the interest on your savings account; the amount you earned last year; how much you received in alimony, child support, workers' compensation, or unemployment compensation; how much you spent on other taxes, doctors and prescriptions, alimony and child support; how many children you have at home. Almost everything that affects the amount of tax you ultimately have to pay goes into the IRS's computer system. Theoretically, this information cannot be shared with another government agency; in actuality, however, access to it may still be granted.

*H*AVE WE LOST OUR PHYSICAL INTELLIGENCE?

One of the reasons we are often so unhealthy physically, according to some scientists, is that our bodies were not designed for the way we live today. The body we walk around with is the same one our ancestors had 30,000 years ago. Societies were hunter-gatherers for 100,000 generations, agriculturists for only 500 generations, industrialized for 10, and computerized for only one. This has resulted in a sophisticated brain being housed in a body that is designed to be on the move all day, facing physical and mental challenges, while subsisting on a diet low in fat, sugar, and salt. In our pursuit of an easier way of life, we have taken a machine designed to run, walk, and be physically active all day and made it sedentary, straining instead the small muscles of the eyes and fingers, injuring the spine through continued sitting, and the wrists through continued flexing. Some doctors feel that an hour at the gym (often, ironically, using computerized equipment) simply cannot restore our physical selves, since often there is little mental or emotional satisfaction in doing routine squats and sit-ups. Our bodies were built for challenging labor and free play. They were not built to be ignored.

Federal Bureau of Investigation

The files of the FBI, with information that ranges from missing children to interstate criminal activity to the last known address of a potentially dangerous individual, are open to law enforcement agencies throughout the country. Although much of the data, such as that gathered from police, court, and prison records, is accurate, some—that provided by informants, for example—may not be. Access to and dissemination of inaccurate or false data can lead to serious errors, sometimes causing innocent people to be arrested or fired from their jobs.

Other Agencies

The Social Security Administration has records of where people have worked, how long they've worked, and how much they've earned. The Selective Service folks know who has registered for the draft—and who has not. The Computer Matching and Privacy Protection Act of 1988 is supposed to keep the government from trying to match records between agencies, but IRS records (which are supposed to be confidential) have been compared with draft registration records. The information you supply when you apply for unemployment compensation is checked against records from your former employer(s). Workers' compensation databases include not only your employment data but confidential medical data as well.

Health Care and Insurance

Hospitals and clinics keep computerized records about their patients' medical conditions, medications, family members, insurance coverage, and ability to pay. Pharmacies frequently use computerized databases to list the patient's medications and allergies. These medical databases can speed hospital admissions, provide crucial data in an emergency, prevent serious drug reactions and interactions, and help physicians to make diagnoses and prescribe medications.

The insurer who pays the bill will most likely report the patient's condition to a medical-insurance clearinghouse, making information available to other insurers.

Businesses

"The last new car you bought was a red Tercel in 1984," says the car salesperson. Although this is the first time you've set foot in the showroom in all those years, she's right—and she also knows how often and for what problems you took the car in to the service department. Computerized databases provide businesses with information about customers' purchases—what they buy, when they buy, how much they spend. A listing from the database of people who buy large, expensive cars every two years can be sold to a mailing list company, whose database, in turn, can provide other businesses with information about personal finances and preferences in clothing, cars, or food.

Politics

Register to vote, volunteer at the polls, or send someone a political contribution: there's your name in a database and more than likely on a mailing list. Political organizations keep—and share—databases on voters, volunteers, and contributors; they may also maintain records on elected officials' voting patterns and base their support (or nonsupport) on those records. Poorly maintained databases can result in voters who have changed registration, receiving friendly solicitations from both major political parties; even death may not remove a potential contributor's name.

GUARDING OUR PRIVACY

Given this proliferation of databases in credit bureaus, banks, department stores, government agencies, political organizations, hospitals, insurance compa-

*P*RIVACY

An increasing amount of controversy has developed around the ability of computers to watch and record us. Caller-ID and e-mail eavesdropping are two of the latest examples. Caller-ID enables a telephone to display and record the caller's telephone number and address. This can be particularly helpful in tracing 911 calls or catching obscene phone callers. But many people are concerned that marketing companies will use this information to hound people. The service can be blocked, but some states disregard the need to offer blocking while others require it. Pennsylvania recently ruled that Caller-ID was unconstitutional since it violated privacy rights and wiretapping laws. Phone companies contend the information is the equivalent of a telephone book and so violates no laws.

The violation of e-mail privacy has been cited by some employees in suits against their former employers. Employees say e-mail was presented to them as an alternative to the U.S. mail system, telephones, or fax. However, all e-mail messages can be printed out, and employees say when they complained of this, they were fired.

nies, and businesses, we must wonder whether there is any such thing as **privacy.**

Each of these organizations has the right, given by us when we deal with it, to develop a profile or history. The bank must know our credit record, the hospital must be aware of all our medical problems, the landlord must know whether we habitually move at midnight. The problem—other than electronic trespass, which is patently a crime—lies in the dissemination of confidential information to others who have no clear right to it (Figure 11–5).

Does the car dealer *need* to know that his customer has asthma or that her sister failed the Bar examination three times? As far-fetched as that may sound, that is precisely the type of information that can be gathered through shared data and used to develop a profile that tells more about a person than any one organization or individual needs to know.

There is obviously a need for information. Credit bureaus, for example, exist to provide financial information that will enable their customers to extend credit wisely. But should they supply it to anyone who asks? Which information should they supply? And how much information do they really need? Is there a need for the credit bureau—or the department store—to know about your mother or your sister-in-law or the fact that 20 years ago you refused to cross a picket line?

Is it necessary for government agencies to keep files on all the country's citizens? Do they have an inherent right to know what we read, where—or if—we worship, and how we vote? There have been some legislative efforts to safe-

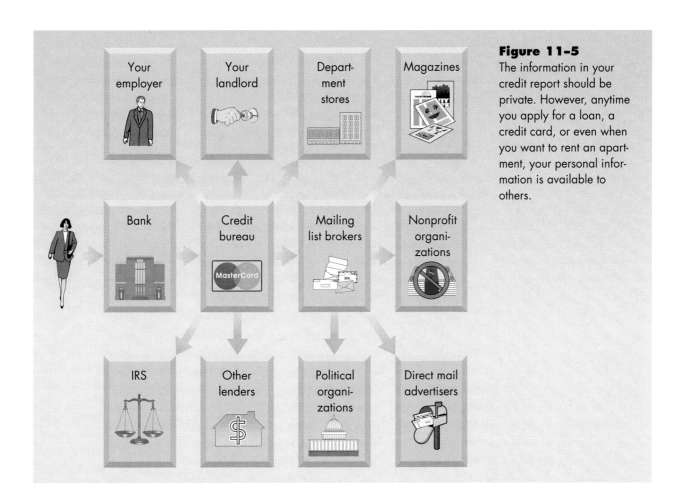

Figure 11–5
The information in your credit report should be private. However, anytime you apply for a loan, a credit card, or even when you want to rent an apartment, your personal information is available to others.

guard our privacy. In addition to the laws just mentioned, the Federal Privacy Act (1974) mandates that people must be allowed to know what information is on file about them—not only with government agencies but with their subcontractors—that they can know the uses of the information, and that they must be allowed to correct errors. None of these laws, however, protects us from the gathering of the data in the first place. And while the Freedom of Information Act (1970) gives you the right to access your federal files, actually getting the information can be a difficult, time-consuming, and—if legal action is needed—costly process.

When files were simply paper files, sharing information was a slower and more complex process. Finding the assessed value of a neighbor's house, for example, might have required taking a trip to the county hall of records and persuading the guardian of the records—which are public records—that you indeed had a need to see them. Now you can access that information quickly—and often with no questions—through your own computer and modem.

The potential for abuse, for invasion of privacy, has increased tremendously with the increase of computerized databases. Ultimately, the right to privacy may have to be addressed in the courts as well as the legislatures.

PEOPLE AND COMPUTERS

The introduction of computers to the workplace was greeted some years ago with cries of fear: The computer was going to replace the typist, secretary, machinist, accountant, executive, and so on. If it didn't take your job away, it was instead going to kill you with radiation and damage your wrist, back, eyes, internal organs, and any other vulnerable portion of your anatomy.

With new technology has come new work-related physical injuries. Even such an innocuous activity as typing at a computer keyboard can be hazardous to your health. Carpal tunnel syndrome and wrist tendinitis are afflictions new to the computer era. Carpal tunnel syndrome is an inflammation of the tendons leading from the fingers and hand to the wrist; this can deaden sensation, incapacitate movement, and cause extreme pain. Though surgery, physical therapy, cortisone injections, and wrist braces can provide some relief, there is no cure other than not to type. Such diseases did not affect people who used manual typewriters because using a manual typewriter requires a different set of movements, which gave relief to the wrist tendons. Manual typewriters also did not encourage the same kind of prolonged use that a computer does. The best method of prevention is to take frequent rest breaks and to adjust the keyboard so your wrists remain straight while typing.

Job Insecurity

The early rush to automate the office did result in the loss of some jobs. The buzzword in the early 1980s was *productivity,* and it seemed that one could achieve it by counting a typist's keystrokes. Some secretarial and typing positions were eliminated with the idea that fewer people, working on wonderfully fast machines, could do the same—or a greater—amount of work. The idea proved erroneous as the workload increased, and in many instances additional—and different—jobs were created. The stress of trying to learn a new skill or to achieve the required number of keystrokes per minute proved too much for some employees, however, and some eventually left—or lost—their jobs.

Part of the problem, then and now, is the lack of training. Software vendors provide manuals, many of which are comprehensible; they may also provide on-site training classes for organizations that purchase multiple copies. Too often, however, the office worker finds a new computer or a new software program on his or her desk and is expected to master it by the close of business that day. Graphical interfaces and menus of commands tend to make using new programs easier, but training is still important—and reading the manual is essential.

Computer Errors and Waste

One obvious result of a lack of appropriate training is operator error. The misplaced decimal point, the incorrect entry of a name or address or Social Security number, or the entry of critical data into the wrong file can lead to errors that range from the ludicrous to the tragic. Entering data carefully, following the program's instructions or documentation, and checking the results for errors that the software may have missed (or caused) are all essential.

The best training in using the computer cannot make up for errors in judgment or a lack of common sense, however. If the billing department's software automatically generates a bill whenever there is a balance, it would be wise to put a bottom limit on the amount. Sending a bill—with interest charges—or threatening a customer with a collection agency when the remaining balance is under a dollar, for example, can lose the company a customer very quickly. It will also cost more than that dollar to send and defend the bill. If the program cannot be modified, sound judgment is required, and the person using the program should be given the appropriate instructions.

Computer waste can also be blamed on improper training. There is no point in having a microcomputer on everyone's desk if half of them are never used because the people behind those desks are afraid to use them or never learned how to use them. On the other hand, it is not necessary to use a computer for every facet of one's life. Some arithmetic calculations can still be done mentally, manually, or on a hand-held calculator. Some notes and memos can and should be handwritten.

Computers for white-collar workers were going to provide the world with paperless offices, said many experts in the 1980s. What they have provided instead has been countless reams of paper, often with information that could have been easily provided either verbally or through the computer network within the office.

Health and Ergonomics: Fact or Fancy?

The wrist brace seems to be a sign of the times. Once worn mainly by athletes and jackhammer operators, we now see it worn by supermarket cashiers, office workers, and others who perform repetitive wrist motions (Figure 11–6). The culprit in most instances seems to be a keyboard that is too high and that requires constant flexion of the wrist. The resulting trauma, whether carpal tunnel syndrome or another disorder, sometimes becomes severe enough to require surgery. Lowering the keyboard is a simple but often ignored preventative measure; some new keyboards have been designed to allow typing with a more natural position for the hands, arms, and shoulders.

Other health-related questions have to do with the placement of the monitor, the chair, and the desk. Will the operator have to squint or stoop? Is his or her back supported properly? Is there radiation from the front of the monitor on our desk or from the back of the monitor behind us? What will the effect be

RADIATION

The jury is still out on whether the radiation produced by computers is harmful to your health. A 1988 study found that a large percentage of women who used computers more than 20 hours a week had miscarriages or abnormal births; but the study has not been replicated, nor did it establish a causal link between computer use and reproductive abnormalities. It is true that the safety standards for computers are lower in the U.S. than they are in Europe. For U.S. companies to produce terminals that comply with Sweden's MPR II standard would raise prices by 2.5 percent. One of the problems is the difficulty of measuring radiation emissions. Another is that it is simply not known how much radiation is actually harmful. Also, emissions are higher from the back of terminals, and they vary depending on the image on the screen and conditions around the computer. One thing that is known is that radiation emissions dissipate rapidly the further you are from the screen, so sitting two feet from the screen will keep you out of any real—or imagined—danger.

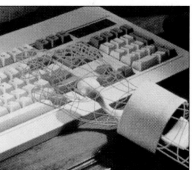

Figure 11–6
Carpal tunnel syndrome has become a serious work-related health issue, and the wrist brace is becoming commonplace. New customizable keyboards and ergonomic designs can help, but true relief requires rest.

in the short term? The long term? Will working in this environment cause unbearable stress? Sterility? Migraine headaches? What about the noise of half-a-dozen impact printers all going at once? Are there harmful fumes escaping from the laser printer or the copy machine? Is the air circulation adequate? How well is the office designed? What are the safety features? Should employers be required to supply furniture designed **ergonomically** (that is, with the comfort and safety of people in mind)?

These are real questions. They deserve real answers.

SUMMARY

- The pervasive use of microcomputers in modern society has created a number of social issues that affect our security, privacy, and well-being.
- The computer can be a wonderfully practical tool, but it can also be misused.
- Computer crime is growing rapidly; electronic trespass, hacking, and espionage all make use of illegal access to private computers and data.
- Viruses and worms are becoming an increasingly serious threat.
- Perhaps the most common misuse of computers is the illegal copying of software.
- Protecting computers and data takes many forms: passwords that prevent access to the system, locks on hardware, secured storage of data disks and tapes, and limited personnel access to equipment.
- Safeguarding data against catastrophic loss is also an issue.
- Personal and private information about individuals can be distributed without authorization to those who have no clear need for it, but would use it for their own purposes.
- Organizations have found it difficult to translate computer use into real gains in productivity.
- Computers create new needs for personnel training and cause organizations to rethink the way they do business.
- As more and more people spend an entire working day staring at a computer monitor and typing on a keyboard, occupational injuries such as carpal tunnel syndrome, back problems, and eyestrain are on the rise.
- Radiation from computer monitors is suspected, although not proven, to have harmful effects on health, possibly including increased risk of cancer and birth defects or miscarriages.

KEY TERMS

computer crimes	electronic trespass	privacy
computer viruses	ergonomically	Trojan horse
data sharing	passwords	worm
electronic counterfeiting	piracy	

REVIEW QUESTIONS

1. List as many kinds of computer crime as you can. Why are they criminal activities?
2. Define electronic trespass.
3. What is data encryption?
4. What is a computer virus? How is one transmitted?
5. What is software piracy?

6. When should personal data be shared between businesses?
7. Define ergonomics.
8. What is electronic counterfeiting?
9. What is a Trojan horse?
10. What rights to privacy are we guaranteed as citizens of the United States?

SELF-QUIZ

1. _____ are one of the oldest means that still work for limiting access to data or programs.
2. _____ are programs on a computer disk that generally remain undetected until their damage is done.
3. Viruses, known as _____, are designed to behave like legitimate software when first used. Once on your system, though, they usually destroy all your data.
4. The effect of a(n) _____ is much like that of a virus: you lose disk space and computer capability.
5. Selling illegal copies of software is called _____.
6. Copying software without paying for it is called _____.
7. With _____ software, there is rarely a charge for the program. There may be a charge for the cost of the disk and a minimal shipping cost if obtained through the mail.
8. Furniture that is designed with the comfort and safety of people in mind is said to be designed _____.
9. Coding data for electronic transmission is called _____.
10. _____ are often spread through shared disks but can also be spread from bulletin boards.

SIMULATIONS

Late one night while surfing the Net, you stumble across a detailed set of plans for making small explosive devices. By using commonly available ingredients and following the instructions available on Internet, you can build an explosive that has about twice the potency of a large firecracker. What do you do with this information? Do you build a big firecracker? Do you report the dissemination of this information to the police or other authorities? Do you print a copy of the instructions and post it around campus? What is your moral position?

Scenario 1: Late One Night

For the past 18 months you have been saving your money to buy a computer. You have worked nights as a burger flipper, days hand-cleaning septic tanks, and weekends cleaning the blood from a slaughterhouse floor—all less than desirable jobs. Finally, you have just enough money to buy a new computer, but not enough to buy the software. A friend of yours, who has a rather large collection of pirated software, has offered you copies of any software you want—free of charge. The dilemma is simple: Do you continue to hand-clean septic tanks for another two months to pay for the software you want, or do you take illegal software from your friend?

Scenario 2: Your New Computer

Internet was established to provide a vehicle through which people could share and exchange information and ideas freely, but it has created a whole new set of issues relative to the right of free speech. Some people have used their access

Scenario 3: Freedom of Speech?

to cyberspace to make a variety of material, which others define as distasteful, pornographic, and even dangerous, readily available.

You have been hired by the Congress of the United States to develop a policy for use of Internet. Your task is to establish guidelines detailing what can and what cannot be made available over Internet. Remember, the issue is the right of free speech versus protection of society and individuals. In other words, where do you draw the line? Prepare a detailed report.

HANDS-ON COMPUTING

1. Computer viruses are widespread. But they can be minimized by using virus protection software. Check all of your disks with a virus detection program to ensure that your disks are not infected. This procedure protects not only your computer but also other computers in which you use your disks.

2. One of the best ways to protect yourself is to back up your disks. As a general rule, the more important the data on a disk, the more often you should create a backup. Use either DOS or Windows to create a backup copy of your disks. It is a good idea to check your disk for viruses before making a backup to ensure that the backup is clean.

A Brief History

Although computers as we know them have existed only since the mid-1930s, people have used computing devices for centuries. We have always looked for ways to be more productive, to gain knowledge, and to improve the quality of our craftsmanship. Whatever the reason, the quest for and use of computing have a long and distinguished history.

Some critics take the view that learning about the origins of computing is unnecessary. Certainly learning a bit about the history of computing devices will not improve anyone's word processing skills or help anyone become a better programmer. However, learning a bit about the history of computers will provide an understanding of the progression of computers and possibly some insight into tasks that computers can perform. For example, in 1981 IBM introduced the IBM-PC for about $3,000. Today, the price of a new personal computer with the latest technology is still about $3,000, but the speed and capabilities of a $3,000 computer have increased more than 100-fold.

This chapter briefly reviews the developments that led from early devices to today's powerful microcomputers. These developments were not independent events, nor are these events a chronological story of technological developments. Each computer, or computing device, evolved as a result of the developments that preceded it. Each computer is also a result of the personalities and conflicts that make up any human endeavor. Therefore, to understand the development of computing, we must understand the effects of these machines on the lives of people.

EARLY CALCULATING DEVICES

Mechanical tools characterized the earliest forms of computing devices. Instead of the electronic devices we know today, primitive calculating devices (except for the abacus) were based on gears and levers. In one sense these early calculating devices were not computers at all because they were not electronic. However, the logic behind many of these devices formed the basis of today's computers. In fact, a study of early calculating devices reveals the change from the mechanical to the electronic.

The Abacus

Somewhere around 3000 BC the Chinese developed a frame and bead device, called the **abacus,** for adding large sets of numbers. Although no one knows the exact origin of the abacus, it is believed that this device grew out of a calculating method developed in ancient Babylon. It is said that ancient Babylonians used a series of lines in the sand and stones on a wood platform to perform calculations.

What made the abacus such an important device was not its accuracy, although it is an amazingly accurate instrument. The abacus became popular because it did not require an educated operator. You don't need to be able to read and write or have a great deal of knowledge about a numbering system to calculate with an abacus. In early Babylon and China, as well as in the rest of the ancient world, most people were uneducated, and the abacus proved to be a most useful calculating device. The abacus is still popular in many parts of the world. In fact, in contests between expert abacus users and electronic calculator users, abacus experts frequently win.

Pascaline

The abacus remained the primary device for calculating throughout much of early human history. Although there were other devices for measuring and predicting the motion of stars and planets, the first mechanical calculating device was not invented until the 17th century. For hundreds of years, scholars have credited Blaise Pascal with the invention of the first mechanical calculating machine in about 1642. However, more recent historical findings indicate that a German professor named Wilhelm Schickard built a primitive calculator in 1623. This was the same year that Blaise Pascal was born. Unfortunately, not much is known about Schickard so many people still honor Pascal as the inventor of the first mechanical calculator.

When Blaise Pascal was a young man, he worked for his father, a French tax official. Pascal's father had to prepare documents that contained several columns of figures. Blaise thought there must be a better and easier way to handle the tedious work of adding and balancing figures. In 1642, at the age of 19, Blaise Pascal invented a calculating device using levers and gears to add and subtract numbers mechanically. He called this mechanical device the pascaline, which proved to be a rather remarkable and accurate machine for the limited tasks of adding and subtracting.

You might think that people of the time would have welcomed this new technology with open arms. After all, the pascaline could do the work of many clerks with amazing speed and accuracy. However, many people were afraid of the pascaline. Some felt it was too complex and difficult to use. Some bookkeepers were afraid that such an efficient machine would eventually cause them to lose their jobs. For these reasons, Pascal was able to build and distribute only about 50 working models of the pascaline.

In many ways, the concerns felt by people in Pascal's time were the same concerns that many people have today. Today, some people believe that advancing technology will eventually take away their jobs. In addition, many feel that computers are too difficult and complex for them to understand.

Later in the 17th century, a German philosopher and mathematician, Gottfried Wilhelm von Leibnitz, further enhanced the pascaline. Leibnitz developed a machine that could multiply, divide, and calculate numerical roots. This machine was the forerunner of modern hand-held calculators.

Jacquard's Loom

One of the most significant developments in computer technology came from the weaving industry, an important industry in the early 1800s. During that era, Joseph Marie Jacquard developed a loom in which punched cards controlled the pattern of woven material. In Jacquard's loom, needles fell through a series of holes punched in cardboard cards strung together in succession. The needles lifted threads to weave cloth. The location of holes in the cards determined the design of the material. Some computer historians believe that Jacquard's punched cards were the origin of the punch-card programs that provide instruction to computers. To produce a new design, weavers could simply produce a new set of cards.

Jacquard exhibited and sold his loom to industrialists at the world's fair in Paris in 1801. Within just a few years, the loom had caused many skilled weavers to lose their jobs. Understandably, opposition to the new technology was strong. Once again, people felt threatened by technological progress. In England, for example, a group called the Luddites went around the country destroying many of Jacquard's machines. However, technology triumphed and the weaving industry still uses Jacquard's technique for making textiles.

CHARLES BABBAGE: A PROFILE

Charles Babbage (1792–1871) is frequently given credit for developing many of the theories used in modern computing. In addition to being a mathematician, he was a great technician. He was able to design and build several parts for the difference engine, often disappearing for several days. Because he was so dedicated to his work and spent much of his time in isolation, those who didn't know him well labeled him an eccentric. His friends, however, knew that Babbage was very sociable. He attended many spirited dinner parties at the home of Charles Darwin, where guests lingered until the early-morning hours. Babbage loved to discuss his wish to live in a future time. He is credited with saying that he would give up the rest of his life to spend three days 500 years in the future.

Babbage's Difference Engine

In the 1830s, Charles Babbage, an English mathematician, designed a machine similar to the first modern computer. While studying astronomical data, Babbage discovered many errors in the tables used for calculating logarithms. Clerks, making calculations by hand, produced the logarithm tables, and the errors ranged from simple arithmetic mistakes to errors in computational logic. Babbage asked the British government for money to develop a machine to calculate accurately. The government agreed, and Babbage set out to build a steam-powered engine to compute logarithms and astronomical tables automatically. Babbage, often called the father of modern computing, called this machine the difference engine.

Unfortunately, Babbage's vision of a steam-powered calculating device was too far ahead of the times. The skills and tools necessary to make such an elaborate machine were not available during Babbage's lifetime. Babbage was able to complete only a small working model of his original idea. However, that model was the foundation of modern calculating.

Babbage's Analytical Engine

While working on his difference engine, Babbage was also developing ideas for an **analytical engine** to compute any mathematical function. What made the analytical engine unique was the introduction of a machine memory, which Babbage called a store. This store had a memory capacity large enough to hold up to 1,000 variables each containing 50 digits. A store would hold a series of punched cards, much like those used in Jacquard's loom. Babbage also envisioned an arithmetic calculating section called the mill. He imagined saving programs for the mill on punched cards, in the store. Babbage believed that his analytical engine could also drive a typesetting machine.

All of the analytical engine's operations were to work mechanically and use steam power, as the difference engine did. That is, data and instructions were to be moved from one part of the machine to another through a series of

LADY LOVELACE: A PROFILE

Much of what we know about the analytical engine comes from the works of an Italian engineer, L. F. Menabrea. Menabrea wrote an article depicting the functions and workings of the engine. Ada Augusta, Countess of Lovelace and daughter of the poet Lord Byron, translated this article into English. Lady Lovelace took Menabrea's 20-page article and added 50 pages of notes that described procedures for issuing instructions to the analytical engine. Because she wrote this detailed set of instructions, many consider Lady Lovelace to be the first programmer.

Lady Lovelace believed the principles of the analytical engine and the logic of her set of instructions could predict the outcome of thoroughbred horse races. Unfortunately, she was wrong. Lady Lovelace lost large sums of money, as well as the family jewels, testing her ideas. Her early death at the age of 36 was a great loss to Babbage and perhaps further impeded development of the analytical engine.

switches, levers, and gears. Unfortunately, like the difference engine, Babbage never completed the analytical engine. Babbage's mechanical devices required such precise fittings that it was not possible to manufacture them with the technology available during the 19th century.

Mark I

It was almost a hundred years before Babbage's ideas for an analytical engine could be realized. The problem with Babbage's ideas was the inability to produce a mechanical device, made up of gears and levers, with the accuracy needed for precise computations. The next major piece of the puzzle was found in 1937 when Howard Aiken and Grace Hopper began to design an electromechanical machine called the automatic-sequence-controlled calculator. Their goal was to produce a calculator that used electrical circuits to move instructions and data from one part of the machine to another. The use of electricity made this type of machine much faster and more accurate than the machines of Babbage and others that used mechanical parts. Aiken and Hopper realized their goal in 1944 with the introduction of the Mark I computer.

Aiken was a visionary who recognized the need for a general, all-purpose, programmable computer, that is, a computer designed to perform a variety of tasks. However, he needed more backing and support. Through a friend Aiken met Tom Watson, the founder and then chairman at IBM, and convinced Watson that his ideas could produce such a machine. Watson gave Aiken two-thirds of the $500,000 he needed to build the machine as a grant from IBM and also gave Aiken access to some of IBM's top engineers to develop the Mark I. The Mark I consisted of 497 miles of wire and a series of 78 adding machines and desk calculators. A roll of punched paper controlled this electromechanical computer through a series of relays and switches. The Mark I could perform three additions per second.

An interesting side note to development of the Mark I demonstrates that not all computing developments occur from a technological perspective. After completing the Mark I in 1944, Aiken appeared at a dedication ceremony at Harvard University and, as the story goes, Aiken neglected to mention the contributions of IBM or Thomas Watson. Although Watson never said so publicly, it has long been a matter of speculation that because Watson felt insulted, IBM and Aiken never worked together on another project. What type of computer might have been developed if Watson and Aiken had remained on good terms?

Atanasoff-Berry Computer

Electromechanical computers represented an improvement over mechanical ones, but they too had disadvantages. Electromechanical computers used electricity to flip mechanical relays and switches. Like most mechanical devices, these switches wore out and broke down. In addition to this lack of reliability, electromechanical devices such as the Mark I were extremely large. The Mark I was 8 feet tall, 51 feet long, and 2 feet thick. It weighed five tons and contained more than 750,000 parts.

About the same time Aiken was working on the Mark I, John V. Atanasoff and a part-time graduate student, Clifford Berry, received a $650 grant from Iowa State University (in 1939) to develop a computer. With the $650, Atanasoff paid Berry's salary and purchased all the materials to develop the first fully electronic computer.

The major advantage of the Atanasoff–Berry Computer, or ABC, was that it used 300 vacuum tubes to move electrons rather than slow-moving mechanical parts. By using **vacuum tubes** the ABC could solve complex equations much faster and fit into a much smaller space. The ABC was about the size of a large office desk. Unfortunately, the ABC was limited in the types of tasks it could perform and was not a general-purpose computer.

ENIAC

The ABC never became widely known, but it influenced the development of a machine recognized in 1945 as the first all-electronic, general-purpose computer. John W. Mauchly, and J. Presper Eckert built this computer at the University of Pennsylvania with the help of a government grant. The machine, called the electronic numerical integrator and calculator, or ENIAC, was developed secretly for use by the military.

As with virtually all developments in computer history, ENIAC was much faster than earlier computers. It could perform in one hour what it took the Mark I one week to complete. Unfortunately, ENIAC could not run for more than an hour at a time. The heat generated by the electric power (130,000 watts) needed to operate its 18,000 vacuum tubes caused frequent breakdowns. In fact, some people said turning power on to the ENIAC caused the lights to dim in Philadelphia.

In addition to the technological advances of using vacuum tubes, the ENIAC also represented a breakthrough in controlling computers. Like its predecessors, controlling ENIAC required operators to rewire and reset switches for each operation—a process that often took several operators many hours. Rewiring and resetting switches also caused the various breakdowns and computing errors. Any time humans make changes, the chance for error increases dramatically. In 1946, John von Neumann proposed a method of feeding instructions and data into the ENIAC without extensive rewiring.

Von Neumann was a famous mathematician who became fascinated with ENIAC. In fact, Mauchly once wrote that von Neumann was like a child in a toy store with ENIAC. Von Neumann's interest was as important as almost any other technological development. Computing machines at the time were never given much status in the scientific community. Von Neumann's interest and work on the ENIAC gave the project much-needed status.

Von Neumann's major contribution was a mathematical method for controlling computers. His method used two numbers, zero and one, to represent all instructions and data. This meant operators could control the computer without constant rewiring. This two-value numbering system, called a binary system, is still the basis for controlling virtually all computers today.

Using the ideas of von Neumann and the developments of the ENIAC, Maurice V. Wilks in 1949 designed the electronic delay storage automatic calculator (EDSAC). EDSAC was the first electronic computer to store a set of operating instructions or programs in its memory. In 1952, the electronic discrete variable automatic computer (EDVAC) was developed. The actual design of the EDVAC was started before the EDSAC but because of bitter project disputes the EDSAC was completed first. Both EDSAC and EDVAC used a binary numbering system like von Neumann's to store instructions internally. All earlier computers used external devices to store instructions or programs.

MODERN COMPUTING

The history of early computing devices is rather long. It took more than 100 years for Babbage's ideas to be achieved with the Mark I. Today, changes in computing are much more rapid. In fact, it is not uncommon today for major changes in computing technology to occur in months rather than years.

Because of today's rapid change in computing and technology, the easiest way to understand modern computing is with the use of the term *generation*. Like generations of humans, there are a number of similarities in computers of the same generation. In computer terms, a new generation is usually marked with a major development in computer hardware. However, new developments in electronic engineering also make new computer applications possible. As you will see, the progression from one generation of computers to the next has been rapid.

First-Generation Computers

The early computers, already described, were developed by scholars or inventors with support from the government or wealthy patrons. The inventors themselves operated the computer. On occasion, other scientists, engineers, or the government would use the computer. Further, most early computers were designed for one specific, narrow purpose, for example, census counting with the ENIAC. However, when early computers showed success in specific applications, business and industry began to show an interest. The entrance of computers into the commercial world is one characteristic of the first generation of computers. First-generation computers were developed during the 1940s and lasted through much of the 1950s.

The first computer to find uses in business and industry was the universal automatic computer, or UNIVAC I, developed by J. Presper Eckert and John Mauchly. Eckert and Mauchly, the builders of ENIAC, were quick to see the commercial applications of computers. The two inventors formed a private company and designed the UNIVAC for manufacture. However, lacking the funds to build the machine, they sold their company to Remington-Rand Corporation (now known as Sperry Corporation), and Remington-Rand sold the first UNIVAC to the U.S. Census Bureau in 1951.

Although the government was the first to take advantage of the UNIVAC I, its applications in business and industry soon became clear. This computer was

Table A-1

Characteristics of first-generation computers.

Vacuum tubes
Large programming and support staff
Magnetic drum storage
Punched cards
Machine language
Assembly language

not a machine limited to a single use. It could count inventory, calculate payroll, monitor accounts receivable, and maintain a general ledger. Even though it took a staff of dozens of people to operate the UNIVAC I and other first-generation computers, these machines could do the work of many bookkeepers and accountants. Thus, a company could justify its large initial investment, purchasing the computer and hiring dozens of specialized programmers, by the increased accuracy and speed of work and more effective use of personnel resources. That is, with a computer, accountants and bookkeepers didn't have to spend hours every day checking the accuracy of reports. Their new task was to interpret the data generated by the computer. Thus, the use of first-generation computers in business didn't result in the displacement of a large number of employees, but did result in a redefinition of their jobs.

First-generation computers used vacuum tubes, first established by Atanasoff and Berry. Vacuum tubes are electrical switches that work much faster than the Mark I's mechanical switching devices. A machine with vacuum tubes could perform several thousand calculations per second—slow by today's standards, but breathtakingly fast at the time.

Unfortunately, vacuum tubes generated heat, which caused them to break down. They were susceptible to frequent failures, shorts, and electronic fluctuations or surges. First-generation computers had to be housed in air-conditioned rooms. The rooms also had to be very large, because the computers themselves were huge in order to hold several different size vacuum tubes. A typical first-generation computer was the size of an average living room.

With early first-generation computers, punched cards similar to those used since the 1800s were the primary means of data input and output. Punch-card readers, machines that could read tiny holes punched in a card, could process 130 characters per second (again, slow by today's standards but amazingly fast in the 1950s). First-generation computers did not have memory devices as we know them today. Many early computers used mechanical magnetic drums to store and process data.

First-Generation Computer Software

There were several limitations on the types of tasks that these computers could perform. Most first-generation computers could operate a single program on a limited set of data. At first, all programs were in binary code. Instructions using zeroes and ones are called machine language instructions. Writing programs in machine language was an extremely difficult and time-consuming chore, and the programs often contained errors.

In 1951 Dr. Grace Hopper, a former colleague of Howard Aiken and a career naval officer, developed a new computer language to help solve this problem. Hopper's assembly language made it possible to write shorthand messages, or codes, that replaced whole series of zeroes and ones in machine language. Dr. Hopper developed a program called a compiler that translated assembly language into the binary language of the computer. This development made computer programming much easier. Nevertheless, writing programs for first-generation computers remained a tedious task, and programming errors remained a common problem.

Second-Generation Computers

The second generation, which began about 1959 and lasted until the mid-1960s, was characterized by the use of transistors in place of vacuum tubes. Transistors do the same work as vacuum tubes but are smaller and faster, use less power, are much more reliable, and allow much larger memory for storing instructions and calculating. For example, second-generation computers could perform as many as 230,000 calculations per second versus 3,500 to 17,000 for first-generation machines. Because transistors require far less energy to operate than tubes (about $\frac{1}{100}$ the power), second-generation computers were also much less expensive to operate than their predecessors.

As with first-generation computers, second-generation computers were limited in the types and quantities of tasks they could perform. However, second-generation computers ushered in broader applications for more businesses. Accounting procedures were the most common type of application for this generation of computers. In large businesses and industry, it was common to group jobs in batches—large groups of similar data transactions. For example, a company might collect billing data over a period of a week and save all this data for processing at one time. It would use the same procedure for payroll, inventory, accounts payable, and so on. This type of data processing is called batch processing.

We have already seen that the major distinction between first- and second-generation computers is the use of transistors instead of vacuum tubes. However, several other hardware changes also occurred.

One important change was the expansion and use of external storage of data, or external memory. One of the first types of electronic data storage was based on little, doughnut-shaped ring magnets, called cores. Core memory was much faster and more reliable than the drums used by first-generation computers. In fact, many second-generation computers were described by the amount of core memory available. (The term *core memory* was frequently used to describe the amount of memory in early microcomputers. However, the term was not completely accurate from a historical perspective, since modern microcomputers did not use cores.)

Another important development was the introduction of off-line devices. Off-line devices are not in constant communication with the computer, but are available whenever their services were required. For example, when the computer needs data from a punched-card reader, the card reader is activated, data is read into the computer, and then the card reader stands idle until it was needed again. Data could be sent to an off-line printer, and the computer would be free to begin computing another set of data.

One important off-line storage medium was magnetic tape. Eckert and Mauchly had developed this medium for first-generation computers, but second-generation computers were the first to use it extensively. As with punched

Table A-2

Characteristics of second-generation computers.

Transistors
Magnetic tape
Magnetic core memory
Card readers
Magnetic tape readers
Printers
Batch processing
Introduction of high-level programming languages
Operating systems

cards, computers could send data onto tapes, the tapes stored the data, and later the data could be reentered into the computer from the tapes. Input was much faster with magnetic tape than with cards. Data could be entered at 130 characters per second with cards, whereas a computer using magnetic tape could read more than 6,500 characters per second.

A further advancement begun during the second generation and still important today was the development of magnetic disk storage. Magnetic-tape processing was slower because to retrieve data from a magnetic tape, the computer had to read the tape sequentially. That is, the computer read the tapes from the beginning of the tape to the place where the data were stored. With disks, the computer could access the desired data directly, so disk storage allowed much faster processing.

Second-Generation Computer Software

Programming languages began to develop during the second generation of computing. Programming languages, usually called higher-level languages, control or tell a computer what to do in a language that more closely resembles a spoken language. Thus, higher-level languages have meaning to humans whereas machine language has meaning only to the computer. To make higher-level languages work, computers translate them into the binary code through special programs called interpreters. An interpreter is similar to a compiler in that it translates programming languages to commands directly understandable by the computer. However, an interpreter makes the translation as soon as the command is issued. A compiler converts all commands and consequently alters the program.

The major advantages of higher-level languages is that writing programs is easier and they also help reduce the number of programming errors. However, the computer language that is spoken in business is often different from the computer language spoken by scientists. For this reason, different higher-level languages appeared for specific types of users and applications. Some of the higher-level programming languages developed during this period include COBOL, a business-oriented language, and FORTRAN, developed at IBM for scientists and engineers.

In addition to the development of higher-level programming languages, instructions designed to control the computer's resources also emerged in this generation. With the development of off-line devices, instructions had to be developed to send or receive data to these devices when they were on-line. These instructions are called operating systems. Early operating systems were primitive. More elaborate operating systems would have to wait until the development of third-generation computers.

Third-Generation Computers

The development and use of integrated circuits marks third-generation computing. This generation lasted from about 1964 until about 1970. An integrated circuit consists of thousands of circuits printed on a small silicon card commonly called a chip. The advantage of chips is that a single chip can replace thousands of transistors. By using integrated circuits, computers could perform more than 2,500,000 calcu-

*T*OM WATSON: A PROFILE

The idea of doing more than selling computers was important to IBM's success. IBM sold "solutions to problems." The solutions-to-problems approach or philosophy did not develop with the System/360. This approach had been a major part of IBM's philosophy since the 1930s. IBM developed a strong sales and support staff. Whenever any customer had a problem with a computer, IBM sent a customer representative to help solve the problem immediately. This business philosophy allowed IBM to become the world leader in manufacture, sales, and service of computer hardware. Even though the computer industry has diversified, IBM's reputation continues to have a strong market influence.

lations per second. Integrated circuits are more reliable than transistors because they use less electricity and have a longer usable life.

Another important development with third-generation computers was the introduction of families of computers. For the most part, families use the same chips and share the same operating system or method of controlling the computer. During the 1960s, IBM developed one of the first computer families, a series of mainframe computers called System/360. The IBM System/360, or S/360, consisted of six upwardly compatible computers. Upwardly compatible indicates that programs that ran on small 360 computers also ran on larger 360 machines. Because of this compatibility, a business could start with a small computer and progress to a larger computer without having to change software and retrain computer operators. This feature was especially attractive to many smaller businesses with less money to spend than the large companies. IBM sold more than 30,000 of its System/360 series computers.

Later, IBM developed its 370 family of computers. This series of 20 computers, with supporting hardware and software, was also upwardly compatible. Once again, companies could start small and then move up to larger and more powerful computers.

Today, other companies offer families of upwardly compatible mainframe computers, but IBM was the first to do so. IBM was the end result of a company called Computing-Tabulating-Recording Corporation (CTR), which became IBM in 1924. Sometimes called "Big Blue," IBM became an early participant in computer development with its support of the Mark I. With its families of computers, IBM ensured its position as the leader of the computer industry.

Although many companies bought computers, others still did not feel the need to invest in systems of their own. Another third-generation development, remote computer terminals, allowed these businesses to tie into single, large, mainframe computers. These remote users, such as small businesses, would pay the owner of a large computer a fee for the amount of time the small business used the mainframe computer. A small business might, for example, use a remote terminal to do its billing, or a small school district might use a remote terminal for scheduling rooms or students.

For the most part, employees in both small and large businesses did not lose their jobs to computers during this generation. However, a subtle shift in business management began to emerge. Two things happened. First computers enabled businesses to keep more efficient and accurate records. This led to a

Table A-3

Characteristics of third-generation computers.

| Integrated circuits |
| Expandable computers |
| Disk drives |
| Lower maintenance costs |
| Advanced programming languages |
| Refined operating systems |
| Multitasking |
| On-line access |
| Time sharing |

redefinition of roles within the company. For example, accountants with access to a computer could spend their time interpreting accounting information and making recommendations for the business owner, rather than spending time on manual calculations. With the development of third-generation computers people with much less training than an accountant could maintain accurate company records. Second, before the introduction of general-purpose computers, many small business owners were afraid of losing their bookkeepers. If a bookkeeper left a small business, the owner might not have been able to teach a new employee proper accounting procedures. However, the owner would probably be able to teach a new employee how to enter data into a computer, and the computer would accurately calculate the necessary accounting information. A small business no longer had to rely on the skill and accuracy of bookkeepers and accountants to maintain company records.

One other important development during the third generation was the increased use of magnetic disk devices for data storage. Magnetic disk storage helped perfect the notion of random access. This meant that computers could access data directly from virtually any location on disks rather than have to wait for magnetic tapes or card readers to read an entire data set. Random access increased computing speed, and the functional use of computers expanded dramatically.

Third-Generation Computer Software

Several new programming languages emerged during the third generation. BASIC, an easy-to-learn, all-purpose programming language is an important example. Another is Pascal, also an all-purpose language. Because these programming languages were easy to learn and use, many computer users could tailor computer programs to their own needs.

The refinement of operating systems, which first appeared during the second generation of computers, played an increasingly important role in the development of new programming languages. Recall that an operating system controls many of the computer's resources. That is, with the correct operating system, a computer can communicate with a printer, a magnetic tape reader, or other peripheral devices. Third-generation operating-system refinements enabled computers to process data in a new way. Remember that first- and second-generation computers used batch processing, that is, they performed only one task at a time. Thus, the speed of processing depended, in part, on the speed of input. Sophisticated third-generation operating systems allowed a computer to work on several jobs at once. Each job was completed in small segments. When finished with one job, output went to a disk, a terminal, a printer, or some other computer device. The computer no longer had to sit idle and wait for data to arrive from a slow input device; it could simply work on the next task. Multitasking is the term to describe this development.

This on-line feature of third-generation computers and their operating systems also increased direct access to information stored on a disk. A more refined random access method expanded the applications for third-generation computers. For example, libraries could store huge amounts of data on a disk, and several people could access the data at the same time. Similarly, airlines could store large sets of flight information, and travel agents throughout the country could access this data simultaneously.

New physical devices, software, and operating systems combined to extend the applications of computers to virtually every segment of society. In fact, many small businesses began to profit from the time-sharing, multitasking capabilities of third-generation computers. A company could buy a computer and sell time on the computer to many other small businesses on a pay-for-services basis.

Many felt that time-sharing providers would profit for years. However, the arrival of fourth-generation computers all but put an end to the selling of mainframe computer time to small businesses.

Fourth-Generation Computers

Ultraminiaturization of the integrated circuit characterizes fourth-generation computers (1970s until today). Through ultraminiaturization, or microminiaturization, the equivalent of several hundred thousand transistors are placed on a chip the size of a thumbtack. A microchip or microprocessor can perform millions of calculations each second. Intel Corporation developed the first microprocessor, called the 4004, as a controlling chip for any device that manipulated information. While this first microprocessor was not an immediate success, Intel continued to refine the microprocessor and released the 8008 a year later. Unfortunately, the 8008 had many technical problems and proved to be inadequate for most needs. However, the 8008 formed the basis for the Intel 8080 microprocessor, the chip that ushered in the age of microcomputers.

Microcomputers weighing only a few pounds and occupying only a few square feet can perform as many tasks as the small mainframe computer of a few years ago. Comparisons with the earliest computers are even more striking. The

In the early 1970s three engineers working for Intel, a microchip company, developed a unique chip that condensed the circuitry of many circuit boards onto a single piece of silicon. This chip became known as a *microprocessor*. A microprocessor could perform the same functions as the central processing unit in a sizable mainframe computer. These small, inexpensive chips became the heart and soul of the new microcomputers.

Interestingly, it was not Intel's engineers who developed these new computers. They believed that microprocessors were best suited for controlling traffic lights. Rather, a small-business owner led the way. Ed Roberts had started Model Instrumentation Telemetry Systems (MITS) to build and supply model rocketry light flashers, digital clocks, and small digital calculators. With the company facing bankruptcy, Ed Roberts and William Yates, a former Air Force officer with a degree in aeronautical engineering, set out to design a computer based on a microprocessor.

Meanwhile, a magazine editor in New York had the same idea. Les Soloman was looking for someone to design a kit for a computer based on a microprocessor to sell through his magazine, *Popular Electronics*. Soloman contacted Ed Roberts, who had sometimes advertised in *Popular Electronics*.

Soloman was so excited about Roberts's machine that he insisted Roberts send him the only prototype to examine. Unfortunately, the prototype got lost in the mail, but Soloman, with Roberts's and Yates's notes and schematics, built a replacement. Not knowing what to call it, he asked his daughter for some help. She had recently seen a "Star Trek" episode in which the Enterprise was traveling to the distant star Altair.

In 1975, Soloman published an article in *Popular Electronics*, written by Roberts and Yates, describing the Altair. Included was the address of MITS and an offer to sell the Altair in kit form for $397. Ed Roberts was hoping to sell 400 Altair computers to save MITS. Within three weeks of the release of the article, MITS sold over 600 computers and emerged from near bankruptcy with $250,000 in sales.

The Altair was the first commercially available microcomputer. It also helped spawn a new breed of people who lived for the challenge of developing new machines. These people became known as hackers.

ENIAC, for example, was as large as a tennis court and weighed as much as six full-grown elephants. The main chip in today's more powerful and economical computers is smaller than a dime.

Another major characteristic of fourth-generation computers is their extremely widespread use. We can find computers in virtually every small business, in every school, and in millions of homes largely because they are inexpensive. Instead of paying hundreds of thousands of dollars for a computer, anyone can buy a complete system for $1,000 to $2,500. Rather than having only limited applications, fourth-generation computers are used for a variety of purposes. They score bowling games, calculate grocery bills and maintain inventory, design automobiles, create documents, support medical diagnosis and research, and perform a variety of other tasks. Microcomputers are in the office of veterinarians, auto parts stores, gasoline service stations, lumber companies, and in virtually every kind of small business.

COMPUTER-ASSISTED INSTRUCTION WITH THE MITS COMPUTER

In the summer of 1976, MITS computer corporation of Albuquerque, New Mexico, marketed one of the first microcomputer kits for amateur radio hams. The product was sold as an assembly kit with a control board for disk drives, terminal input/output interface boards, memory boards, power supply, and a CPU with 64K of RAM memory. Several months later, the company introduced eight-inch floppy disk drives and supplemental components.

David L. Jelden, a professor of industrial/educational technology, and Lloyd D. Thompson, a graduate student at the University of Northern Colorado, were very interested in using a microcomputer for individualized instruction at the university. They purchased one of these early kits with two disk drives, 64K memory, and four terminals for under $10,000. During the Christmas vacation of 1976, they assembled the hardware and started research on the feasibility of using a multiuser microcomputer system to deliver individualized instruction. This was one of the first attempts to use a microcomputer to manage and deliver computer-assisted instruction to several users at the same time.

To manage the microcomputer system, about 23K of RAM was needed to manipulate the hardware and control the instructional programs. The remaining RAM was divided into four partitions of 10K each to handle the interactive instructional scripts for each terminal. The instructional scripts were programmed in BASIC and saved on floppy disks; one lesson and its associated test questions (pretest and posttest) were programmed on a single disk. Jelden and Thompson developed 86 interactive instructional lessons on 86 separate disks for classroom use. The disks were changed every week so students had five school days in an open lab arrangement to master the lesson material. However, with only two drives, only two lessons were available for students at a time.

As the usefulness of individualized instruction was confirmed, a mainframe system eventually replaced the MITS system and more sophisticated instructional lessons were developed. According to Professor Jelden, "In retrospect, the utilization of the microcomputer in the classroom for delivery of instructional/testing materials has come full circle. The first large systems were mainframe only, then the MITS microsystems were developed, replaced by the sophisticated mainframe system, which in turn are being replaced by the high-speed, specialized, compact microcomputer systems today capable of delivering color visual, sound, and script modes to students. As a matter of interest, the MITS computer system and its related software, the first dedicated COMPUTER MANAGED SYSTEM for interactive micro delivery, are currently on display in the Computer Museum in Boston, Massachusetts."

WOZNIAK AND JOBS: A PROFILE

Interest in computers and computer software blossomed in the 1970s. Across the country computer enthusiasts formed clubs to share ideas and experiences. The Home Brew Computer Club was to turn out to be one of the most important.

Two members of the Home Brew Computer Club were Stephen Wozniak and Steven Jobs. Wozniak was an electronic whiz kid, a tinkerer who reveled in making electronic devices. Jobs was a visionary who saw computers as a tool that could be useful to almost anyone.

Based on his vision, Jobs wanted to create a computer that was fast, powerful, small, and most importantly, inexpensive. Jobs convinced Wozniak to quit his job with Hewlett-Packard to build such a computer. In 1977, with an investment of a little more than $1,000, Wozniak built the first Apple computer. (Jobs named the computer Apple because he was on a fruit diet at the time.) Within a year Apple Computer, Inc., was formed, and just three years later Apple Computer had sales in excess of $139 million.

The combination of Wozniak, the whiz kid, and Jobs, the visionary, was highly successful in starting one of the giant computer companies. However, that very success forced both Wozniak and Jobs to leave Apple. While there are conflicting reports and views as to what really happened, one view is that Jobs forced Wozniak out because Wozniak lacked a strong business interest and sense. At the same time Jobs hired John Sculley from Pepsi to expand Apple Computer, Inc. Sculley, who believed only one person could be on top, eventually forced out Jobs.

To John Sculley's credit Apple Computer continues to be a strong, dynamic, and profitable corporation. To Steven Jobs's credit, he remained a visionary who went on to invent the NeXT computer. To Stephen Wozniak's credit, he is considered the Henry Ford of microcomputers.

The development of microprocessors was accompanied by developments in other computer hardware. In place of core memory, modern microcomputers use a metal oxide semiconductor (MOS) for internal memory. This is a special chip that can store large amounts of information in a very small space. Semiconductor memory circuits are very similar to the microprocessors etched on silicon chips. Semiconductors are very, very fast; however, they are volatile. That is, whenever there is a power outage, semiconductors lose everything stored in them.

In addition to the developments in semiconductor technology, advances in the use of auxiliary memory or disk storage accompanied fourth-generation computers. Most microcomputers use small floppy disks as a form of auxiliary memory for data storage. With a microcomputer, computer programs must be entered into memory each time the computer is turned on because semiconductors lose information when turned off. However, programs and data can be stored on a disk for use at a later time.

Fourth-Generation Computer Software

Database management systems are an important software development in fourth-generation computing. Database programs allow computer users to store and retrieve data in a variety of formats. Colleges and universities, for example, use database programs to store student information and retrieve the data in a variety of ways—by name, Social Security number, course enrollment, zip code, or any number of other important identifiers.

BASIC and Pascal, developed during the third generation, are ideal for the home microcomputer programmer, and use of these programming languages mushroomed after the development of the microcomputer. In addition, many home-based enterprises, or "cottage industries," developed special software for the microcomputer.

Fifth-Generation Computers

What will mark the beginning of the fifth generation of computers? Are we in the fifth generation? Computer historians disagree. Some contend that in the fifth generation every home will have some form of microcomputer. This microcomputer may be of the type already familiar to all of us. It may be a new type that controls or regulates heat, electricity, security, and other functions such as cooking or water purifying. It may enable people to work at home, do their schoolwork at home, or shop at home. Others contend

Miniaturized integrated circuit
Microprocessor
MOS memory
Silicon
Data communications
Modems
Floppy disks
Hard disks
Microcomputers
Diverse applications software
Expanded operating systems

Table A-4
Characteristics of fourth-generation computers.

that we will not reach the fifth generation until computers can deduce, infer, and learn, that is, until computers have intelligence.

Whatever happens in the next generation of computers, it will be an exciting development. New technologies will solve many of today's problems. However, as with all advances in technology, there will be new limitations and new problems.

The Computer Time Line

3000 BC	The earliest abacus.
1623	Wilhelm Schickard introduces an early mechanical calculator.
1642	Blaise Pascal introduces the pascaline.
1801	Joseph Jacquard invents Jacquard's loom based on a series of punched cards.
1830	Charles Babbage begins work on the difference engine.
1834	Charles Babbage begins work on the analytical engine.
1906	Lee De Forest invents the vacuum tube.
1924	CTR Corporation becomes IBM.
1939	The initial work on ABC begins with John V. Atanasoff and Clifford Berry.
1944	The introduction of Mark I.
1944	Eckert and Mauchly invent the notion of data and information storage.
1945	ENIAC goes into operation.
1946	John von Neumann begins work on using commands rather than rewiring to control computers.
1947	Scientists at Bell Labs invent the transistor.
1949	Introduction to EDSAC.
1951	Introduction of UNIVAC.
1952	Thomas Watson becomes president of IBM.
1957	IBM introduces FORTRAN.
1961	Introduction of time-sharing computers.
1964	IBM introduces System/360.

1971	Intel invents the microprocessor.
1975	The Altair appears in *Popular Electronics.*
1977	First Apple computer.
1981	IBM introduces the IBM-PC.

REVIEW QUESTIONS

1. Describe several early computing and calculating devices.
2. Identify the pioneers instrumental in the development of computing devices.
3. Describe the development of computing devices from early machines to today's microcomputers.
4. What technological advance characterizes the development of first-generation computing?
5. What technological improvement characterizes the development of second-generation computing?
6. What technological advancement characterizes the development of third-generation computing?
7. What are the characteristics of first-generation computing?
8. What are the characteristics of third-generation computing?
9. Describe the development of the pascaline.
10. Describe the first general all-purpose computer.
11. Why are transistors so valuable in a computer?
12. What invention made microcomputers possible?
13. What is the ABC?
14. Why is it important to examine the history of computers?
15. Was the development of modern computers an independent event or was it evolutionary? Why?
16. What was the major problem with first-generation computers?
17. What was Charles Babbage's contribution to the development of computers?
18. What is machine language?
19. What was the first computer built around a microprocessor?

SELF-QUIZ

1. The automatic sequence controlled calculator was also known as
   a. the Mark I.
   b. ENIAC.
   c. UNIVAC.
   d. the pascaline.
2. Charles Babbage developed the
   a. Mark I.
   b. ABC.
   c. abacus.
   d. analytical engine.
3. Modern data processing techniques were first employed in the armor making industry.
   a. true
   b. false
4. Using punched cards to provide information for computers was associated with
   a. the pascaline.
   b. the abacus.
   c. Jacquard's loom.
   d. the difference engine.
5. Who is regarded as the father of computing?
   a. Charles Babbage
   b. Joseph Jacquard
   c. Thomas Watson
   d. Clifford Berry

6. The use of transistors is associated with which generation of computers?
   - *a.* first generation
   - *b.* second generation
   - *c.* third generation
   - *d.* fourth generation

7. Significant development of programming languages occurred during which generation of computing?
   - *a.* first generation
   - *b.* second generation
   - *c.* third generation
   - *d.* fourth generation

8. Third-generation computers were characterized by the use of
   - *a.* punched cards.
   - *b.* vacuum tubes.
   - *c.* integrated circuit.
   - *d.* semiconductors.

9. Core memory is associated with which of the following generations of computers?
   - *a.* first generation
   - *b.* second generation
   - *c.* third generation
   - *d.* fourth generation

10. An early calculating device, perfected by the Chinese during the 12th century, was a frame with beads called the _____.

11. _____ invented the first mechanical calculating machine.

12. Jacquard developed a loom in which _____ controlled the pattern or design of woven material.

13. _____ is generally regarded as the father of computing.

14. The _____ is generally considered the first all-purpose computer.

15. First-generation computing is characterized by the development and use of _____.

16. Using a system of zeroes and ones to write instructions for the computer is called _____ .

17. Second-generation computing is characterized by the development and use of _____.

18. Third-generation computing is characterized by the development and use of _____.

HANDS-ON COMPUTING

1. To understand the history of computers, we must understand the impact of computers on society. Search the classified advertisement section of a newspaper and identify all the jobs that involve some computer knowledge. Be sure to consider not only computer programming jobs but also jobs that use computers in a support role.

2. Describe the similarities between operating a player piano and operating Jacquard's loom. Be sure to consider the relationship between the notes on a piano and the needles that control the pattern of woven material.

3. Visit one or two local businesses and ask how they use computers. Try to visit a local newspaper, a travel agent, a grocery store, and a bowling alley or some other businesses that might have vastly dissimilar computer applications. Be prepared to present a summary of your visits to the rest of the class.

4. Describe the similarities and differences in the data input strategies used in computing devices since the development of Jacquard's loom.

5. Describe how the development of computing devices affected the workforce. How are computers likely to affect the workforce in years to come?

6. It is fun to think about how history might have been different if computers had been available in earlier times. What might the western United States in the early 1880s have been like? How might the Egyptians have used computers? Think of some possible effects on other historical eras.

7. Search through the Sunday newspaper and list advertisements for computer hardware. Make another list for computer software and another for training classes.

8. How have microcomputers affected college and professional sports? Be sure to consider ticket sales, scouting reports, play making, and scheduling.

Index